THE LIFE AND AFTERLIFE OF HARRY HOUDINI

Center Point
Large Print

**This Large Print Book carries the
Seal of Approval of N.A.V.H.**

THE LIFE AND AFTERLIFE OF HARRY HOUDINI

JOE POSNANSKI

CENTER POINT LARGE PRINT
THORNDIKE, MAINE

For Margo, Elizabeth,
and Katie

CONTENTS

THE LIFE AND AFTERLIFE OF HARRY HOUDINI

Would I have liked Houdini? I don't know. Are you supposed to like heroes?
—Patrick Culliton

LOS ANGELES,
NOVEMBER 30, 1915

L adies and gentlemen," Harry Houdini sang, for in those days he did sing. Houdini's voice in many ways was more magical than any escape or illusion. He spent a lifetime cultivating it, smoothing it, flattening out the Hungarian accent, cleaning up the New York street grime, transforming every *da* into *the, dees* into *these,* and *ain't* into *are not.* By the time he became famous—and by 1915 he was famous in more countries than any performer on earth—you could hear European high society in the street urchin's voice. One newspaper writer said he spoke "Parisian English," a passing reference that meant so much to Houdini that he clipped and saved the article and proudly showed it to friends for the rest of his life.

Houdini did not just clean up his voice. He amplified it, not by shouting but by releasing it into the audiences, as if his words were the birds from his first magic act. His voice cut through applause and crosstalk like a siren. Even at the crescendo of his performance, when the startled *ooh*s and *ahh*s had surged into a cacophony of clapping and wolf whistles and shrieks of joy, Houdini's voice still rose above. Everyone heard him vividly, as if he were in the next seat.

"I never spoke to the first row," Houdini recalled. "My method of addressing an audience, as a result of experience, was as follows: I would walk down to the footlights, actually put one foot over the electric globes as if I were going to spring among the people, and then hurl my voice, saying: 'ladies and gentlemen.' "

So, he began that day of the Jess Willard fight.

"Ladies and gentlemen," Houdini roared, "I need three more men."

Los Angeles in 1915 was still a frontier city with fewer than a half million people; this was before the movies changed everything. It was the first night of Houdini's two-week engagement at the Los Angeles Orpheum Theater, which was at that moment the center of vaudeville on the West Coast. On Houdini's stage, seven volunteers scurried about like building inspectors. Men pulled at chains and knocked on wood; they circled about the stage looking for trap doors and loose panels and escape routes.

Since the dawn of magic, going back to Moses and the pharaohs, magicians have needed volunteers to scrutinize and examine and confirm that everything is as it appears. Magic isn't magic without belief. Most performers require no more than one or two volunteers. Houdini (being Houdini) demanded ten. It is perhaps a coincidence that ten men make a minyan, a quorum for prayer in the Jewish faith of Houdini's father.

"It so happens," Houdini continued, "there is a man here tonight who doesn't know that I am aware of his presence. But he is equal to three ordinary gentlemen. I ask him to come forward."

The crowd restlessly looked around the theater.

"He is," Houdini said, "Jess Willard, our champion!"

With that, two thousand people in the theater gasped. Willard, the giant of 1915! For seven long years, the heavyweight champion of the world had been Jack Johnson, a source of great embarrassment for much of America as he was black. Johnson particularly enraged white supremacists because he was flamboyant and independent and unapologetic. He raced cars and opened nightclubs. He married three white women. Promoters searched the world for a white boxer, any white boxer, who could defeat Jack Johnson. This pursuit gave birth to the term "the Great White Hope."

Johnson pummeled all the White Hopes, laughing all along. Promoters grew so desperate to find a white boxer capable of beating Johnson that they coaxed the once champion James Jefferies out of retirement. Jefferies was thirty-five years old and had not fought in six years. The Johnson-Jefferies bout was billed as the Fight of the Century.

"I am going into this fight for the sole purpose of proving that a white man is better than a Negro," Jefferies said. Many Americans wanted to believe him. Gamblers bet overwhelmingly in his favor. But the Fight of the Century turned out to be no fight at all. Johnson battered Jefferies round after round before, mercifully, knocking him out in the fifteenth.

"The fight is over," former champion John L. Sullivan wrote sadly but unequivocally in the *New York Times*, "and a black man is the undisputed heavyweight champion of the world."

After Jefferies's humiliating defeat, Johnson continued to thrash an increasingly inferior parade of Great White Hopes. Then came Jess Willard. He was a big (six feet seven, more than 250 pounds) and genial cowboy from Pottawatomie, Kansas. He did not start boxing until he was twenty-seven, and even then, he did so reluctantly. He always let his opponent strike first. Willard was excessively strong—he once killed a man in the ring—but he was also awkward and placid. Willard announced that he planned to take a pounding from Johnson for ten or twelve rounds and then would make his move. Few thought Willard had the heart to last that long. The fight was in Havana on April 5, 1915. The betting odds were 3 to 1 for Jack Johnson.

But everyone—Johnson included—under-estimated him. Willard and Johnson smashed away at each other in the scorching heat of Havana. In the words of one ringside reporter, Willard took a beating that "would have put any ordinary fighter down and out." The fight went on and on until the twenty-sixth round, when Willard landed a right cross that snapped Johnson's head back. The champion crumpled to the canvas. Willard had just become the biggest man in the world.

Now, less than eight months later, Willard sat in the balcony of the Orpheum Theater in Los Angeles and watched silently as Harry Houdini called to him.

"I will leave it to the audience," Houdini shouted. "You see they want you."

The roars grew louder and rowdier. Even after four minutes of uninterrupted cheering, Willard would not stand. Only after it became clear that the cheers would not fade did he reluctantly wave his hand, silencing the crowd.

"Aw, go on with the show," he shouted to Houdini. "I paid for my seat."

"But Mr. Willard . . ." Houdini said.

"Give me the same wages you pay these other fellas," Willard said as he pointed to the other volunteers, "and I'll come down."

Houdini had not expected resistance. When told that Jess Willard was in the audience to see him, he assumed the champion would consider it a great honor to share the stage with him. No other possibility ever registered with Houdini. Willard had to be joking.

"I will gladly pay you what I pay these men," Houdini replied. "Come down. I pay these men nothing."

The crowd laughed and cheered again, but Willard was unmoved. He was not joking. "Aw go on with the show, ya faker, ya four-flusher," he growled. "Everybody knows you're a four-flusher."

It is unclear if Willard knew that those would strike a nerve. A four-flusher was a popular insult in 1915; it referred to poker players who boasted loudly and bet big when they had only a four-card flush. He might have meant it as a joke. Houdini did not see it that way. He believed that Willard was calling him a fraud. And nothing cut the man as profoundly.

Houdini glared at the heavyweight champion of the world. The tension was thick with irony. Willard was an enormous boxer who did not see himself as a fighter. Houdini was a small vaudeville performer who saw himself as nothing else.

"Jess Willard," Houdini cried out, his trained voice now deeper and filled with menace, "I have paid you a compliment. Now I will tell you something else. I don't care how big you are or how strong you are."

Everybody in the crowd held their breath.

"I will be Harry Houdini when you are not the heavyweight champion of the world," he shouted.

With this, the silence broke, and the crowd roared, but Houdini could not hear or see his audience. He saw only Jess Willard's red face, and he heard his own rushing blood.

"I will be Harry Houdini," he thundered, "when people have forgotten you were ever a heavyweight champion."

The crowd erupted—"a hydra-throated monster," Houdini would call those cheers—as Willard trembled with fury and shook his massive fist. He offered Houdini a thousand dollars to come to the balcony and say those words to his face. But no one heard him. They only saw a beaten giant. As the clamor climbed higher, the defeated Willard quietly slipped out of the theater.

Harry Houdini stood on stage and reveled in the sound of his own immortality.

THE TRUEST BELIEVER

At sixteen, John Cox determined that he was destined to be Houdini's disciple. He promptly announced it to the papers. "That's what Houdini would have done," John says, and we laugh because it's true, nothing mattered more to Harry Houdini than getting into the papers. We munch on sandwiches in Hollywood's Musso & Frank Grill, a historic place where F. Scott Fitzgerald wrote parts of *The Last Tycoon*, William Faulkner slipped behind the bar to make his own mint juleps, and Joe DiMaggio walked in with Marilyn on his arm.

"I wonder if Houdini ever ate here," I say absentmindedly, quickly realizing that I have made a mistake in wondering because now John Cox's eyes fade out, and he is obviously gone. It's not right to say that John spends every waking minute thinking about Houdini; he's a levelheaded guy with a job and a life. But it is right to say that John would like to spend every waking minute thinking about Houdini. Today is a day off, and on days off, John can let his mind go. Our conversation hits a lull as he considers the timeline, works out the calculations, and ponders if Harry Houdini had ever been in Musso & Frank Grill.

"I guess he wasn't ever here," John says finally and with some disappointment in his voice. "Musso & Frank opened in 1919. That was the year that Houdini left Hollywood. So, I would say it is highly unlikely that Houdini was ever here."

The conversation picks up again, and I soon forget all about it. John does not. The next day, he calls. "I had a brain fart," he explains. In the heat of the moment—and he cannot believe he did this—John briefly forgot that while, yes, Houdini did leave Hollywood in 1919, he of course came back for a short while in 1923. He even performed a swimming pool escape at the Ambassador Hotel, less than five miles away from Musso & Frank. John is mortified. Nobody on earth knows more than about Houdini's schedule than he does. He can place Houdini on just about every day of his adult life. For John, forgetting about Houdini's return to Los Angeles in '23 is like LeBron James missing a breakaway dunk or Neil deGrasse Tyson forgetting to put Jupiter down in a listing of the planets.

"So, the good news in all of this," John says, and you can almost hear him sing, "is maybe one day we'll be able to put him inside Musso."

"Well," I tell him, "you did become Houdini's disciple after all."

He shrugs.

"No," he says. "That's Patrick."

• • •

Why Houdini? That is our question. Why is it that everyone still knows, still cares about, still idolizes Ehrich Weiss, a vaudeville escape artist who died at a time when the Orthophonic Victrola phonograph was still being called "the miracle of the age"? How is it that this little man who slipped from handcuffs and jumped off bridges and shook himself loose from straitjackets still inspires wonder and awe in our cynical and jaded technological world?

Make no mistake: Houdini still arouses wonder and imaginations. On this crazy journey, I spoke with a man in India who was handcuffed, locked in a box, and thrown in a fire because of Houdini. I spoke with a woman in China whose first English word was *Houdini*. I met a man in Texas who became a magician because he saw Houdini in a dream.

There are more than five hundred books about Houdini, from sweeping biographies (*The Making of America's First Superhero*) to jarringly specific ones (*Houdini's Texas Tours 1916 & 1923*). There are psychological profiles, magical instruction books, and large coffee table books. There are Houdini-inspired novels, graphic novels, comic books, chapbooks, pop-up books, and self-help guides (*The Houdini Solution: Why Thinking Inside the Box is the Key to Creativity*). A Houdini golf instruction book teaches you how to help your golf ball escape from danger. An arcane but surprisingly touching book titled *Houdini's Mailbags* offers a detailed study of the US Postal Service mailbag Houdini escaped from in 1907. There are others that are difficult to categorize such as the baffling but intriguing novel, *Escaping from Houdini (Stalking Jack the Ripper)* and a thriller called *Houdini: International Spy.*

We haven't yet gotten to the Houdini children's books, so many children's books, dozens and dozens of them, filling every school library across the world, from *Who Was Harry Houdini?* to *Orangutan Houdini* to *Hurry Up, Houdini!* to *I, Houdini*, about a particularly elusive hamster.

Films? There are more than a dozen documentaries about Houdini and several full-length movies. Television? Houdini has been featured in multiple television movies, a not-too-great miniseries, and more television shows than we can begin to list. Then there are Houdini paintings, sculptures, anime, photographs, posters, and we cannot forget the stage plays performed in numerous languages: *Houdini: The Musical, Houdini, A Circus Opera, The Houdini Deception, The Houdini Exposure, The Houdini Box, Being Harry Houdini, Der Grosse Houdini, Rosabelle, Believe,* and *Houdini's on First.*

The Microsoft chess engine was called Houdini.

So is the most popular 3-D software on earth. A California Fair Employment and Housing project is named after Houdini. A rap group is called Whodini. The Android app ODINI was built by computer hackers. There's a color named after Houdini, a medium dark shade of blue-magenta, according to the Dutch Boy paint company. Stores sell Houdini wine openers, Houdini locks, Houdini puzzles, Houdini board games, Houdini magic sets. You can eat at a Houdini pizza shop, wear Houdini sportswear (under a Patagonia Houdini Air Jacket), drink a Houdini cocktail, escape from a Houdini escape room, secure your baby in a car seat with a Houdini seat clip, light the way with a Houdini flashlight, freshen your surroundings with a Houdini air purifier, make up your face using Houdini eyeshadow. All the while you can listen to any hundreds of songs that mention Houdini.

You probably have a piece of Houdini trivia memorized without even realizing it. Whenever Houdini's name comes up in conversation—and, strangely, it still does come up—you might be able to dazzle your friends by knowing Houdini's real name, Ehrich Weiss, or by telling a story about his turbulent friendship with Sherlock Holmes's creator Arthur Conan Doyle, or by recounting his epic battle with Margery the medium, or by suavely mentioning that Houdini was the first man to fly a plane in Australia.

Or you might know something about how he died.

Why do we know any of this? We are closing in on one hundred years since his death, and yet when a thief in Bangkok slips out of his handcuffs and eludes a dozen police officers, what do they call him? Houdini. A baby in Mundaring, Australia, continuously escapes a crib to the dismay and panic of her parents, and the newspapers dub her "Houdini Baby." A dog keeps slipping out of the yard and creating havoc in a neighbor's gardens in Melbourne, Florida, and is similarly called "Houdini Dog." (This is unoriginal; newspapers in San Diego, Des Moines, Rome, Amsterdam, and North London also call particularly troublesome pooches "Houdini.")

"What sort of Houdini child do you have?" asks Houdini Solution Ltd., a New Zealand company that makes baby safety devices. "A harness Houdini? A bedroom Houdini? A put-things-in-the-toilet Houdini? . . . We have the products that will help keep that Houdini of yours contained and safer."

FC Barcelona, the most famous soccer team on earth, overcomes a late deficit in a game. The headlines call them Houdini. Donald Trump gets tangled in a seemingly endless series of scandals and emerges unscathed. How does he do it? The reporters explain: "He is Houdini." In Missouri, a man's car flips over eight times after a fiery crash, and he walks away from the wreckage unharmed.

"I don't know," his wife tells reporters. "He must be Houdini."

An Alabama man on death row dodges execution seven times. Houdini. A baseball relief pitcher gets out of a bases-loaded jam in the World Series. Houdini. The Russian chess genius Sergey Karjakin escapes from a seemingly inescapable trap. Houdini.

Houdini is always there, ready to be summoned. He is in headlines around the world every single day, a fact that would no doubt thrill the man endlessly. Five lions escape from Kruger National Park in Komatipoort, South Africa. The lion spotters call the most elusive one Houdini. India finds itself in a delicate military standoff with China; a commentator says that the generals will need "the skills of Houdini." In Moose Jaw, Canada, the city council finds itself entangled in a mess involving curbside garbage pickup. "The council," a local reporter writes, "has been in a straitjacket, unable to pull a Houdini."

> his marvelous feats were but warm-ups
>   for the big break
> Ah Houdini. he tried it. he didn't do it. he
>   died before it. quick. but he died game.
> And he'll be back he'll be back he'll be
>   back . . .

That's Patti Smith, the so-called Punk Poet Laureate, in her chapbook "Ha! Ha! Houdini!"

> The lean make me feel like Houdini
> (Houdini)
> Yeah, the lean make me feel like Houdini
> (got lean)
> The lean make me feel like Houdini
> (got damn)
> Ayy the lean make me feel like Houdini
> (uh)

And that's Smokepurpp, a nineteen-year-old rapper from Miami who exploded on the hip-hop scene after getting millions of plays on the internet. The lean is a drink spiked with Promethazine, Sprite, and, improbably, Jolly Rancher candies. Smokepurpp's proposition seems to be, if I can decipher his meaning, that the lean makes him feel like Houdini.

The influential pop artist Joseph Cornell contained his gorgeous and haunting works inside small boxes. Why? He saw Houdini escape from them.

The Academy Award–winning actor Adrien Brody says that he learned to be obsessive about his craft from Houdini's obsession for his own.

The street magician David Blaine attempts ever more dangerous and insane things—now he's trapped himself in a sheet of ice, now he's going for the record for consecutive hours staying awake, now he's burying himself alive. Why? He saw a poster of Houdini when he was a child.

Why Houdini? This is our driving question. Why does he live on? Why does he still alter lives? Why are so many people drawn to him? There were more prominent stars—more prominent magicians even—in his day. But who thinks of Rudolph Valentino or Al Jolson or Douglas Fairbanks or Buster Keaton? Who thinks of Howard Thurston now?

"Walk into a second-grade classroom, and they know Houdini," the magician and historian Mike Caveney concedes (for he is no Houdini fan). "Who else from that time do they know?"

Why Houdini? I went in search of the truest believers. I found one in John Cox. He said there was someone else, someone on an even higher plane.

I had to go and find Patrick Culliton.

Patrick Culliton is an actor. If you watched any television dramas in the 1960s or 1970s, you've seen him; his portfolio is a potpourri of TV nostalgia. Patrick played a roller coaster operator in *Cannon*, a kidnapper in *Most Wanted*, a policeman in *Land of the Giants*, a patrolman in *The Rockford Files*, and at different times he was a reporter, sheriff's deputy, waiter, and someone named "Russell" on *Barnaby Jones*. He made it into a few miniseries, too, and he had a credited role in the star-studded movie *The Towering Inferno*.

Inside Houdini World, though, Patrick's acting career is of little concern. Even among Houdini's most passionate believers, Patrick represents something else, something strange and mystical and a little bit intimidating. Patrick Culliton is the truest believer.

What does it mean to be the truest believer? Well, you begin with the books. Patrick has written several of them, all about Houdini, *The Tao of Houdini* and *The Secret Confessions of Houdini* and *Houdini's Strange Tales* among them. These are books only in the most literal ways, which is to say they have covers and they have pages, and there are words and pictures inside.

But Patrick's books are more like dented and torn cardboard boxes you find in a dusty attic, a whirlwind of stories and odd facts and letters and rumors and whispers about Houdini that he has collected over the years. The most Patrick of all his books—and the hardest one to find—is a massive thing inside a blue vinyl cover with the title, *Houdini: The Key*, embossed on the front. Patrick calls this, "the sum of everything I have learned about Houdini in my life."

I obsessively spent months trying to get a copy of *Houdini: The Key*. It was like chasing the wind. There are so few copies in print that whenever one did show up on eBay or some magic auction site, it would sell almost instantly for hundreds and hundreds of dollars.

Finally, I went to Culliton himself.

"Dear Patrick," I began an email, and I explained the quest, explained why I would like to talk with him, told him how much I would like to get his book. A few days later, he responded.

> Dear Joe,
> I wish you the best on your Houdini book. I am on to other things and don't voluntarily do anything with Houdini— much as I still admire him.
> You should do fine without me.
> Patrick Culliton

At the bottom of *Houdini: The Key*, two author names are listed.

The first author is Patrick Culliton. The second is Houdini's Ghost.

CHILDHOOD

LIES AND ILLUSIONS

My birth occurred April 6, 1874, in the small town of Appleton in the state of Wisconsin, U.S.A.

Harry Houdini lied obsessively, though he did not think of it as lying. "Magic," one of Houdini's friends and rivals Karl Germain said, "is the most honest profession. A magician promises to deceive you. And he does."

What, after all, is magic? Is it lying when you pretend to saw the lady in half? Is it lying when you shuffle the cards so that they stay in place? A magician floats between lies and illusions, and no one did so quite like Houdini. With him, it's hard to tell where the lies and illusions end, and where real life begins.

Take the sentence that leads us off. It is the opening line to the most candid autobiographical piece Harry Houdini ever wrote, a piece simply called "Harry Houdini by Harry Houdini." He wrote it for the *Magical Annual of 1910*. It was edited by another friend and rival, Will Goldston.

As you will see, most of Houdini's friends were also his rivals, most of his rivals were also his friends.

"Harry Houdini by Harry Houdini" has been

endlessly quoted by Houdini scholars, cynics, admirers, and biographers. In it, he describes and deflects the pain of his childhood and the early challenges of his career in vivid detail. This is Houdini at his rawest and most candid.

Now, read that sentence one more time:

> My birth occurred April 6, 1874, in the small town of Appleton in the state of Wisconsin, U.S.A.

Not one of the details is true.

Harry Houdini was not born on April 6. He was not born in the small town of Appleton, nor in the great state of Wisconsin. He was not even born in the United States of America.

Why say his birthday was April 6 when it was March 24? Why say he was born in the United States when he was born in Budapest and did not come over the ocean until he was four? Why did Houdini consistently punctuate his autographs with a cheerful "Appleton, Wisconsin," as if that was his beloved hometown, when he actually lived in Appleton for less than four years?

The best answer is that for Houdini, the illusion never ended and real life never began. The boy born as Ehrich Weiss became Harry Houdini the way James Gatz became Jay Gatsby and Dick Whitman became Donald Draper and Norma Jeane Mortenson became Marilyn Monroe.

Houdini never stopped mythologizing himself. He hired the best writers—including pulp fiction legend H. P. Lovecraft—to immortalize his larger-than-life story. This, from the promotional book he had produced, *Houdini: The Adventurous Life of a Versatile Artist*, is fairly typical:

> Buried in the brain of Houdini is an unknown power he alone possesses that makes their prisons as powerless as Japanese screens and renders their multiple-locking handcuffs, leg irons and all the other prison paraphernalia no more binding than store twine.

Houdini's public mythmaking was big and bold and over-the-top, but he was no less vigilant in private. He never stopped being Houdini, not for a single minute of any day. Houdini once wrote a touching letter to the daughter of his onetime Appleton neighbor Miles Brown.

> I will never forget your father or your mother. Many a happy ride he gave me when I was a youngster, and from what my mother told me, he was in the house the day I was born.

Of course, Miles Brown was not in the house at all because Houdini was not born in Appleton, but myths had to be fed and secrets kept. This is the magician's code. This was Harry Houdini's code.

Houdini kept the secret of his birth so close that it wasn't until 1971, after decades of conflicting research and fierce debate, that the Society of American Magicians decided to find out the truth. They formed the Houdini Birth Committee, a notable collection of historians and magicians, who worked on it for a year, traveling the world, interviewing Houdini associates, and gathering letters, birth documents, and insurance policies.

The Houdini Birth Committee concluded that the boy called Erik Weisz was born in Budapest on March 24, 1874, and didn't make it to America until Independence Day in 1878, where the spelling of his name was changed to Ehrich Weiss.

And you know what this extraordinary bit of research changed? Almost nothing. Houdini's grand illusion was so well performed, so brilliantly executed, that even when faced with birth certificates and family testimony, many people still argued that Houdini was born in Appleton. Some still argue his birthplace today.

Houdini undoubtedly would tell you that's as it should be. What are lies? What are illusions? Erik Weisz might have been born in Hungary, but, as he plainly and unequivocally told us, *Harry Houdini* was born April 6, 1874, in the small town of Appleton in the state of Wisconsin, USA.

Walk right out and tell your tale to the audience, Houdini used to advise young magicians. And perhaps many will believe it.

THE ORIGIN STORY

Ehrich Weiss was a clever and mischievous child; a genius in ways that he and his family could not yet grasp. This is the Harry Houdini origin story, the tapestry that Houdini and his writers and his truest believers weaved through the years. Is it a lie? Is it an illusion?

The story goes that as a baby, Ehrich rarely slept, but he never cried. His mother, Cecilia, watched on with awe as the boy stared peacefully at the ceiling for hours at a time looking for all the world as if he was pondering life's richest mysteries.

When he was barely old enough to walk, the child wandered into the kitchen, drawn by the smell of his mother's Apfelkuchen—apple cake. He ate it all. This happened again and again until Cecilia decided to put an end to it by locking her treats in a box. This, as you already guessed, did not work. When Cecilia returned to the kitchen, the lock was intact, but an enormous chunk of the Apfelkuchen was missing. Cecilia tried a different lock, then another, another, some with keys, some using combinations, none of it mattered. Each time Cecilia came back to the kitchen, she found the bolt in perfect working order and another piece of cake gone.

Ehrich had no memory of these small miracles, but as he grew older, he felt certain that he was special and destined to do something thrilling and supernatural, something that soared high above his family's miserable existence. He thought his destiny might be in the circus, so he practiced tightrope walking and swinging on a trapeze. He strengthened his legs by hanging from tree branches. He worked on tumbling. At nine, he put on tights and performed for the first time as Ehrich, Prince of the Air in the traveling circus of his friend Jack Hoeffler. Houdini's memories of his childhood act were ever changing; sometimes he remembered doing a trapeze act, sometimes he remembered walking a tightrope, sometimes, most joyously, he remembered being a contortionist who would dangle upside down and pick pins off the ground with his eyelids.

All along, Ehrich Weiss was hopelessly fascinated by locks. School was a bore. Life at home was hard. Food was scarce. But locks? They held a cosmic hold on his imagination. He had to know everything about them, how each model and sort opened and closed, how keys fit, how combinations worked. Ehrich recalled spending his young life wandering through junkyards and picking up and studying bolts and detainers and keys and latches. Locks spoke to Houdini, and Houdini understood.

When Ehrich was eleven—and now we get to

the crescendo of the origin story—he worked as an apprentice for a locksmith in Milwaukee. It was a tedious job, until the day the city sheriff brought in a hulking man clamped in a pair of handcuffs. The judge had thrown out his case for lack of evidence. He was a free man. But the sheriff had lost the handcuff keys.

"Hack this guy out these cuffs, won't you?" the sheriff said, and the locksmith began to file away. It is grueling work to saw off a pair of handcuffs, and after a few fruitless moments the sheriff said, "Hey, why don't you let the kid work on those cuffs, and we'll get a beer?"

The locksmith decided this absurdity was a good idea, because that's how it works in dreams and origin stories, and so Ehrich was left with an enormous and irritable prisoner in handcuffs. He tried filing through the cuffs, but he made no progress. He grew nervous.

And then all at once, it happened: the flash of light, the big bang moment of Harry Houdini's life. He suddenly knew just what to do. Ehrich reached for some wire. He followed his instincts and bent and shaped the wire just so. Then, as the prisoner looked on curiously, Ehrich grabbed the prisoner's hands, shoved the wire into the handcuff lock, twisted and turned just so and, impossibly, the handcuff cracked open. Ehrich picked the other lock even quicker. The free man stared wide-eyed at Ehrich. "He is the only person," Houdini later said, "who knows my secret."

Houdini told this charming origin story again and again—of the baby who stole his mother's apple cakes, the restless boy who longed for an otherworldly life, the young man who one day picked the locks and set an innocent man free. He told the story, and the newspaper writers wrote it, and Houdini's wife Bess retold it after he died, and biographers repeated it after she died, and at some point, like all great magic, it no longer mattered what was a lie and what was an illusion.

THE SILVERMAN BOXES

There's a Houdini quote that you can find splattered all over the internet, it's in just about every Houdini quote collection, and it goes like this: "The greatest escape I ever made was when I left Appleton, Wisconsin." It's a funny and seemingly revealing quote, which is why it's too bad that Houdini almost certainly never said it. Tom Boldt, who runs the Boldt Company in Appleton and knows more about Houdini's connection to his hometown than anyone, finds those words to be counter to everything we know about Houdini.

"I've never seen anything that would tie Houdini to that quote," he says. "On the contrary, as you know, there's plenty of evidence that Houdini had fond memories of Appleton, often communicated with Appleton friends, and returned several times as an adult—not exactly the behavior of someone who wanted to escape the town."

Boldt does have a fun theory about the quote's origin: He thinks it was said by a different Appleton native, the award-winning actor Willem Dafoe, who never hid his distaste for his hometown. Boldt is probably on to something; Dafoe said something similar in a magazine interview when asked about Houdini. "Yes," he said, "we both escaped the favelas of Appleton."

Houdini did not see it that way. He was deeply proud of his connection to Appleton; he once told fellow native and famed writer Edna Ferber that, together, they had put it on the map. He loved Appleton. And Appleton loved him back. Every few years for more than a century, the people of Appleton have looked for ways to honor Houdini and their own place in his story. The height of the frenzy came in the 1980s, when developers tried to build a mall called Houdini Center. That fell through, but Houdini Plaza, a pedestrian walking area, was opened between Oneida and Appleton Streets. A sculpture celebrating Houdini's first successful illusion—"Metamorphosis"—was put at the heart of the city. The history museum was rechristened the Houdini Historic Center, and it featured an interactive Houdini exhibit, a sort of Houdini amusement park but without rides. The local paper, the *Appleton Crescent-Post*, began a public campaign to insist that, despite the Birth Committee findings, Houdini indeed had been born there. In 1988, at the height of the mania, Houdini Elementary School was opened.

Throughout, there was also a daily Houdini walking tour to point out the thrilling Houdini-related sites throughout town. This was hampered only slightly by the fact that there aren't any Houdini-related sites in the city; Houdini only lived in Appleton from ages four to eight. This didn't prevent guides from taking tourists down College Avenue and saying that the young Ehrich Weiss used to run up and down the street and magically unlock the storefronts, creating much joyful mayhem.

Houdini fever has died down since the 1980s, and the town generally accepts his rather tenuous connection to Appleton. But he remains a constant presence. Houdini Plaza is still a popular pedestrian walkway. Houdini Elementary continues its "longstanding 'magical' tradition of being innovative."

While the Houdini Historic Center is now called the History Museum at the Castle, there is still a charming and engaging Houdini exhibit that offers fun facts and lets you try a few of Houdini's escapes. And on the second floor of the museum, in a back room, there are seven fascinating boxes that attempt the most astounding magic trick of all.

In these boxes, somewhere, is the real child-hood of Harry Houdini.

These are the Silverman Boxes.

Kenneth Silverman taught literature at New York University. He wrote significant and weighty books in his literary life, including biographies of the writer Edgar Allan Poe, avant-garde composer John Cage, and inventor Samuel Morse. He won a Pulitzer Prize for his book on the Puritan preacher Cotton Mather. He also wrote what many consider the finest cultural history of the American Revolution.

Before all that, though, he was Ken Silvers, master of illusion.

And once you are Ken Silvers, master of illusion, there's no turning back.

"Magic," Silverman's childhood friend Dick Brookz says, "doesn't ever die once it gets inside you." Silverman and Brookz grew up in New York together in the decade or so after World War II, and they were two of many to fall under the spell of a beloved professor and magician named Abe Hurwitz. Thankfully, there are always people like Abe Hurwitz, people who want nothing more than to bring a little more magic into the world. He did just that, teaching magic to children while working at the Brooklyn Hebrew Orphanage. In time he expanded his reach, traveling to schools around New York City. During the Depression, New York Mayor Fiorello La Guardia named him the city's official magician.

Hurwitz started a club that he called the Peter Pan Magic Club. Silverman and Brookz both joined along with Hurwitz's daughter, Phyllis, who would later change her name to Shari Lewis and become America's most beloved ventriloquist. Silverman too changed his name, to Ken Silvers, and he began performing at birthday parties. He was hired to play in a candy commercial, where he magically poured out hundreds of M&Ms from what appeared an empty box. After that, he performed on the Catskills Borscht Belt circuit. He told Dick Brookz that he loved the life of a magician, but that it did not feel like his life, and so he went to Columbia and then began his life as a teacher and writer.

He soon became known for his dogged and relentless research; once on the trail he would not let go. He visited countless archives in multiple countries. He found important papers in the basement of a Veterans Administration hospital. He wandered yard sales. He loved the chase.

"Someday," he told Dick Brookz, "I'm going to take on the big one."

"You mean . . ." Brookz said.

"I'm going to write the definitive biography of Harry Houdini."

The definitive Houdini biography! It hadn't been done. It couldn't be done. There had been a half-dozen or so attempts by the time Silverman heard the call, and all fell well short of definitive. The first book came out in 1928, two years after Houdini's death: *Houdini: His Life Story*. The author, Harold Kellock, was a newspaper editor who always seemed to be staking out for a quick payday. In 1928, Kellock also wrote a book about Parson Weems, author of the first George

48

Washington biography, which is remembered mostly for its countless invented stories, including the one about Washington chopping down the cherry tree. Kellock's Houdini book drew from Parson Weems's example.

To be fair, though, Kellock was mainly hired to take dictation. *Houdini: His Life Story* is the story of Houdini as seen through the dream-filled eyes of his wife, Bess. Because of Bess's own talents for inventing captivating stories—she often matched her husband's imagination—it's charming, warm, and great fun to read. How true is it? Houdini's brother, a magician who called himself Hardeen, was asked to sign an early copy. He obliged and added the jaunty dedication: "This book is full of lies."

Walter B. Gibson—a magician and writer who created the radio sensation *The Shadow*—knew Houdini personally. Gibson began writing Houdini books in 1927, just one year after the magician's death, and didn't stop for the next fifty years. He wrote *Houdini's Book of Magic and Party Pastimes*, *Houdini's Escapes*, *Houdini's Magic*, *Houdini on Magic*, and *Houdini's Fabulous Magic*. He basically ran out of titles. His books were not biographies, exactly, they focused on the magic. But in explaining the magic, Gibson offered many insights into Houdini.

"On one occasion," Gibson wrote in *Houdini*

on Magic, "I took him to a magician's meeting in my car, which that season was a Ford Model T coupe with a front seat of only two-person width and with the door-catches inconveniently placed behind a person's elbow. When he tried to twist around and work the catch, Houdini found it stuck, and in all seriousness, he demanded, 'Say—how do you get out of this thing?' It wasn't until I had reached across and pulled the knob for him that he began laughing because he, of all people, couldn't get out of a Ford Coupe."

In 1950, the writing team of Samuel Epstein and Beryl Williams wrote a rip-roaring biography called *The Great Houdini* that was not in any way constrained by facts or research. The haunted novelist William Lindsay Gresham wrote a strange but fascinating book called *The Man Who Walked Through Walls* that was as much about Gresham as about Houdini.

In 1969, Milbourne Christopher, a magician and prolific writer about the art, made the first serious effort to write the definitive biography. He called it *Houdini: The Untold Story*. The book has its merits. As one critic wrote: "It is a straightforward factual narrative devoid of padding."

But there was something soulless about it.

"Christopher was a very fussy guy; very fussy, prissy guy," the wonderful magic inventor Jim Steinmeyer says. "He was a famously terrible performer. Very tone deaf as a performer, and he had slight delusions of grandeur. Christopher tended to think he was building things up, but you always ended up feeling, 'this isn't very good.'

"I just don't think he ever would have understood the kind of rough-and-tumble show business of Houdini. Christopher always had money and was always above all that kind of stuff. And so, Christopher wrote a completely bloodless book . . . It's not a bad biography because he's got lots of information there that at that time was original. But it was a completely pointless book."

Ken Silverman set out to write something different, a soulful book that would break through the myths, pierce through the lies, and bring the real Harry Houdini back to life. You can feel the weight of his ambition by reading the full title of the book:

HOUDINI!!!: The Career of Ehrich Weiss. American Self-Liberator, Europe's Eclipsing Sensation, World Handcuff King & Prison Breaker—Nothing on Earth Can Hold Houdini a Prisoner!!!

Even if he accomplished nothing else, Silverman certainly set a record for most exclamation points in a book title.

The punctuation only hints at Silverman's passion for finding the real Houdini. He sought out every public and private Houdini collection in the world, exploring every one that was open to him, and pleading again and again with those who refused to let him in. He spent a month at the Library of Congress poring through scrapbooks Houdini left behind. Silverman read thousands of letters and diary entries. He found tens of thousands of Houdini references in newspapers, magazines, and books. He reached out to anyone who might have known Houdini, might have known someone who knew Houdini, or might have known someone who knew someone who knew Houdini. He investigated every tiny clue that might offer a revelation into the character of Houdini. And he always wanted more.

"I located more of his letters, scrapbooks, and photographs than I managed to get a look at," Silverman wrote bitterly in Notes to *HOUDINI!!!* "Very frustrating. Most collectors generously allowed me to see and quote from the material they owned. But, to my frustration, two collectors with sizable Houdini holdings gave me only limited access, and two others refused to let me see anything at all. May they live and be well, these folks. But they can't take their collections with them."

The remains of Ken Silverman's great search are in these seven boxes at the Appleton History Museum at the Castle. Inside these boxes are copies of articles, programs, letters, and book pages. There are loose sheets of paper with rumors written on them. Half-written thoughts are scribbled on scraps of paper. Most of it is a dusty mess, entirely disorganized, but as you pick through, you can begin to see not just the story of Houdini, but the story of Ken Silverman, the wild goose chases he went on, the rabbit holes that engulfed him, the storylines he abandoned. There are dozens of pages, for instance, on James Thurber's fascination with Houdini. Thurber, the beloved humorist who wrote *The Secret Life of Walter Mitty*, spent a great deal of time thinking about writing a Houdini book. Silverman obviously spent hours chasing this thread, but it led nowhere. Thurber did not make it into the finished book.

The best part of these boxes, though, is Ken Silverman's collection of index cards. There are thousands of them, each personally typed by Silverman himself, chronicling every aspect of Houdini's life.

If you go to the *P* section, for instance, you find:

Paris
Personality
Pets
Places
Plagiarism

These cards were Silverman's roadmap and his daily journal. They are filled with the joy of discovery, and they are also filled with the rage of frustration. Silverman had come into this project with the intention of finding the ultimate escape artist. In some ways he did, but he also found that some parts of Houdini always stay hidden. While Houdini walked through brick walls, Silverman ran into them. Every myth has a conflicting story, every story has a conflicting myth. What was real? What was made up? Silverman, the ultimate finder of truth, kept trying.

"Myths," Silverman wrote to himself on one card. "Endless number of supposed interviews with HH in the press clearly the concoctions of reporters, press agents, managers and HH himself. They told and retold the stories of his origins and beginnings, his unceasing invention, again and again changing the details when he first learned to pick locks, how he ran away from home, his circus days, etc. Impossible to tell how much of it, if any of it, can be believed."

Silverman's exasperation blazes through the boxes. He would type out facts that he felt sure were real and then, later, scribble on those cards "No" or "Untrue" or "Unlikely." He crossed out entire paragraphs and wrote on top, "Probably didn't happen." He had two "Myth" sections in his files—personal myths and work-related myths—and you can almost feel Silverman's pain as he reluctantly moved a compelling Houdini story from an active file into a myth file. He had to repeatedly remind himself not to naïvely believe what he saw. But how do you avoid believing what you see?

"Houdini's half-dozen surviving, sworn passport applications show a startling disagreement in detail," Silverman wrote on one card. "His height is variously given as five-feet-five-and-one-quarter, five-feet-six, and five-feet-seven. His eyes variously appear as 'brown,' 'blue' and 'grey,' his complexion as 'dark' and 'fair.' His birthplace in the earliest application is given as 'Buda-pest,' and after that as 'Appleton.' His birth-date is given incorrectly as 6 April 1874 or, even more incorrectly, as 6 April 1873. His occupation is given variously as 'Actor,' 'Performer,' 'artiste' and 'juggler.' On the earliest passport he appears as a naturalized citizen; but just three months after that, when getting a new passport at the American embassy in London, he swears to having been born in Appleton, Wisconsin."

The Silverman Boxes show that Houdini's greatest escape wasn't from handcuffs or strait-jackets or Appleton. It was from the shackles of reality.

Houdini's friend and rival, the magician Howard Thurston, would tell his audiences every night: "I wouldn't deceive you for the world." It was an audacious and brazen thing to say since he was, in fact, blatantly deceiving his audience as magicians do. But Thurston's stylish and graceful magic was not about deception. He gently, and with good humor, led viewers into that shadowy world between dreams and daylight.

Houdini did none of that. He came at you straight on. Lock me up! Go ahead! I'll get out! He dared the world to hold him down, to lock him out, to guess his secrets: NOTHING ON EARTH can hold Houdini prisoner!!! Ken Silverman tried to break through Houdini's illusions. He tried to pin Houdini down. He tried to lock Houdini in one of the Silverman Boxes.

And did it work? When Silverman was done, his *HOUDINI!!!* was 465 pages, and the notes on sources ran another 181 pages. Twenty-plus years after it was written, *HOUDINI!!!* remains the gold standard, the most thorough, the least exaggerated, the most truthful, the least aggrandized Houdini biography of them all, the book our friend John Cox calls "The Bible."

Do you know how many of those 465 pages were dedicated to the childhood of Ehrich Weiss? Five.

Nothing on earth, not even Ken Silverman, could hold Houdini prisoner.

"HH's greatest personal failing, his profound deceit," Silverman admitted to himself, "was also his greatest professional strength."

THE RUNAWAY CHILD

"My father was a skunk," Dorothy Dietrich says. We talk about Houdini's childhood while Dorothy eats Chinese food and Italian food and seafood. It's an international plate. We are at the Royal Buffet in Scranton, Pennsylvania, where the only thing more overwhelming than the variety of food choices is the sound of screaming children, deluged grandparents, and aggrieved servers.

"My father was really a bad guy," she continues. "He was a drunk. He beat us. We were all afraid of him. I remember feeling afraid all the time."

We are talking about the time Ehrich Weiss ran away from home and talking about how that changed Dorothy Dietrich's life.

Dorothy is an icon of magic. She is the first female magician to saw a man in half on television. She did that back in the 1970s, when everyone in America fought over the Equal Rights Amendment, not long after Billie Jean King blew people's minds by beating Bobby Riggs in the great Battle of the Sexes tennis match. She became the first woman to do a lot of magical things on television—first to saw a man in half, first to catch a bullet between her teeth, first to escape a straitjacket while dangling from a burning rope (the last while a leering Tony Curtis continuously commented on her beauty). She was the inspiration for Henley Reeves, the Isla Fisher character in the *Now You See Me* movies. Fisher came to train with Dorothy to prepare for the part.

"She is amazing," Fisher says. "I studied her intensely."

"She *is* amazing," says Dick Brookz, who is sitting to Dorothy's left. You will remember Dick from his childhood friendship with Ken Silverman. He did not follow his friend into real life. He has been, at various times, known as Dick Brooks, John Brave, Bravo the Grate!, and Bravo the Great (no exclamation point). He added the *z* to his last name so that it would stand out on Google searches. Dick is Dorothy's longtime partner, promoter, handler, manager, assistant, public relations director, and scheme developer. These two have gotten into some serious Houdini schemes over the years, as you will see.

"My father would come home," Dorothy continues, "and we had no idea if he was drunk or not. If he wasn't drunk, it might be okay. But if he was drunk, someone was going to get it. He was so mean. I remember one night, he came home—it had to be three in the morning—and he started beating up my mother. In the middle of it, he seemed to realize that I was watching, and he reached up and grabbed my hair and threw me off the top bunk of the bed. He just threw me across the room, like I was a rag doll. I was afraid every minute of every day."

She vividly remembers plotting ways to kill her father. "I thought, *You know what, he's drunk all the time, he wouldn't even know if I stabbed him to death. And who would miss that skunk? We've got a lot in the back there, let's just bury him back there. Who would even know?*"

She smiles wanly. She obviously did not kill her father.

"Houdini saved me," she says.

Ehrich Weiss was twelve when he ran away from home. Nobody knows the reason, not for sure, but it surely had something to do with his father, the Reverend Doctor Mayer Samuel Weiss. Houdini was a mama's boy all his life. His mother, Cecilia, was his muse, his inspiration, his rock, and his lifelong cause. He struggled for her. He succeeded for her. He judged his success through her eyes. He died when she died. He searched for her the rest of his life. Even the sleight-of-hand wizard Dai Vernon, who had almost nothing good to say about Houdini, marveled at the depths of Houdini's love for Cecilia. In the middle of a typical Vernon attack on his rival's character, he once conceded, "Houdini was a very good and kind man to his mother. That much must be said."

Houdini's relationship with his father was

cloudier. Mayer Samuel migrated to America in 1876, when Ehrich was a toddler. Why did he come? This is a popular and much-disputed question in Houdini World. Bert Sugar and magician the Amazing Randi cowrote *Houdini: His Life and Art* and speculated that Mayer Samuel, overtaken by wanderlust, answered a German newspaper ad for a rabbi opening in Appleton. Houdini wrote that Mayer Samuel was awarded the trip for his scholarship by the millionaire Baron Rothschild. Houdini's brother, Hardeen, offered the most dramatic hypothesis. He wrote in an unpublished autobiography that Dr. Weiss had gotten into a vicious argument with a Hamburg prince—probably over an anti-Semitic slight—and it led to a duel.

"Father," Hardeen wrote, "insulted by Prince Eric—challenged to dule [*sic*]—which was fought following morning and Father killing his opponent then fled to London and stayed there for a short time after which he took sailing vessel to New York. After reaching New York kept going to Appleton, Wis. where he sent for Mrs. W., and soon after her arrival Houdini was born on 6th April 1874. And he was named Ehrich Prach after Prince Ehrich."

Houdini, as we now know, wasn't born in America, and he was alive when Mayer Samuel left Hungary. Hardeen had his brother's distaste for letting the facts get in the way. Still, the story is so good that there remain Houdini chasers who believe in the duel and continue to seek evidence to support it.

The most likely story is that Mayer Samuel, like many Jews throughout Eastern Europe in the nineteenth century, felt thwarted by rampant anti-Semitism and was drawn to the chance for freedom in the United States. He had wanted to practice law, but there was no such opportunity in Hungary, where Jews were not even considered full citizens until 1867. Two million Jews immigrated to America between 1870 and 1920 in search of opportunity. Mayer Samuel was one of them.

Mayer Samuel was probably in America for two years before he ended up in Appleton, a surprisingly progressive and tolerant university town—so much so that Catholic, Episcopal, Methodist, and Baptist congregations helped raise the money to build the city's first temple for a few dozen Jewish families. Mayer Samuel was hired as the Zion Congregation's first rabbi before construction was even finished.

He certainly looked the part. The local paper on several occasions talked about his "venerable appearance."

Buoyed by his place of honor in the Appleton community along with a generous $750 a year salary, Mayer Samuel sent for his family in Budapest. Cecilia, Ehrich, and four brothers came over the Atlantic on the SS *Frisia* and arrived in New York on July 4, 1878. They reached Appleton a couple of months later. Ehrich was four. And as he would remember it, the next four years would be the happiest of his childhood. Mayer Samuel was a respected rabbi. Ehrich attended school. He had numerous friends. The family ate well.

And then, in August of 1882, Mayer Samuel was fired and sent Ehrich Weiss's life careening.

No one knew at that moment that Mayer Samuel would never again have a steady job.

"Some of the leading factors in the congregation, thinking he had grown too old to hold his position, supplanted him for a younger man," Houdini wrote in "Harry Houdini by Harry Houdini." "And one morning father awoke to find himself thrown upon the world, his long locks of hair having silvered in service, with seven children to feed, without a position, and without any visible means of support."

The reason for Mayer Samuel's dismissal is vague. For years, it was thought to be the language barrier—he never did grow comfortable with English and led prayers in German instead. But Appleton historian Tom Boldt argues that the man who replaced Mayer Samuel—a Rabbi Solomon—was German too and, as Boldt says, "I doubt he was able to speak English any better than Rabbi Weiss."

A more likely reason comes from a member

of Rabbi Weiss's congregation, Beatrice Ullman Frank, who said that while he was a good man, he was out of touch with the times. The congregants wanted a rabbi who didn't just speak the language of the new world but also understood and represented the new world. Mayer Samuel, she said sadly, was of another time.

Mayer Samuel never fully recovered from his firing. After failing to find work in Appleton, he moved the family to Milwaukee and sold himself as a rabbinical jack of all trades, offering his services as a cantor leading prayers, a rabbi working in the community, a mohel performing circumcisions, and a kosher butcher. There were few customers. He tried opening a Jewish school. He sometimes traveled to speak, once going to Louisville, Kentucky, to talk about how "The human soul will never die." But there was never enough work. The family moved from apartment to apartment in Milwaukee, shack to shack, staying barely one step ahead of the landlords. When a particularly brutal Wisconsin winter hit, the family appealed to the Hebrew Relief Society for coal. Ehrich quit school and took on odd jobs, shining shoes, delivering messages, and selling newspapers.

When thinking back to those times, Houdini wrote bitterly: "Such hardships and hunger became our lot that the less said on the subject, the better."

The less said on the subject, the better. This was more or less Houdini's policy about his father as well. Even in his later years, long after Mayer Samuel had died, he played the role of the dutiful son. Every year, on the anniversary of his father's death, Houdini found a synagogue, lit a yahrzeit candle in his memory, and said the Mourner's Kaddish. He rarely spoke about his father, though he did on occasion praise his father's legacy and scholarship (once, when asked to name his favorite writer in a questionnaire, Houdini wrote "My father").

"I think he has given me my success," Houdini told a *Cincinnati Star* reporter in 1916. "When he died, he asked me to pray for him every night. He would watch over me and assure my success. I have followed his request."

Beyond such traditions and platitudes, though, it is striking how little emotion Houdini showed when discussing Mayer Samuel. He often said that his greatest ambition in life was to support his mother, but he seemed every bit as determined to be the opposite of his father. Mayer Samuel could not speak English; Houdini worked tirelessly to perfect his own. Mayer Samuel could not find work; Houdini never stopped working. Mayer Samuel could not support his family; Houdini fought for every dollar and said that his most significant achievement was his ability to support and spoil his mother.

Houdini regularly told only one story about his father: The story of the day Ehrich Weiss turned twelve. He remembered his father calling him into a room. This version appeared in Houdini's 1926 souvenir program:

> "My boy," Mayer Samuel told his son, "I am poor in this world's goods but rich in the wonderful woman God gave as my wife and your mother—rich also in the children we have brought into the world and raised to sturdy manhood. Promise me, my boy, that after I am gone your dear mother will never want for anything. Promise that you will make her declining days as carefree and comfortable as I have tried to make them."
>
> "And," Houdini remembered, "with all my heart and soul I gave that promise."

The next morning, the story goes, Ehrich Weiss ran away from home.

And this story, unlike so many others, is true. He definitely did run away from home. One of the most famous Houdini collectibles is the postcard he sent to his mother:

> Dear Ma,
>   I am going to Galvaston [sic], Texas, and I will be home in about a year. My

best regard to all. Did you get my picture?
If you didn't write to Mead Bros., Wood
Stock, Ill.

Your truant son,
Ehrich Weiss

In fact, Ehrich did not go to Galveston. Even
Houdini was baffled by why he wrote that (he
scribbled "I was on my way to Texas?" on the
card before putting it into a scrapbook). Instead,
he went to Kansas City. Silverman theorized he
actually might have run away twice. We do know
that at one point he found himself in Delavan,
Wisconsin, about sixty miles southwest of
Milwaukee. He probably went there to catch on
with a circus; at the time Delavan was the winter
home for more than twenty circuses including
one named for P. T. Barnum. But he couldn't
find work and was instead taken in by a couple,
Thomas and Hannah Flitcroft. For many years
afterward, he sent Hannah Flitcroft gifts from
around the world.

In all, the runaway was a failure. He shined
shoes and found odd jobs and tried to make
enough money to help support the family. He
could not. He returned home in time to join
his father on what would be the last gambit
of Mayer Samuel's life: they moved together
to New York to try and finally make a life in
America.

"I can't tell you the power of Houdini running away, how much that changed my life," Dorothy says. We are now at Dorothy and Dick's Houdini Museum of Scranton. The slogan here is "The Only Building in the World Dedicated to Houdini," which isn't technically true. There are Houdini museums in New York, Budapest, Appleton, Toronto, Las Vegas, and elsewhere. But Dick and Dorothy would argue, with good reason, that there is no building in the world quite so dedicated to Houdini as theirs.

Dorothy and Dick are both cheerfully obsessed with him. Dick's obsession comes from his father, who had seen Houdini perform and shortly afterward started stockpiling collectibles. Dick picked up from there. In his colorful life, Dick Brookz has been a standup comic, a magician, a talent manager, a professional blackjack player, and a taxicab owner. He founded New York's Magic Towne House (once among the most famous magical theaters in the country). He and Dorothy bought a soap opera acting school. More than once, Dick was on the brink of stardom, but fame brushed past. Dick says he has no regrets.

Dorothy's connection to Houdini takes a bit more explanation. One day, after deciding that there was no way to escape her abusive father, she made a fateful decision. She stood by the side of the road, waited for a truck to come barreling forward, and she jumped in front of it. Her timing was off. The truck screeched to a stop.

"The driver was pretty mad at first," Dorothy says. "But then he sat down next to me on the curb, and he talked to me. I don't think I'd ever had an adult just talk to me like that. He asked me why I would do something like that. I said that I wanted to die. I didn't go into details about my father or anything else. I just said I wanted to die. I don't remember if I was crying. I'm sure I was crying.

"He told me that I couldn't do that to someone else, that if he had hit me and killed me, he would never have been able to live with that. I had not thought of that. And then he said something to me that I have never forgotten. He said, 'Don't do this. I know you can become something. I have faith in you.' "

Dick looks over at Dorothy.

"Well," he says, "the guy sure was right about that."

And it was right around that time that Dorothy saw a magician perform in the theater-like auditorium at her school.

"I don't even remember what tricks he did or if he was any good," Dorothy says. "I only remember how beautiful it was. Red velvet curtains. I'll never forget the red velvet curtains.

"He performed, and what I remember is that the wiseguys in the class, the ones who never shut up, they had this look on their faces. Wonder. That's what it was. I think I was more amazed at the looks on those boys' faces than I was by the magic itself. I wanted to make people feel like that. I went to my teacher after that show and said, 'What is that? I want to be that.' And the teacher said, 'No, no, girls don't do magic.' "

She barely even heard what the teacher said, she was so excited. Dorothy rushed to the library and searched for a book about the only magician she had ever heard of. She looked everywhere but couldn't find anything about him.

"Can I help you, dear?" the librarian said.

"I'm looking for a book about a magician," she said tentatively. "Whodini?"

"No, dear, it's Houdini with an *H*," the librarian said, and she took Dorothy over to find the one Houdini book in Erie Public Library. It was called *Houdini on Magic*, by Walter B. Gibson. Dorothy raced home to read Houdini's own words about jail escapes, handcuff escapes, the Chinese Water Torture cell, interaction with other magicians, efforts to expose spiritualists. It mesmerized her. And Dorothy taught herself how to do some of Houdini's simple tricks like the Hypnotic Match Box and the Card in Egg and the Coin Balanced on a Sword. She learned the secret to Sawing a Woman into Twins, the trick she would later change into Sawing a Man into Twins.

But beyond the tricks, beyond the illusions,

beyond the mystery and excitement of Harry Houdini's life, there were seven words that exploded her imagination, and she read them to herself over and over and over.

"Young Ehrich ran away with the circus . . ."

That, she realized, was her answer. Dorothy Dietrich was not much older than Ehrich Weiss when she approached an older boy in the neighborhood and asked him to take her to New York City. She had saved up some money. She had a knack for doing various kinds of magic. She sensed that she was pretty. She would figure out the rest later.

"You figure, here's this guy—Ehrich Weiss—who leaves home at twelve years old, and he becomes Houdini," she says. "So, I thought, *that's what I should do*. It really was like that. It seemed normal. If that guy did it that many years ago, what's the worst thing that could happen to me?"

She realizes now that many horrible things could have happened to her, but her confidence never faltered. Dorothy was born with several of Houdini's traits: she was resourceful and relentless. Most of all, she was fearless. She found a job as a magician for the Westchester Department of Parks. One thing led to another led to another. The novelty of a woman magician intrigued a lot of people. In time, she performed on television and in big theaters. Eventually, she and Dick opened up the Houdini Museum of Scranton, where they perform daily in the summer and by appointment the rest of the year.

"Sometimes," she says, "I think Houdini lives inside me."

BAHL YAHN,
THE STRONG MAN

Harry Houdini loved to write fiction. He was dreadful at it, but he was earnest. And in his earnestness, he sometimes wrote more profound truths in fiction than he did when writing autobiography. There's a silly Houdini story titled "Bahl Yahn the Strong Man." It is, I believe, the most revealing thing Harry Houdini ever wrote about himself.

The story of Bahl Yahn begins with a band of Hindoo musicians performing for soldiers in the East Indies. One of the musicians is a young and impossibly light woman; impossible lightness seems to be her most notable trait. She is so light that a soldier begins to throw her in the air. The soldier is powerful and throws her so high that the crowd applauds his remarkable strength.

And then, in a sudden and rather upsetting plot twist, he drops her. The fall paralyzes the woman, and she would never be able to walk again (Houdini saw "Bahl Yahn" as a sweet bedtime store for kids, by the way).

The woman's bravery after being paralyzed moves the soldier, and he falls in love with her. The woman and the soldier—neither named in the story—have a son. He is named. He is Bahl Yahn.

72

Who is Bahl Yahn? Well, it isn't hard to tell. Bahl Yahn's father dies in the fourth paragraph of the story, much in the same way that Mayer Samuel died in the fourth paragraph of Houdini's story. Before he dies, the father tells Bahl Yahn: "You must grow strong and tall and always take care of your mother if anything happens to me," which, you might remember, is just what Mayer Samuel told Houdini just before he died.

And Bahl Yahn begins his adventure.

Around 1888, Mayer Samuel and Ehrich moved to New York; Mayer Samuel thought he might be able to get a job as a rabbi. The Jewish population of New York was exploding, jumping from eighty thousand to more than one and a half million between 1880 and 1920. Mayer Samuel ordered heartbreakingly optimistic business cards that read "Minister of the Congregation: Adath Jeshurun." It means "A Community of Approach."

"All religious services a specialty," the business card said. "Marriages and Funerals, also practical Mohel."

But there was no congregation. There was no work at all for a German-speaking rabbi. His life and health rapidly declined; he developed cancer of the tongue. The Reverend Doctor Mayer Samuel Weiss died on October 5, 1892, when Ehrich was eighteen. He left behind a wife, six children—two of them adults—and a mound of debt. Houdini recorded in his diary the heartbroken words of his beloved mother on the day Mayer Samuel died:

"*Weiss, Weiss, du hast mich verlassen mit deiner Keinder*!!! *Was hast du gethan?*"

Which translates to:

"Weiss, Weiss, you left me with your children!!! What have you done?"

In Houdini's story, Bahl Yahn takes his mother with him to the country, where he finds a good job working on a farm. Bahl Yahn does not want to leave her at home while he works, so he designs a chair that he can wear on his back—a sort of reverse BabyBjörn baby carrier—and he carries his mother around as he tills the fields. "She sat like a queen on his back while he worked," Houdini wrote, "for he was strong enough to carry her and work, too."

But such a blissful life cannot last. One day, some men see Bahl Yahn in the field and, noting how big and strong he is, offer him money and drink to carry water to their boat. Bahl Yahn gently places his mother under a tree and brings the water to the boat. He finds the sweetish, spicy drink that the men give him to be delicious, but it makes him woozy. In time, Bahl Yahn passes out.

When Bahl Yahn regains consciousness, he is lying in a boat, bound in ropes, and the only thing he can see are the stars overhead.

• • •

Houdini didn't like talking about his youth in New York any more than he liked talking about his childhood. "I prefer to pass rapidly by those hard and cruel years when I rarely had the bare necessities of life," he wrote, echoing his earlier words about Milwaukee.

He spent much of those hard and cruel years playing sports; he was an athletic marvel. His height, like most other Houdini things, is much disputed. Some sources list him no taller than five feet three while others have him as tall as five feet eight. Patrick Culliton explains the discrepancy by making the dubious but undeniably colorful argument that Houdini grew taller late in life, that he had spent so much time suspended upside down, escaping straitjackets and water torture cells that he stretched himself out.

Fortunately, in this case, unlike with most Houdini details, we have an answer. The results of Houdini's 1926 physical—obtained by the ever-tenacious John Cox—reveal that Houdini's standing height was a shade over five feet five, or 5 foot, 5.276 inches if you prefer precision (165.8 centimeters if you prefer metric precision).

But he was all muscle. Ehrich boxed competitively and later told a reporter that he would have won an Amateur Athletic Union boxing title at 115 pounds had it not been for an illness. As a runner he won an AAU one-mile race when he was officially too young to compete. He swam competitively.

As his powerful body developed, so did Ehrich's sense of himself. One of my favorite photographs is of a seventeen-year-old Ehrich Weiss wearing shorts and a Pastime Athletic Club running top, his left arm on a staircase rail, his right arm on his hip.

Eight athletic medals are pinned to his shirt.

The photo is a little bit blurry, but even so, you can pick up the seriousness of the young man. He glares straight ahead, no hint of a smile on his face, and he seems to be flexing every muscle in his body. "It is the picture of a scrapper," Ken Silverman wrote, "who feels he can never do enough, who wants all the medals there are and more."

But what makes the photograph so wonderful— what lets us peer inside Erhich Weiss and see the blossoming of Harry Houdini—is that he had only won three or four of the medals on his chest. The rest were fakes he had made for the occasion.

Bahl Yahn was brought to America, where he became a strongman for the circus. They paid him with new clothes and good food and an endless supply of the sweetish, spicy drink. Bahl Yahn no longer thought of the days before the bottle. He forgot his dear mother, whom he'd left under the tree. He cared only about the next drink.

One day at the circus, Bahl Yahn saw an elderly woman holding hands with her grandson. Something about that scene stirred emotions in Bahl Yahn. He realized that he had forgotten something important, but he could not make himself remember. He slept fitfully for two nights. On the third day, Bahl Yahn stopped drinking. He began to exercise again. When boys and girls came to the circus, they found a much happier Bahl Yahn.

Finally, Bahl Yahn escaped the circus. He fought a man for a five-hundred-dollar prize then slipped away, boarded a ship, and sailed home. It took many weeks, but when Bahl Yahn the Strongman returned to the farm, he found his mother in the care of neighbors. He returned to work in the fields with his mother on his back. "Ah, my son," she said, "it is good to feel your strong back beneath me, your strong arms around me."

Bahl Yahn replied that it is all well and good to have a stiff back and strong arms, but real strength comes from "refusing that which tastes good to the tongue but cuts out the heart and makes one forget duty and promises."

To which his mother smiled and stroked his hand happily.

Bahl Yahn did not become a children's classic despite Houdini's grandest hopes. Funny thing,

Houdini came up with this odd and awkward tale for kids when he had a real story, a true story, that is much sweeter. It happened in New York, when the Weiss family was at their lowest point. Mayer Samuel was dying, and he had lost all hope. "My father," Houdini wrote, "kept pacing up and down the room murmuring, 'the Lord will provide' . . . something to that effect."

"The Lord will provide" comes from the book of Genesis, it is the name Abraham gave that place where he was ready to sacrifice his son Isaac in the name of the Lord. These words offered hope for so many Jewish people after they immigrated to America, when it seemed that all was lost. The Lord will provide. The words comforted religious men like the fathers of Asa Yoelson and Izzy Beilin and Ehrich Weiss. They were rabbis and cantors and believers; their sons were not. The sons faithfully believed in their own power to provide, their own power of work, will, talent, and self-promotion. Asa Yoelson sang on street corners for pennies before changing his name to Al Jolson, becoming one of the world's great stars. Izzy Beilin played piano in saloons before changing his name to Irving Berlin and writing the great American songbook—"God Bless America," "White Christmas," and "Blue Skies" among more than one thousand other classic songs.

Ehrich Weiss shined shoes and was a messenger

boy before changing his named to Harry Houdini and becoming immortal.

The three would meet along the vaudeville circuit and form the Rabbi's Sons Theatrical Benevolent Association, a nod to their upbringing and the faith of their fathers. But they all broke away. They lived secular lives, and they married non-Jewish women, and not one of them put any faith at all in their fathers' old-world faith. Houdini, in particular, lived a life in defiance of what he saw as his father's "The Lord will provide" impotence. When asked to reveal his motto, he offered his own version of a different biblical verse: "Do unto others before they do unto you."

All his life, he raged against his father's inertia. That Christmas of 1891, while Mayer Samuel prayed for help, Ehrich worked tirelessly as a messenger boy for a department store. One day, he came up with a moneymaking scheme. He wrote down a couplet on a piece of cardboard and attached it to his hat so that everyone could see.

Christmas is coming
Turkeys are fat
Please drop a quarter
In the messenger boy's hat

"Everyone laughed seeing this poem on me," Houdini remembered, "and quarters, dimes and half dollars fairly rained into my hat. And at the end of the day a godly sum of money was there, all in silver."

Once he had gathered all the glittering coins—more than he had ever seen—Ehrich had his second bit of inspiration. He hid the coins on his body, putting them up his sleeve, behind his ears, under his collar. He slowly walked home, jingling with each step, and after he entered the house, he raced to find his beloved mother, just like Bahl Yahn did.

"Shake me," he said. "I'm magic."

Cecilia wanted to know what he meant by this nonsense. But he insisted, and she began to shake him, and coins fell from every direction. "Harder!" he yelled, and she shook him harder, and more coins fell, and Cecilia and Ehrich and all the rest laughed with delight. Houdini called this the greatest day of his young life, the first day he could remember genuinely making his mother happy.

"When she counted the coins," Houdini wrote, "she had almost enough for the rent."

There's a magic trick Houdini loved to perform all his life, particularly for children. It is called The Little Messenger. He would produce a tiny, handmade doll—Houdini's Little Messengers remain prized collectibles—and ask the child for a message to deliver anywhere in the world. The child would whisper something into the doll's ear. Houdini would wave his hand in a grand fashion. And nothing would happen. The messenger remained in his hand.

"But of course," Houdini would say, "we have to pay the messenger."

With this, he would ask the child to pay the messenger with an invisible coin. And in the next instant, the messenger disappeared.

METAMORPHOSIS

Here's why I can't find a copy of Patrick Culliton's book *Houdini: The Key*. He only published 278 of them. Why 278? Because Houdini's address in Harlem, the home where he lived most of his life, was 278 West 113th Street. If Houdini had lived at, say, 1050 Second Avenue, I'd probably have a book right now.

The more I learn about the book, the more desperately I need it.

"I believe this book is a key," Patrick writes on his website, "because the notes and references, not to mention the 940 illustrations, will unlock a thousand doors for anyone researching Houdini and his methods."

Sigh. I need a thousand doors opened. I scan Patrick's website. It is . . . interesting. The site clearly was built back in the days when America Online was cutting-edge and, I guess, people still used the abacus. The front page contains a bunch of hyperlinks in different colors. That's the whole design. Some of the links are Houdini related such as The Greatest Houdini Letter Ever, and Patrick Culliton's Notes on Houdini's Vanishing Elephant.

Others relate to Patrick's own life and the famous people he met.

"How I Met Muhammad Ali."

"How I Met the Music Man."

"How I Met the Lone Ranger, Clayton Moore."

Among the hyperlinks, Patrick has posted a photograph of himself as a young man. It is what you might call a typical actor headshot. Patrick has the top two or three buttons of his shirt unbuttoned, and he has a hairy chest, and he stares directly into the camera, making love to it, as the old line goes. He was handsome in a Hollywood way. You definitely have seen him before.

I write to Patrick Culliton again. I get no response.

TORRINI

Eight o'clock has just struck; my wife and children are by my side. I have spent one of those pleasant days which tranquility, work and study can alone secure. With no regret for the past, with no fear for the future, I am—I am not afraid to say it—as happy as a man can be.

And yet, at each vibration of this mysterious hour, my pulse starts, my temples throb, and I can scarce breathe so much do I feel the want of air and motion. I can reply to no questions, so thoroughly am I lost in a strange and delirious reverie . . .

. . . The reason for my emotion being extreme at this time is that, during my professional career, eight o'clock was the moment when I must appear before the public.

—Author Overture from
The Memoirs of Robert-Houdin,
Ambassador, Author, and Conjurer

Harry Houdini took his name from a man once considered the greatest of all magicians, the very Father of Modern Magic, Jean Eugène

Robert-Houdin. And to understand how this came to be, we must first understand a man called Torrini, the most enchanting character of the most enchanting book of magic ever written. *The Memoirs of Robert-Houdin* was first published in English in 1859. It was an immediate sensation and has remained so among young magicians for one hundred fifty years. The book probably inspired more magicians than any other. *The Memoirs* changed Ehrich Weiss's life.

In it, Jean Eugène Robert-Houdin tells the story of his life. He was the son of a clockmaker in the French city of Blois and a brilliant young man who graduated from the University of Orleans at eighteen. His father dreamed of him becoming someone important, a successful lawyer. The young Robert-Houdin, being a dutiful son, did study law for a time, but he could not stomach that life. He was a tinkerer, an inventor, and an artist. He became a clockmaker like his father.

This led him to magic in a bizarre way. One day, he went to a bookstore to buy a two-volume set called *A Treatise on Clock Making*. When he got home, he realized the shopkeeper had mistakenly given him a different set of books called *Scientific Amusements*. Robert-Houdin opened the first and fell under its spell.

"The way of performing tricks with cards—how to guess a person's thoughts—to cut off a pigeon's head, to restore it to life," Robert-

Houdin wrote. "I devoured the mysterious pages, and the further my reading advanced, the more I saw laid bare before me the secrets of an art for which I was unconsciously predestined . . . This discovery caused me the greatest joy I had ever experienced."

Robert-Houdin first began to practice the tricks he saw in the book. He quickly moved on to his own magical inventions. He did all of this until the story takes a strange turn; Robert-Houdin went to a fair in a nearby village, ate some of the food, and came down with a severe, even life-threatening case of food poisoning. He grew so delirious from fever that after leaving, he threw himself from a carriage. When he awoke, he saw a man who told him to be silent and to drink from a cup he held.

The man was named Torrini.

Torrini, Robert-Houdin learned, was not his real name. He had been born as Count Edmond de Grisy and he once had been the grand magician of Europe, performing for royalty and commoner alike. According to some magic historians, the Count de Grisy performed for Pope Pius VII, dropping and breaking the watch of a cardinal and then bringing it back to life. Others credit him as the first magician to saw a woman in half.

"He was the only son of a French loyalist noble, the Count de Grisy, who was ruined by the great political and social revolution of the last century," wrote Thomas Frost in his 1881 book *The Lives of the Conjurors*.

"Torrini was a skillful performer with cards," wrote Henry Ridgely Evans in his 1906 classic *The Old and the New Magic*. "He invented a trick called 'the Blind Man's Game of Piquet.' While blindfolded, he would play piquet and defeat adepts at the game."

What happened to Count de Grisy? Only after many days did Robert-Houdin learn the terrible secret.

The Count had a son, Giovanni, the light of his life. Count Edmond and Giovanni often performed together, and their greatest trick was called the Son of William Tell. In the Swiss folk story, William Tell was arrested and sentenced to death but was offered the chance to save himself by shooting an apple off the top of his son Walter's head with a bow and arrow.

Count Edmond and Giovanni twisted the tale. Instead of a bow and arrow, the father pulled out a pistol, but instead of shooting it himself, he offered it to someone in the audience. And the apple did not go on his son's head; Giovanni held it between his teeth. The Count told the audience member to take careful aim (Count Edmond was always surprised by how readily they aimed) and then fire at the apple (he was equally surprised to find that they did not hesitate to shoot).

After the smoke cleared, Giovanni stood upright.

The apple was removed from his mouth and cut open; the bullet was lodged inside.

The trick's setup was relatively simple. The pistol was loaded with blanks. And through clever misdirection, while the audience's attention was focused elsewhere, Count de Grisy switched the whole apple with one that already had a bullet lodged inside. It was perfectly safe. The count and Giovanni performed the Son of William Tell many times, all over Europe. It was, Torrini said, a sensation. Until one particular day.

"The pistol was fired," a broken Torrini finally told Robert-Houdin, "and the spectator, with cruel adroitness, had aimed so truly that the bullet crashed through my son's forehead. He fell forward with his face to the ground, rolled over once or twice, and—"

Torrini could not finish the story. Somehow a real bullet had been loaded into the gun. Giovanni was dead. The count fell on his son and shrieked in agony; he was pulled away by a mob. The courts were cruel. They sentenced Count Edmond de Grisy to six months in prison. And only when he was released did they tell him that his beloved wife, Antonia, had been so overwhelmed by grief that she died of a broken heart.

For a few bleary months, the Count de Grisy lacked the strength to live. He had lost everything. He was destitute. He was broken. Almost all of his friends had turned their backs on him. But one did not. Antonia's brother Antonio pleaded with Count de Grisy to reengage with the world.

"How?" the count asked.

Antonio pleaded with him to perform again. The count was never so alive as when he performed. He was so forceful in his pleas that finally, the count agreed to become a magician once more, but he could never again perform under his own name. And so he became Torrini.

Torrini traveled from town to town and performed for a few coins. No one knew of his dark and tragic past until he came upon Robert-Houdin, feverish and near death. Torrini understood that he had to nurse this young man back to health and teach him the secrets of magic. It was his penance.

And this was Robert-Houdin's first step into his destiny as the Father of Modern Magic.

The Memoirs of Robert-Houdin is a hypnotic book. It brings a romance to magic that no book before and perhaps no book since has matched. Robert-Houdin tells of his adventures, his triumphs, his inventions. He recounts the most famous magical performance since Moses turned his staff into a snake, when "at the special request of the French Government" he went to Algeria to show the Marabout priests that French magic was more powerful than their own. Many have written that Robert-Houdin's magic quelled a potential revolt, which isn't exactly right, but when it comes to the wonders of *The Memoirs of Robert-Houdin*, people can't help but get carried away.

Reading the *Memoirs* even now, you can feel the excitement, the awe, the eagerness that Ehrich must have felt: What on earth could be more glamorous than to be a magician like Robert-Houdin? What could be exciting, more intoxicating, than to put on a tuxedo—for Robert-Houdin insisted that magicians wear evening clothes and not wear the garish costumes of magicians past—and, with your own hands, create magic?

Robert-Houdin wrote that it was Torrini who created that excitement for him.

"Remembering Torrini's principles," he wrote, "I intended to have an elegant and simple stage, unencumbered by all the paraphernalia of the ordinary conjurer. Real sleight of hand must not be the tinman's work, but that of an artist's, and people do not visit the latter to see instruments perform."

The parting of Robert-Houdin and Torrini in the *Memoirs* is as touching and haunting as anything in magical literature.

"The moment of our separation had arrived," Robert-Houdin wrote. "And my old friend had been arming himself for it during several days. The parting was painful to us all; a father quitting his son, without hope of ever seeing him again, could not have displayed more violent grief than did Torrini when pressing me in his arms for the last time. I, too, felt inconsolable."

What role did Torrini play in Ehrich Weiss's life? In the days after Ehrich read *The Memoirs of Robert-Houdin*, he and a friend came up with a name for their magic act: the Brothers Houdini. They took Robert-Houdin's last name (they thought the name was pronounced hoo-DEEN rather than the actual ooo-DAHN) and simply added an *i*. Why the *i*? The common tale is that they believed adding an *i* to a name would mean "like." They thought Houdini meant "like Houdin."

But magical inventor Jim Steinmeyer has a more compelling theory. "It seems more logical," Steinmeyer says, "that 'Houdini' was a combination of the names of the teacher and his pupil, Torrini and Robert-Houdin. It's sort of obvious for someone who had read the *Memoirs* and patterned himself after Houdin and his mentor."

All of which leads us, at last, to the magical reveal, to that moment in the trick where you realize that everything you just saw was nothing more than a brilliant illusion.

There was no Torrini.

There was no Torrini. There was no Count de Grisy. There was no son killed by a bullet, no wife who died of a broken heart, no mentor nursing our hero back to life. The *Memoirs* was all a beautiful fiction, all of it, even the story of Robert-Houdin getting the wrong book at the bookseller. It was all a magic trick developed in the fertile and creative mind of Jean Eugène Robert-Houdin.

Robert-Houdin duped historians, who for the next century wrote about Torrini as if he had existed. He fooled his future biographers who continued to write about Torrini's influence on Robert-Houdin. And he tricked Harry Houdini. In time, Houdini would turn on Robert-Houdin. Late in his life, he would spend countless hours trying to unmask his hero and model. But that's later.

First, though, he was inspired. The magical words of Jean Eugène Robert-Houdin awakened in Houdini countless possibilities. He took on the name of two heroes, of Robert-Houdin and Torrini, and for the rest of his life he never fully grasped that one was telling sweet lies and the other never existed at all.

THE NAME

When I started all this, I had no idea where it would go. But I suppose I always hoped that, at some point, it would lead to walking through a cemetery in the rain.

The only trouble is that I have no idea whatsoever what we are looking for. My guide, John Cox, will not tell me. He promises only that it will be worth it.

"It's a surprise," he says every now and again and looks around to place himself. His sneakers squish through the mud. There is unmistakable glee on his face.

John Cox is an impossibly friendly middle-aged man with looks and mannerisms that make him blend into the scenery. You can imagine him standing at a bar and finding himself unable to get the bartender's attention. John was once a Hollywood screenwriter—his big credit is as cowriter for a Mila Kunis film called *Boot Camp*—but it wasn't the life he expected, so he quit writing and took on a more manageable and stable job at SGI Cinema Quality Control Services. He and his team review digital movies (mostly versions sent from the United States to other countries) and make sure that everything lines up and they are ready for release. He routinely watches the same movie (or, more technically, Digital Cinema Package) ten or twenty times. His record is *Zootopia*, which he watched seventy-four times, if you include spot checks.

He took that steadier job, in large part, so he could spend his time doing the only thing he has ever really wanted to do: study Harry Houdini.

"There is a tree, I know there's a tree," John says as we wander the cemetery somewhat aimlessly. There are, in fact, many trees at the Forest Lawn Memorial Park in Los Angeles. This is one of the most famous burial grounds in America. Samuel Goldwyn used to say that his studio, Metro-Goldwyn-Mayer, had more stars than there are in heaven. Forest Lawn now has more stars. Spencer Tracy is here, Errol Flynn, Sammy Davis Jr., Clark Gable, Carole Lombard, W. C. Fields, Nat "King" Cole, and Jean Harlow. The "It Girl," silent movie star Clara Bow, is here, as are two of the Marx Brothers, Elizabeth Taylor, and the baseball manager Casey Stengel. Walt Disney's grave is here as is Humphrey Bogart's. The beloved comedy team George Burns and Gracie Allen rest under one gravestone that says, "Together Again." L. Frank Baum, who wrote *The Wizard of Oz*, has a huge tombstone here. And Samuel Goldwyn himself is buried in among stars.

Many of the graves are hidden away in private

gardens, away from the prying eyes of the public, but Mary Pickford's headstone is enormous enough to be seen over the fencing. She was, perhaps, the biggest star of Harry Houdini's time. They called her "The Girl with the Curls," and the "Queen of the Movies." She won the second ever Academy Award. Now her gravesite, massive as it is, goes mostly unnoticed.

I offer John this thought as he leads us around the cemetery: Mary Pickford is all but forgotten, and Harry Houdini is as famous as ever. This sort of thought would normally get him talking at length, but he's so distracted by the mission that I'm not sure he actually hears me.

"This is definitely the wrong tree," he says, and he heads back to the car to look again at the map he had made the first time he came.

When John was twelve, he handcuffed himself and jumped into the family pool. He obviously did this because of Harry Houdini, but—and this may seem like a subtle point—not because he wanted to become an escape artist like Houdini. He did it so he could try to understand what it feels like to be Houdini.

You might ask: Well, what's the difference? And you should know the difference is everything to John Cox. He doesn't want to be Houdini and never did, but he wants to understand Houdini as no one has ever understood him. Few people have ever gotten that. Family, friends, classmates, everyone always assumed that John would someday become a magician. When he was eleven and got good grades in school, he asked his parents for a straitjacket. He used it to perform an escape on the short-lived *Toni Tennille Show*. But he didn't perform on TV for attention (well, okay, he might have liked the attention) or to build his career as a magician. He performed because, well, how could he know Houdini if he didn't know what it was like to escape from a straitjacket in front of a live audience?

"There was never really a great ambition to become a magician," he says. "That never felt right. I was always just wanting to do it because Houdini had done it and kind of experience it in that way. I should show you some of the articles."

There are indeed newspaper articles about the young John Cox's love of Houdini. After all, nothing mattered more to Houdini than to get his name in the newspaper, so nothing mattered more to John. The most compelling of the John Cox stories is one in the *Los Angeles Times* headlined "Hobby Turns Teen into Houdini Disciple."

"People say we are put here for a reason," the sixteen-year-old John Cox said. "And if someone said I was put here for Houdini, I'd believe it."

"Funny," John says. "I remember that was the one where I was announcing that I had retired from performing and wanted to spend my life researching and studying Houdini. I was calling myself a Houdini disciple. My hook was 'I'm in a line of Houdini disciples who worked to promote Houdini's name.' "

John pauses for a moment and smiles.

"I had this whole crazy philosophy," he says, "but the craziest part is that I think I was right."

He is right. John is the creator, proprietor, editor, designer, and writer of a website called Wild About Harry, the most comprehensive Houdini site in the world. Becoming the most comprehensive Houdini site might sound like a fairly easy thing to do, but it is a much more competitive field than you might think. Other contenders would include The Houdini File, and The Magic Detective, and Houdini Circumstantial Evidence, and Houdini & Hardeen, and Interval Magic, and dozens of others. These are not just history sites rehashing old tales or recounting Houdini's great escapes. They are surprisingly fresh and alive; they break ground, find new information, tell new stories. To people who run these sites all over the world, Houdini is not a figure of the past. He is a living, breathing, and modern phenomenon.

John goes several fathoms deeper than anyone else. He has averaged more than one story per day for the first ten years of Wild About Harry, and he's only growing more engaged. In any given week, he will write a dozen original stories about Houdini. His site has received more than five million pageviews. Some posts are rabbit hole investigations into Houdini curiosities. When did Houdini first perform his Prison Cell and Barrel Mystery illusion? What is the true story of a Houdini photo that just sold at auction? Some are explorations of Houdini's personal life where John will dig in to learn more about, say, the magician's relationship with Bess or try to grasp Houdini's sense of humor. John goes on adventures; he was granted a tour of Houdini's New York house. He reviews Houdini books, fact-checks Houdini television shows and movies, introduces exciting discoveries about the man's life. He also spends extraordinary effort creating the most extensive timeline of every single year Houdini lived.

He alerts his readers about Houdini events all over the world, and it's stunning how many are happening. Someone puts on a one-person Houdini play in Chicago. A magician reenacts a Houdini escape in Pittsburgh. A Houdini museum in Budapest has a ribbon cutting. A group in Cleveland puts on a Houdini séance. I came upon John's site when he advertised a Dining with Harry Houdini cooking class in Austin, Texas, which I attended. Chef Louis Ortiz taught everyone how to make chicken paprikash, Hungarian goulash, and custard bread pudding, three of Houdini's favorite dishes. A magician brought a set of handcuffs and did a quick escape act. Several Houdini stories were told and refuted.

I don't know for sure. But I think going to the class is what convinced John to let me into Houdini World.

"There are other Houdini disciples," John says. "Patrick Culliton is now the great Houdini disciple. Patrick is the king. But I sort of feel like maybe I've become what I said I was going to be."

It was a movie that changed John Cox's life, the 1953 Technicolor movie *Houdini* starring Tony Curtis and Janet Leigh as Houdini and Bess. In fact, it changed many lives. It crashed through America's sensibilities. "There was nothing else like it," the director Barry Levinson says. "Nobody made movies like that; it was revolutionary."

My own fixation on Houdini began with that movie as well. There's a scene in it that I have probably thought about at least once or twice every month: Houdini and his wife, Bess, are at a dinner for magicians. It is a critical juncture in the movie when Houdini has reluctantly given up magic for Bess. After dinner, the president of the magicians' organization announces a prize for anyone who can escape from a straitjacket (all of this is Hollywood invention).

"These are regulation straitjackets which have been loaned to us for this occasion by Bellevue Hospital," the man says. "No inmate has ever escaped from one of these . . . As you can see, ladies and gentlemen, one has to be a little crazy just to put on one of these."

Tony Curtis pleads with his on- and off-screen wife Janet Leigh to let him enter the contest. Bess repeatedly refuses. He begs. The rest of the crowd joins in. Finally, in exasperation, Bess lets Houdini go on the stage, and the contest begins. The other magicians roll around on the ground frantically and futilely; they make no progress actually getting out of their straitjackets. One of them fights the jacket so hard, he flies off the stage and crashes into the audience.

And this is the part that stays with me: Houdini just stands there. He stands motionless, staring at a spinning crystal ball attached to the chandelier, as if hypnotizing himself. Beads of sweat pour off his forehead. Finally, his right hand pushes through the bottom of the jacket. He reaches around and unhooks the latch in the back of the suit. And he is free. The audience of magicians goes wild with delight. Janet Leigh's Bess rushes over to give him a big kiss.

"You know, Mr. Houdini," the magic club president says, "no one has ever escaped from a straitjacket before. I've been a magician for over forty years, been to quite a few places, seen quite a few things in my time. But there was always some explanation, some trick. Tonight, there was none. There couldn't have been. Yet you got out."

The scene is not only made up, it's deeply flawed. Houdini did not escape from straitjackets by standing motionless. Quite the opposite; he was always sure to helplessly flop around much more than necessary, making it look like getting out was the hardest thing the mind can imagine. But the authenticity of the scene never mattered to me; it has burned in my memory. I tell this to John.

"Yes," he says as if he understands perfectly. "It's a powerful scene."

John then says there wasn't any one scene that grabbed him; it was the whole movie, everything about it. He remembers the date he first saw it—November 16, 1975. He was at his mother's boyfriend's house. Everyone else wanted to go to dinner, but a young John insisted that they stay until the movie was over. He remembers the place and the time and the moment so vividly that he can go back to it any time he likes. And so he does.

John is self-aware enough to note that while he remembers everything about seeing Tony Curtis as Houdini, he cannot recall the day or month or even the universal emotions he felt when his parents divorced.

"I know it was around the same time," he says,

and he stops as if something has occurred to him for the very first time.

"I wonder," he says, "if that was part of the thunderclap."

At that instant, Houdini overtook his life.

"I sometimes wonder," he says, "well, we weren't religious at all. I never knew the existence of Jesus or anything like that. Houdini was the first I heard of a miraculous human being. I don't know, the idea that he could be put into anything and escape, wow, that really stuck with me."

The day after John saw the movie, he begged for someone to take him to the bookstore at the mall, where he bought two books about Houdini. A month or so later, the most famous magician of the time, Doug Henning, memorialized Houdini by escaping from the Chinese Water Torture Cell on a television special. Then came 1976, which happened to be the golden anniversary of Houdini's death, and there was a Houdini television movie (Patrick Culliton played in it).

And by then John Cox was possessed. He thought about Houdini more or less every minute of every day. When John's father asked what he wanted to do on their weekend visits together—with everything on the table, ballgames, beach visits, trips to the mall, anything he wanted—John insisted they travel the dusty bookstores along Hollywood Boulevard in search of a book or pamphlet or poster that connected him even more closely to Harry Houdini.

"Looking through those bookstores to find a Houdini treasure," he says, "are some of the happiest moments of my life."

It is ironic that a movie as blatantly fabricated and stylized as Tony Curtis's *Houdini* is the one that set off John on this path. He spends much of his life now exploding Houdini myths. His most-read blog post was an epic takedown of History Channel's lamentable Houdini miniseries; John was so devastated and furious about the many myths it perpetuated that he had to break up his scathing review into two parts.

"After one night," he wrote at the end of part one, "HISTORY's Houdini miniseries starring Adrien Brody is on track to be the least accurate Houdini biopic ever made, and that's saying something."

And yet, the History Channel's Houdini was practically gospel compared to Tony Curtis's *Houdini*, which got almost nothing at all right. In fact, *Houdini* created the most powerful myth of all by showing Houdini die while trying to escape the Pagoda Water Torture Cell, the movie version of Houdini's Chinese Water Torture Cell.

Spoiler alert: This is not how it happened.

And yet, even now, John still loves Tony Curtis's *Houdini*.

"I jokingly call it the biblical version of

Houdini's life," he says. "It's not true in any of the details, but it is true, if you know what I mean. If you look at the superstructure of it, it's all true. He was a struggling magician for many years, met Bess, went to Europe, became a star, did jail escapes, straitjackets, became involved in spiritualism, and died suddenly at the height of his fame. He travels into a place of more intensity and fame than anyone who has ever gone before him, and in the end, he annihilates himself horrifically in front of people, in front of this wonderful woman, because he went too far. That is the story of Houdini. The story is true even if the details are not.

"You know what I love about it? He's so likable I think that's the part people miss about Houdini. He was not always an easy guy to deal with, but he was just so likable that people were drawn to him. It is in Technicolor. It's fun, and it's dark, and it's wonderful. It is, in many ways beyond the obvious details, the closest anyone has gotten to what I think Houdini was really like."

Back in the cemetery, John finally finds the grave marker. He shouts out something that sounds like "Eureka!" and gleefully calls me over. I look down at the ground, and there is a small marker, mostly covered in mud and grass. I get on my knees to wipe away some of the dirt so I can read it:

Dr. Jacob Hyman
1871–1942
UNTIL THE DAY BREAK
AND THE SHADOWS FLEE AWAY

Yep, this is the place. And the strangest part of all is I know exactly why he has brought me here.

Jacob Hyman is the man who (probably) came up with the name Houdini.

Let's talk about the name for a minute. Houdini! Would Ehrich Weiss be as remembered if he had lived exactly the same life but was named something else, something more or less grand, something like "The Great Ehrich" or "Weiss the All Powerful?" Maybe not. Howard Thurston faded away. The Harrys—Kellar and Blackstone—are mostly forgotten. Nevil Maskelyne and Eugene Laurant and Max Malini are known only to magic nerds. They were all famed magicians around Houdini's time; many magicians today would say that some or all of them were greater than Houdini.

But that name, Houdini, has rung through the years. Why? For one thing, there's something about three syllable names: Skywalker, Da Vinci, Kennedy, Unitas, Beyoncé, Dumbledore, Houdini.

The first of those three syllables, the eternal question: Who?

The second and third syllables: *dini*. Italian. Exotic.

Put them together: It's fun to say. Filled with mystery. Enchantment. But there's something more. Think of a game show or family trivia game and a question is asked, and you know the answer, you know it, you can see the person in your mind, but the name is just out of reach, just beyond your grasp ("I know it starts with an *E*!").

That could never happen to Harry Houdini.

The name is unforgettable.

Jacob Hyman and Ehrich Weiss did not plan any of this. They were poor kids who only hoped to quit their jobs at Richter's Sons' neckwear factory. They liked magic. They admired Robert-Houdin. They added the *i* to the end of his name and called themselves the Brothers Houdini. Ehrich Weiss (or Ehrie, as friends called him) became Harry Houdini. Jacob Hyman became the less lyrical J. H. Houdini.

They came up with the name together. But if you look closely at how things played out, it seems pretty clear that Jacob Hyman was the one who actually thought of it. Ehrich and Jacob only performed as the Brothers Houdini for a short while. Then they broke up, but each continued to do a magic act, each still calling himself Houdini. While Harry performed in sideshows and dime museums in the mid-1890s, Hyman went into the army. But once he returned home, Hyman began to perform again, and naturally insisted on calling himself J. H. Houdini.

This drove Harry blind with rage. He had worked relentlessly to make a small name for himself as Houdini. There had been more failure than success along the way, and Harry saw Hyman's return just as he was beginning to have some success as a betrayal of the worst kind. In 1899, Harry and Bess took out a savage ad in the *New York Clipper*.

OPEN LETTER TO THE
UNSCRUPULOUS FAKIR
Stealing our hard and well-earned Name and Reputation. We Warn You to Stop stealing our name or we will REACH you in a MANNER that will cause you to back out of the business with your FAKE ACT with Greater Rapidity than you entered it.

HARRY AND BESSIE HOUDINI

P.S.—And You Know We Can do so.

No, Harry Houdini did not play; if he thought someone was trying to steal from him (and he often thought someone was trying to steal from him), he lashed out with a fury that, looking back, seems just a little bit excessive. Here, Houdini seemed so racked with rage that he just began randomly capitalizing words.

But Jacob Hyman he did not scare easily. He

read the Mafia-like threat and promptly wrote a counter-letter to the *New York Dramatic Mirror*:

> The name "Houdini" originated with an act known as the Brothers Houdini, of which I am one of the original members. I have never received any financial remuneration or ever agreed not to use the title "Houdini," and in view of the foregoing you will certainly admit that I have as much right to the use of it as anyone under those circumstances.

To this, Houdini responded: "Perhaps he has. But he has no honor."

Houdini's bitter but quick concession strongly suggests that Hyman was the one who thought of the name. Houdini made very few concessions for anything or anyone. In the end, Harry Houdini ended the magic career of J. H. Houdini in what would become a trademark move: He sent his brother Leo to publicly challenge Hyman to escape from a particular type of handcuff. Hyman accepted the challenge, failed to get free, and suffered such embarrassment that he soon left magic and studied to become a doctor. In time, he moved to the Beverly Hills and married a once-famous silent film star named Lyda Wilcox.

In their later years, Hyman and Houdini reconnected and became close friends again.

That story repeats itself again and again through Houdini's life. His friends became rivals. His rivals became friends.

Jacob Hyman was hardly the last magician to use some of the magic of the name. Dozens of Houdini imitators through the years did not just shamelessly copy the act, they also stole parts of the name: Oudini and Howdini and Hardini and so many others. But even more, magicians whose acts were nothing at all like Houdini's have tried to channel some of the brand's power. There have been great sleight-of-hand magicians like Cardini and Slydini. Numerous modern magicians have come up with their own twist like Haydini and Mahdi Moudini and the Great Tomsoni.

In Norfolk, Nebraska, in 1937, a twelve-year-old boy named Johnny Carson read a magic catalog and was instantly smitten. He dedicated his life to magic. He called himself the Great Carsoni.

And it still continues today. In Washington Heights, a Marine named Tomas B. De la Cruz decided to try and use his sleight-of-hand talents and become a full-fledged magician. He called himself Smoothini, the Ghetto Houdini, and performed in bars. Later, after gaining some fame on the television show *America's Got Talent*, he slightly changed the name and began performing as Smoothini, the Hip-Hop Houdini.

And to think it all began here, with this man,

Jacob Hyman. John and I stare at this tiny grave marker for a while. "You would never expect to find such a big piece of magic history right here," John says. We jog back to his car to get out of the rain.

THE EARLY DAYS

By all accounts, including their own, the early magic shows of the Brothers Houdini were pretty terrible. There were numerous brothers who joined Harry. Jacob Hyman was the original, his brother Joe Hyman filled in for a while, and then Houdini's actual brother Dash (who would rename himself Hardeen) became a regular. Hardeen remembered the early act:

"The act started, I recall, with the flower in the buttonhole—Harry's buttonhole, of course. It included the trick of taking a handkerchief out of a candle and some card tricks."

Even in 1893, this was the sort of clichéd magic act you might see at a children's party.

But the Brothers Houdini had one thing going for them. They had Metamorphosis.

"The sensation in the lecture room," wrote the *Buffalo Commercial*, "was the pair of trick artists called Houdini Brothers. Their illusion, entitled 'metamorphosis,' is more mystifying than Herman's latest Chinese puzzle. In plain view of the audience, a man was securely bound with ropes, put in a case, and less than a minute afterward the case was removed, and another man found tied with the same rope. The transformation is puzzling and should not be missed this week."

The writer added: "Another novelty was the automatic giantess, Miss Matilda Cornstalk, who walked, danced and kicked higher than any other female."

Harry Houdini was nineteen years old when he got this first extended newspaper mention, and it deepened his faith that he was going to become a star. This is one of the most endearing things about him: Houdini refused repeatedly to accept that he was ordinary. He never wavered on his future as a great man, even when he was just a poor magician who spoke broken English and had a crummy act except for one ingenious trunk escape.

It is fair to say that without Metamorphosis, Harry Houdini might have gone the way of Miss Matilda Cornstalk.

Houdini did not invent Metamorphosis. Trunk escapes had been around for almost a half century. Their genesis is fascinating. You would never think about it, but when you see that familiar sight—a tied-up magician escaping from a trunk—you are watching a bit of Americana. You are going back to a time before the Civil War, to the beginning of what was called the American Spiritualism Movement.

That movement began with the Fox sisters. In

1848, Kate and Margaret Fox claimed an ability to speak with the dead. The Fox family lived in an old house in Hydesville, New York. Neighbors thought the house to be haunted, and the family admitted that they often heard strange sounds; sometimes, they even saw various pieces of furniture move on their own accord.

In the spring, Kate made a connection with the spirit in the house. She snapped her fingers, and the spirit startled her by knocking in response. Kate then asked the spirit to guess her age and twelve raps followed. She asked the spirit to guess Margaret's age. Fifteen raps followed.

Word of the Fox sisters miracle spread quickly, and people came from all over to see Kate and Margaret communicate with the spirit. And, sure enough, all of them heard the strange and eerie knocking sounds that so vividly echoed from the spiritual world. Before long, the Fox sisters taught the spirit to speak in code—each knock might represent a letter or a number. In time, the spirit would rap out entire words and phrases, messages from the beyond.

The Fox sisters gained followers and zealots. Many of the most famous people of the day—including writers William Cullen Bryant and James Fenimore Cooper, influential newspaper editor Horace Greeley and abolitionist Sojourner Truth—made the trip to Hydesville. The Fox sisters began to travel the country and to speak to other spirits before huge crowds. "The Fox family found that the rapping business would be made to pay," P. T. Barnum wrote in *The Humbugs of the World*. "And so, they continued it, with varying success, for a number of years."

They were so convincing—or, perhaps more to the point, people wanted to believe in them so badly—that even after exposers proved that the sisters made the rapping sounds by cracking joints in their knees and feet, and Margaret admitted to the ruse, many continued to believe. Spiritualism gained a small but persistent foothold in America, one that would rise particularly after American wars, when communicating with the dead seemed more urgent. Houdini's life continually intersected with the spiritualism movement.

What does this have to do with trunk escapes? The Fox sisters inspired imitators, hundreds of them, and the most famous of these were the Davenport brothers of nearby Buffalo. Ira Davenport Sr. was a police officer with delusions of grandeur, and he believed that if the Fox sisters had the power to speak to the dead, his own sons Ira Jr. and William must have the same power. To prove it, he held a family séance. Sure enough, the table shook. Spirits knocked.

Ira Sr. was pleased. He quit his job and took the boys on the road in 1854. The Fox sisters had been performing demonstrations for five years and had the speaking-to-spirits market more or less cornered, so the Davenports needed a different gimmick. They introduced the Spirit Box. It was a large wooden box—six feet high, seven feet wide—that was placed on top of sawhorses so that you could make sure no one escaped through a trap door in the floor.

There were various musical instruments inside the box—a horn, a tambourine, a guitar, and so on. The Davenports then entered the box and sat in chairs. Volunteers were called to the stage to tie them to those chairs. The brothers would encourage the volunteers to tie the rope tighter, to tie the arms and legs and midsection until they felt confident that there was no possible escape.

After the brothers had been immobilized, their father closed the doors of the Spirit Box. Immediately, eerie music began to play. Someone was inside playing the horn and tambourine and guitar, separately at first, then together, a ghostly concerto. The music would stop suddenly, and the doors flew open. The Davenport brothers were tied up tight, just as before. There seemed no other explanation: spirits were playing the music.

For a time, the Davenports' popularity exceeded even that of the Fox sisters. Then they made a mistake: they traveled to Europe where people, for whatever reason, were not buying into spiritualism. It was a disaster. Crowds howled and magicians lined up to expose the Davenports and send them back to America. One of those was Jean Eugène Robert-Houdin himself; he wrote a widespread exposure of the Davenport brothers, one that doesn't hold up very well.

"His explanations are sort of dumb," Jim Steinmeyer says. "He supposes, for example, that they can bring their fingers in, make their hands narrow, and slip ropes directly off their wrists. Houdini, rightly, laughs at him about this sort of thing later. But, of course, escapes like this were new at the time. Robert-Houdin had no experience with them."

This was the point. The Davenport brothers had unintentionally come upon a new and exciting magical form. After they returned home, two European magicians—France's Commandeur Cazeneuve and England's John Nevil Maskelyne—became famous for their trunk escapes. Maskelyne, in particular, was directly inspired by the Davenport brothers; he had seen them perform and within a year had created an illusion intended to reveal their secrets. Maskelyne found that people were less interested in learning the secrets and preferred to be amazed watching someone escape from ropes and a box. By the time Houdini came around to magic, there were dozens of trunk escape magicians.

One of those magicians was a now-forgotten man named Joe Godfrey.

You can search and search the vast array of

Houdini books—even Ken Silverman's extraordinary biography—and not run across the name Joe Godfrey. He went entirely unnoticed until the ubiquitous Patrick Culliton discovered him. It is one of the cooler discoveries in Houdini lore: it seems likely that the unknown Joe Godfrey launched the career and life of Harry Houdini.

Joe Godfrey was a small-time magician who went by the name of Godfrey, the Man of Mystery. He mostly worked dime store museums around Pennsylvania in the late 1880s and early 1890s. He began receiving a few newspaper notices in early 1893, which—and this is probably not a coincidence—was exactly when the Brothers Houdini were starting.

What was Godfrey, the Man of Mystery's act?

Well, that's the thing: he was Houdini before Houdini.

"His cabinet act is a marvel," wrote the *Pittsburgh Daily Post* of Godfrey. "It has never been duplicated in this city, although several persons have attempted to imitate it."

The cabinet act was essentially a one-man presentation of what Houdini would turn into Metamorphosis.

"He defies anyone to produce locks or handcuffs that he cannot get out of," the *Wilkes-Barre Record* reported. Challenging people to bring inescapable handcuffs? This was at the heart of Houdini's act for a quarter century.

"Godfrey, the Man of Mystery, laughs at prison irons and shackles, and ropes cannot hold him," said the *Scranton Republican*. These lines almost perfectly foreshadow two of Houdini's most famous slogans: "Love, in company with Houdini, laugh at locksmiths," and "Nothing on Earth Can Hold Houdini a Prisoner."

Godfrey was doing the act that Houdini would later make world famous. But others were doing similar things—what makes Godfrey so special?

And that's the connection Culliton made, purely by accident. Culliton used to own Houdini's Metamorphosis trunk, and he tried to find out everything he could about it. One day, he was talking with Houdini's friend Walter Gibson, and Culliton asked what he had asked others: how in the world could an eighteen-year-old without a dime in the world afford to buy the trunk to perform a trick like that?

Gibson offered a name that Culliton had never heard before. He said that Houdini probably bought it cheap from Joe Godfrey when the Man of Mystery decided to give up magic.

The discovery of Joe Godfrey is precisely the sort of thing that thrills and delights Houdini World. There's a constant hunger to find new information about the magician, any new tidbit that might open up his life in even the smallest way. The discovery of Joe Godfrey was a breakthrough among the Houdini zealots. The timing matched up perfectly. Godfrey disappears from the scene at exactly the time that the Brothers Houdini arrive.

Later, Culliton found another connection. He discovered a story written by Houdini's brother Hardeen:

"On the bill of the Palace Grimsby I note a man billed as Godfrey, the Man of Mystery," Hardeen wrote. "It can't be possible that Godfrey is the American that once performed the 'cell and handcuff,' act about 12 years ago at the old Worth's Museum. Must find out as I know him very well. The last I heard of Godfrey was of him having lost his voice and selling out his entire outfit."

A small-time magician loses his voice and sells off his magical trunk and perhaps handcuff secrets to an eighteen-year-old boy who is ambitious, desperately hungry to become rich and famous and, mostly, known. The boy turns out to be Harry Houdini. It's one heck of a story.

The trunk act may have been pretty old, but the Brothers Houdini made it new. First, Houdini gave it that regal name Metamorphosis. And then they performed it with pure speed. "Three seconds," Harry would shout to the crowd. "That's all it takes. In three seconds, you will see a miracle."

The miracle went like so: Houdini asked volunteers to come to the stage to tie him securely, using rope at first and later handcuffs and chains. (In the early years, Houdini actually asked volunteers to tie up his partner, but Harry soon learned that people wanted to see him escape.)

Before they tied up Houdini, he often put on a dinner jacket borrowed from someone in the crowd; this was an early indication of his imagination at work. The volunteers would tie him up, place him in a sack, pulling the drawstring on top of the bag to bind Houdini inside the Metamorphosis trunk. The trunk was then locked. At this point, Houdini's partner turned to the audience and said, "Watch closely for the effect." The curtain was pulled, there was a first clap and a second clap, and on the third clap, Houdini emerged, free of the ropes and chains.

Houdini and the volunteers would quickly unlock the trunk, pull out the bag, and reveal Houdini's partner inside, tied up precisely as Houdini had been—and, yes, he was wearing the audience member's jacket.

"In many ways, he's doing a cheap, ambitious young amateur's version of the Indian Mail," Jim Steinmeyer says. "Houdini didn't have the stagecraft. He didn't have the right equipment. But he was athletic and ambitious and came close to the original feeling of the trick, even surpassing it, through pure effort and will. Yes, trunk escapes had been done. But never quite with that amount of effort nor so successfully fast an effect."

Metamorphosis was not a full act. Houdini needed to do more, and he tried everything. He did card flourishes. He made birds appear out of handkerchiefs, and handkerchiefs appear out of birds. One intriguing act was called the Butterfly, though even Houdini experts like Steinmeyer and John Cox have no idea exactly what it was. According to an advertisement in the *Philadelphia Inquirer*, "the king of wonder-workers, assisted by Mlle. Ola, will present Europe's latest sensational illusion . . . the evolution of a caterpillar into a gorgeous butter-fly, illustrated in a most realistic fashion."

It did not last long.

For five grueling and often heartbreaking years, Houdini tried everything he could think to try. Only Metamorphosis connected with audiences. The other acts fell flat; even some of the illusions he later would make famous like the Needle Trick and the handcuff challenge sparked little interest. But at least there was Metamorphosis, and he would perform it as often as twenty times a day. His partners changed continuously— first it was Jacob Hyman, then his brother Joe, then Houdini's brother Hardeen. But one day all that stopped. That was the day Houdini began performing Metamorphosis with a tiny young woman with a high-pitched voice.

Harry Houdini had met Bess.

ACID ON THE DRESS

Ugh, that acid-on-the-dress thing," John Cox says. "Please tell me that you're not going to put that acid-on-the-dress story in the book."

You can't blame John: he has become the unofficial Harry Houdini fact-checker, which means he spends countless hours knocking down myths and half-truths. Any time some crazy new rumor about Houdini's life comes along—he was a spy, he was impotent, he had affairs—John gets a call and has to do the fact-checking. He fact-checked Acid on the Dress: it isn't true.

But in some ways, it is more telling than the truth. Bess loved that one. Bess told it, again and again, all her life, embellishing it a little bit, then a little bit more, changing this detail, adding that one. It's the story that Bess Houdini wanted people to believe.

And it goes like so: When Bess Rahner was almost eighteen, there was a magic show at the small high school she attended. Bess was entirely innocent then, all but unaware of the larger world. Summer was beginning; Coca-Cola was available in bottles for the first time. Pullman car workers were on strike. Grover Cleveland was president of the United States. "Say 'Au Revoir'

But Not Goodbye" was the most popular song in the land.

Bess was raised as a strict Catholic, which meant that magic shows—entertainment of any kind—were considered "wicked and unfit for the eyes of young women." It isn't clear how Bess convinced her mother to attend the magic show with her, but they sat together in the front row. The magician came out; he was, as you guessed, a handsome twenty-year-old Harry Houdini. He performed some sleight-of-hand magic to the delight of Bess and the quiet disapproval of her mother.

"I had never dreamed of such wonders," Bess would say. "To me, the performer was a marvelous genius."

Then the marvelous genius made a spectacular blunder. He knocked a beaker of acid off the table by mistake. Why was there acid on the table in the first place? Unclear. The acid spilled on Bess, ruining her dress. Bess's mother was so outraged that she stood up and began to dress down Houdini right in the middle of the show, even threatened to have him arrested. Houdini was mortified, his face cherry red, and he mumbled feeble apologies.

Then Bess whispered in his ear, "Don't mind Mother, I think you're wonderful."

"Do you?" Houdini asked with surprise and delight in his voice. Their eyes met and held, and for Bess, it was as if they were the only two people in the world.

A week later, Houdini showed up at Bess's house armed with a beautiful pink dress his mother had made. After Bess put it on, she sneaked away to be with Houdini.

"The dress is wonderful!" she shouted.

"You are wonderful," Houdini replied.

And they were off, wandering New York, two kids already deeply in love. They somehow ended up at Coney Island, and Bess was dizzy with joy. As night fell, Bess realized the hour, and she began to cry. She could not go home; the punishment would be too awful to imagine.

"If you were my wife," Houdini said, "they wouldn't dare punish you."

With that, before either one of them fully understood what they were doing, they walked into a pawn shop. Bess bought her own wedding ring (Houdini was predictably broke), and they went to find John McKane, the irredeemably corrupt but good-hearted boss of Coney Island. They were not allowed to get married without Bess's mother's permission, but McKane did not see their youth. He saw only the love on their faces. He arranged for the marriage. It was June 22, 1894.

That's the story. You can see why it drives John Cox mad; it isn't just untrue, it's entirely implausible. It's ridiculous. The story also falls apart with even the lightest fact-check; for instance, it would have been hard for the good-hearted boss of Coney Island to have arranged for their marriage because he was in jail that year for election fraud and assault.

The real story is that Bess was hardly that naïve. She was a stage performer (a member of the song-and-dance Floral Sisters), and she probably dated Hardeen or Joe Hyman (or both) before even meeting Houdini. But, alas, that story lacks magic. And Bess Houdini's life, she always believed, was magical.

Harry and Bess actually did have a whirlwind courtship. It certainly was less than three weeks and might have lasted just three days. They might have been married at Coney Island, though one of the more persuasive theories in Houdini World is that they did not get married at all but just pretended for their parents' sake.

One other part is true: as a Catholic, it was an act of rebellion for Bess to marry a Jew. She would say she did not speak to her mother the first twelve years of their marriage.

"In our simple Catholic upbringing," Bess would say, "a Jew was a person of doubtful human attributes. It was long before the growth of tolerance . . . but Ehrich was kissing me, and nothing else mattered beyond the spring in our hearts."

It was also an act of rebellion for Harry, the son

of a rabbi, to marry a Catholic, but his mother, Cecilia, accepted Bess as a daughter the first time they met.

And how did Harry feel about all this? Houdini was an inscrutable mix of romantic and cynic when it came to Bess. Friends noted that Houdini seemed to save his strongest emotions for his mother. When talking about Bess to reporters, he often played up the professional side of their relationship. "No one can realize what a great help she has been to me," he told one, then joked: "She started as my assistant, and I married her to save expenses."

Then again, he left mushy love notes for Bess all his life—she kept finding them for years after he died. And he always credited Bess for his success. The magician's life was particularly rough on Bess, who sometimes longed for a more stable existence. But no matter how little money they had, how few opportunities came around or how dire things became, she never stopped believing in the unlimited future of Harry Houdini.

"I would absolutely have given up the handcuff act had it not been for her encouragement," he said, and this is undoubtedly true.

SIDESHOW

Born with the pride of Lucifer, and a thirst for glory that amounted to an obsession, Houdini took the knocks of mischance with an optimism many could envy. He was simply convinced that he was great. Great at what, he had not yet decided.
—William Lindsay Gresham,
The Man Who Walked Through Walls

We need a guide to take us through Houdini's sideshow years, and William Lindsay Gresham is perfect. Gresham grew up on Coney Island. Technically, he was born in Baltimore, raised in Brooklyn, but it was Coney Island that captured his imagination and set his life in motion. Coney Island was where Gresham saw his first sideshow. It altered his life.

There, he saw "a stately Italian," as he wrote in *Monster Midway: An Uninhibited Look at the Glittering World of the Carny*, "who wore, attached to his abdomen, the body of a vestigial twin, the size of a two-year-old.

"I thought it would be wonderful to have a vestigial twin. I wouldn't have to work as hard as my father did, bossing around people in a factory all day . . . Bitterly, I realized it was too late for me to be gifted like the Italian gentleman, but hope surged up within me that someday I might get tattooed all over and so qualify."

That hope—that irrepressible hunger to become a tattooed sideshow carny—never left Gresham. He lived a tormented life. He joined the Communist Party and then grew disillusioned by it. Like Rick from *Casablanca*, he fought in the Spanish Civil War on the side of the loyalists. He attempted to hang himself with his belt and probably would have died if the hook in the wall had not given way. He drank heavily and self-destructively, and he could be violent. He was also just odd. In the dust jacket of his hugely successful 1946 novel *Nightmare Alley*, there is a sentence that reads: "Friends claim that they used to catch him strolling down Broadway on a summer evening magnificently clad in shirt, slacks and bedroom slippers."

Gresham was one of the lost souls of New York.

Writing alone brought him clarity and meaning. He hoped, at first, to become another Mark Twain, but his mind drifted to darker places. Gresham was a hard-bitten man drawn to the edges of madness. He could not write *Tom Sawyer*, so instead he wrote *Nightmare Alley*, the story of Stanton Carlisle, a womanizing carny who uses his sideshow mind-reading skills to become a spiritualist preacher but ends up being a drunken carnival geek. The unrelentingly dark story has become a classic of *noir* fiction and also a movie starring Tyrone Power. *Nightmare Alley* briefly made Gresham famous.

But Gresham found success even harder to deal with than failure. He felt intense pressure to write a book that could match the power of *Nightmare Alley*, and the effort all but destroyed him. He worked on his next novel for years before growing so depressed and angry that he burned everything he had written along with all his notes. His drinking grew worse, his behavior more unpredictable. His son, the writer Douglas Gresham, recalled the warmth his father exuded when sober. But as time went on, Bill Gresham was rarely sober.

"When Dad drank; he drank heavily," Douglas writes in his memoir *Lenten Lands*. "He became volatile. He became explosive. He would roar around the house, uncontrollable and at times dangerously violent. Once he broke a bottle over my head; he smashed to matchwood a good guitar when he repeatedly failed to master a difficult run . . . Inside the house was a sick, constant uneasiness, an awareness that nastiness lurked."

These days, Gresham is remembered—if at all—as the cheating and abusive husband who drove away his wife, the poet Joy Davidman. After Davidman caught Gresham cheating with her cousin, she left for England and fell in love with the writer C. S. Lewis (that love affair is retold in the play and movie *Shadowlands*). Gresham, meanwhile, was left behind in the United States to deal with the endless sequence of demons that haunted his life.

Through it all, he never stopped longing for the carnival life. He became a fortune teller. He volunteered to be the target in a knife-throwing act. He taught himself how to eat fire. He grew fascinated with witchcraft. And he studied magic. Houdini, in particular, enthralled him. When Gresham was a boy, he attempted to do various Houdini escapes—once almost strangling himself in the process.

Gresham was a broken fifty-year-old man when he decided to finally write his Houdini book. *The Man Who Walked Through Walls*, however, was not written for love. It was written for money, and the book is something of a mess. Gresham admitted in a letter to a reader that "Finding out the truth about a legend-builder like Houdini is like trying to chew your way through a coconut." He could not do any newspaper research because his eyesight had deteriorated to the point where he could not read type that small, so he wrote from memory, imagination, a handful of interviews, and the instincts he gained from what he called his "years as a fact-detective editor."

This led to some unexpected turns. For instance,

at one point late in the book, Gresham goes on a tangent about how difficult it was for Bess to adjust to life after Harry died. Then, inexplicably, he wrote this:

> One of the most destructive experiences a writer can have is to sell a novel to the movies after years of a grinding, hand-to-mouth existence. Like a deep-sea fish, accustomed to the pressures of the deep, when brought to the surface suddenly by a net, he often explodes when the pressure is removed.

Bess Houdini has nothing at all to do with this paragraph. She was not a writer. She had sold no novels to any movies. William Lindsay Gresham was writing about himself. Throughout the book, it seems, *The Man Who Walked Through Walls* is as much about Gresham as it is about Houdini.

"It isn't a brilliant research project," Jim Steinmeyer says. "But it's brilliantly written. You get the feeling that Gresham knows Houdini, knows him in a way that other writers do not. I think there's a reason for that. Other people wrote about Houdini as the great man. But Gresham wrote about him as a sideshow performer. And that, at his core, is what Houdini was. A sideshow performer."

Three years after *The Man Who Walked*

Through Walls was published, Gresham wrote his last book, one about weightlifting, and then he contracted cancer of the tongue. Shortly after the diagnosis, he checked into the Dixie Hotel near Times Square, a somewhat seedy place where Gresham had made many of the sideshow acquaintances who fascinated him all his life. He checked into room 2023.

And there he overdosed on sleeping pills and killed himself.

Sideshow performers captivated Harry Houdini in much the same way that they captivated Gresham. Houdini admired showmanship and commitment. The freaks, as they were called, were willing to tell any story, take on any identity, and endure any indignity for smatterings of applause and a few dollars and the show business life. Houdini could relate to that.

As you follow him through those early years with Bess, those years long before he became famous, you can see the Houdini character forming. He escaped from a barrel in Detroit on the same card as Texas Ben, the "phenomenal cowboy pianist who never took a lesson but can play any classical piece after hearing it only once," and Leah the Whittler, who could make "the most marvelous things out of wood using only an ordinary pocket knife."

In Pennsylvania, Houdini traveled with Whitlark

and Kaminsky, better known as the frogmen, along with Master Claudie May and his school of educated dogs.

Houdini opened for Steward, the legless and armless genius, and Frac Da Cameo, an intrepid gymnast. He shared the stage with Mazeppa, the talking horse ("The Wonder of the 19th Century!"), and the Dewitts, America's Refined Muscle Duo. On one dime store card, he followed John Rauth, the man with the longest head, and Carlos Davids, the human centipede. He performed with Count Orloff, the Human Window Pane ("You can see his heart beat!") and the world-famed Tyrolean Yodelers ("From the Alps Region of Romantic Switzerland.")

In 1895 and 1896, Houdini briefly co-owned a burlesque show called the American Gaiety Girls, where he worked closely with May Morgan, a 122-pound woman who offered to wrestle any woman in the crowd. He also worked with Cooper and Stewart, two "wholesale dealers in blackface comedy."

Houdini spent time with Charles Hermann Unthan, "The Armless Wonder," who could play the violin and the coronet, hit bull's-eyes with a rifle, and hustle at cards. He came to know Miss Emma Shaller, also known as "The Ossified One." Emma was four feet six and weighed forty pounds but, according to the advertisements, "performs the duties of everyday life just the same as any other lady, and yet is nothing more than a living shadow." Houdini became weary of Colonel Goshen, the giant with a twenty-four-and-a-half-inch neck. At one point, Houdini bought a gun for protection from Bill, the Dog Boy.

For a young and ambitious man like Houdini, there were lessons everywhere. A Japanese acrobat taught him how to swallow an ivory ball and regurgitate it on command. George Dexter, a barker at Hubert's Theater on Fourteenth Street in New York, taught Houdini the proper way to slip from ropes. But none of the sideshow performers fascinated or taught Houdini more about show-business than Thardo, Defier of Snakes. Not much is known about Thardo, Defier of Snakes; Houdini is the only known person to refer to her, and it is possible that he simply mixed up the name. He might have been confusing her name with Edward Thardo, who once traveled with Howard Thurston and was billed as "Thardo, the Mexican Knife Thrower, and Contortionist." There was also Claude Thardo, a vaudeville singer and comedian who made the papers after abandoning his wife.

Houdini's Thardo was "a woman of exceptional beauty, both in form and feature." She had a simple act. Thardo allowed poisonous snakes to bite her. Houdini wrote about her with great relish:

It was Thardo's custom to give weekly demonstrations of this power, by which the medical profession was invited, and on these occasions, she was invariably greeted with a packed house. When the moment of the supreme test came, an awed silence obtained; for the thrill of seeing the serpent flash up and strike possessed a positive fascination for her audiences. Her bare arms and shoulders presented a tempting target for the death-dealing reptile whose anger she had aroused. As soon as he buried his fangs into her expectant flesh, she would coolly tear him from the wound and allow one of the physicians present to extract a portion of the venom and immediately inject it into a rabbit, with the result that the poor creature would almost instantly go into convulsion and would soon die in great agony.

As hard as it is to believe considering the power of the act, Thardo soon disappeared from show business. But this was the lesson from the sideshow days that left the biggest impression on Houdini: audiences are fickle. You can't keep doing the same thing or they will leave you behind.

The Houdinis took their Metamorphosis trunk around the country, and audiences did eventually lose interest. When the husband-wife magic gigs dried up, they tried to make it as "The Rahners: America's Greatest Comedy Act." When that failed, Harry left behind the Houdini name and made a go as a sleight-of-hand magician called Harry Raynohr and a hypnotist called Professor Murat.

For a few days, he took on his most famous sideshow gig as Projea, the Wild Man of Mexico. This job required him to growl while trainers threw raw slabs of meat at him. After Houdini became famous, movies and books often played up Houdini's stint as Projea; the Tony Curtis movie begins with Houdini as Bruto, the Wild Man (where he is "saved" by Janet Leigh's Bess). In real life, Houdini's stint as Projea, the Wild Man of Mexico ended when he was hit in the eye by a piece of meat.

There simply wasn't a job in show business that Houdini considered beneath him. For a time in the late 1897, Harry and Bess performed as spiritualists for a traveling medicine show, the California Concert Company. The company put on shows to sell medicine that was "a cure-all for all mortal ills!" Looking back, it seemed that most people were in on the joke. "The week's engagement was pretty successful financially," Kansas's *Garnett Journal* wrote, "and we have not yet heard of any deaths resulting from taking their medicines."

Two lasting things came out of the California Medicine Show. First, Houdini became friends with Joe Keaton, who was the father figure in a vaudeville act that mostly involved Joe and his wife Myra falling down and smashing into walls and performing various crude acts of slapstick comedy. Joe and his wife Myra had an eighteen-month-old son named Joseph, and Houdini watched in awe as young Joseph fell down a flight of stairs and then walked as if nothing had happened. "That was a real buster!" Houdini said (according to the elder Joe), and the boy, who would go on to become one of the biggest stars in silent films, would forever be known as Buster Keaton.

The second was more personal. The Houdinis turned out to be quite good at spiritualism. Houdini was smart and quick on his feet, and Bess was trustworthy. And they worked at it. Before the act, Houdini wandered around local cemeteries to learn as many secrets about the town as he could. He paid attention to everything. He once saw a boy riding wildly on his bicycle, and that night he told the boy's mother that the spirits were warning about a future accident involving her son. A couple of days later, the kid crashed and broke his arm, securing Houdini's reputation.

Spiritualism was financially successful. Houdini said that they lived like royalty for a couple of weeks. But even when facing poverty and desperation, spiritualism offended Houdini. There was something blatantly dishonest about it. And this is the part that Gresham understood so vividly. On the one hand, yes, Houdini was a perpetual liar, but he lied to build his own legend.

Spiritualism was a different kind of lie, one that broke with his personal ethics. "The sideshow," Gresham writes, "has its own rules." Houdini did not want to alter people's lives. He did not want to give people false hope. He lived to entertain and to tie minds into knots and to leave the audience breathless and content and ready to buy another ticket for the next show. He walked away from spiritualism even when it was the best-paying opportunity he had.

And then, after he became rich and famous, he sought to destroy spiritualism altogether.

KING OF CARDS

Let's talk about playing cards. There is a pack on my desk as I write this. I pick it up every now and again to practice cutting the deck with one hand—I am no good at this. I might work on the color change, turning the red jack black, turning the black ace red—I am no good at this either. I put the deck down, write a few words, but it calls to me, always, challenging me to improve my in-the-hand riffle shuffle or to cut four queens out of the deck, a feat that I never get even close to right.

Few things in the world can be more magical— or, I suppose, less magical—than fifty-two playing cards, four suits, two through ten, jacks, queens, kings, and aces. On the less magical side, you have your Uncle Johnny, who asks you to pick a card, any card. Is this your card? How about this one? But to watch an artist at work with cards—to watch the late Ricky Jay or the fantastic younger close-up magician Joshua Jay (no relation) or the man many consider the greatest card magician on earth, Juan Tamariz— is to experience perhaps one thousand years of history. People have used playing cards through the centuries to tell fortunes, to decide fates, to challenge each other in drinking games and, in the case of Ricky Jay, "to penetrate the thick pachydermatous outer watermelon layer." Jay gained his fame originally with his unique ability to throw playing cards fast and far—he wrote a book called *Cards as Weapons*—but his art was sleight-of-hand magic. He would work with cards for hours every day, shuffling without shuffling, mixing without mixing, cutting and nullifying, seeking a particular kind of perfection, all the while his hands were surrounded by mirrors so that he could see how it looked from every angle.

"Watching Ricky just work with cards," Jay's friend, actor Joe Mantegna says, "was like watching a great ballet dancer or a great baseball pitcher work."

"Nothing," Ricky himself said, "brings more joy than just working with a deck of cards."

Card tricks draw in the most diverse group of people. Take Jen Kramer. She is a professional magician who does a magic stage show at the Westgate Hotel in Las Vegas. Her act involves much more than just card tricks. But she, like many of the most successful magicians, is, at heart, a card magician.

This is unusual for several reasons, including an obvious one: Jen is a young woman obsessed by an art form that has long been the domain of men. It isn't just that a vast majority of magicians have been men (and the vast majority of their assistants were women); the very cliché at the heart of card magic is that boys who can't find dates do card tricks. The legendary director Orson Welles, one of those boys who would spend countless hours working on his card magic, told the archetypal story of the time he tried to win a woman's heart with a card trick:

> I remember once doing a miracle rather in the style of Houdini, a humble little miracle that cost me seventy-five dollars to do in honor of the young lady I was courting. And this was the miracle. I asked her—it was three o'clock in the afternoon, Central Park—if she would take a card, any card. All ladies know how boring this is, but I didn't know it was boring, and I asked her to take a card.
>
> She took the card I wanted her to, and I asked her if she would like it in her purse or in my pocket or would like it written in the sky? She said written in the sky. And I pointed à la Houdini, to the heavens. And she looked up and there, sure enough, written in the heavens over New York, was the seven of hearts. I had hired a sign writer, a skywriter, one of those airplanes with the smoke, given him seventy-five dollars to write the name of the card in the sky.

And as I say, she said, "Well, you must have seen it up there before you did the trick."

But Jen Kramer's insistence on becoming a magician is unusual beyond her gender. She's also brilliant, a Yale-educated New Yorker, the daughter of two lawyers. She has a joke in her act that goes something like this: "If you happen to see my parents, can you please tell them that I'm a neurosurgeon? That's the story I'm going with; I do the card tricks to keep the fingers nimble."

In truth, she knew she would be a magician from the time she was ten years old. That was when her Uncle Steve—it's always an uncle, isn't it?—gave her one of the classic books of sleight-of-hand magic, Jean Hugard's *The Royal Road to Card Magic*. It is one of those books that separate magicians from the rest. Many hobbyists think it might be fun to do a few magic tricks and so they pick up the book. They then read the ultra-specific directions—"Stand with your left side to the audience holding the deck upright in your left hand, the bottom card facing the onlookers, between the first phalanx of your thumb on one side, a little below the middle of that side, and the first phalanges of your index and middle fingers on the other side"—and decide that doing card tricks does not sound all that great, and they move on.

But a few really do see the royal road. Jen was one of those people.

"I can remember sitting on the floor in my childhood bedroom," she says, "and I'm reading the same passage four or five times to figure it out. 'Do I take the third finger or the fourth finger and put it at a forty-five-degree angle?' And I loved it. I loved every minute of it. The harder it was, the more I loved it."

Card magic fit the ordered way her mind worked. When Jen was eleven, she and her parents were on a train heading into New York. There were no seats left, so she walked up and down the aisle for hours, performing card tricks for the other passengers. She loved the looks on their faces, and she realized for the first time that magic wasn't about fooling people, not exactly. If she did it right, she sparked wonder in. That did it.

When Jen graduated from high school, she chose Yale (over Stanford, Princeton, and all the biggies) because it reminded her most of the Hogwarts School of Witchcraft and Wizardry from the Harry Potter books. She started the Yale Magic Club more or less the day she arrived. Every class she took was in preparation of becoming a magician. And as soon as she graduated, she moved to Las Vegas because that's what you do if you are serious about becoming a stage magician.

What does all this card talk have to do with Houdini? Well, everything. When Jen Kramer was young and still dreaming of magic, she would look up at a poster that she had on her bedroom wall.

"That poster was probably in the room of every kid who ever wanted to be a magician," Jen Kramer says. "It's a cliché. I'll bet ninety percent of the kids who dream of becoming a magician have that poster on the wall, and we stare at it endlessly."

She was right. Joshua Jay had the same poster on his wall. The marvelous Australian magician Cosentino had the same poster on his wall. Almost every person I spoke with had the same poster on their wall.

The poster is of Harry Houdini as the "King of Cards."

"The irony is," Joshua Jay says, "Houdini was probably pretty terrible with cards."

Houdini was in the room for perhaps the most famous card trick in the history of magic. In many ways, he played the pivotal role in the story. But—and this is important—Houdini didn't actually perform the trick.

The year was 1922, and Houdini was famous beyond even his grandest dreams (and he'd always had grand dreams). He was forty-eight years old, and he had escaped from countless chains, from hundreds of prisons, from death traps and impregnable fortresses. He had walked through walls and entertained kings and made elephants disappear. He had made Hollywood movies. Three years earlier, Funk & Wagnalls *New Standard Dictionary* added a word:

> houdinize, vt—to release or extricate oneself from (confinement, bonds, or the like) as by wriggling out.

Houdini's fame made him the center of attention in every room, and so it was on this day. There were several others milling around. One of those was a twenty-eight-year-old Canadian who was almost entirely unknown, only just beginning to make a name for himself in the backrooms of New York magic shops. His name was Dai Vernon.

Houdini and Vernon would, each in his own way, become perhaps the two most influential magicians of the century.

We know about Houdini's influence, his everlasting fame, and his overpowering impact among so-called laymen, which is the magicians' term for muggles.

But if you go to a magic convention filled with young magicians—I am at one now, Magifest in Columbus, the oldest magic convention in the United States—Houdini is all but absent. Vernon is the hero here. His spirit hovers over everything and everyone. At this very moment, the lobby of the Crowne Plaza is filled with hundreds of magicians, young and old, each with a deck of cards, each showing off their best ambitious card routine, they're twisting the aces, they're doing a series of perfect Faro shuffles (a skillful move that requires cutting the deck precisely in half and then pushing the cards together, so they perfectly intertwine). This is Dai Vernon's world.

"If you want to be an artist," Vernon used to tell young magicians, "you must devote your life to it." That's what Vernon did. He was born in 1894, twenty years after Houdini, and from a young age he was drawn to the artistry of prestidigitation, a word that through the years has often been used interchangeably with "magic," but is, in fact, slightly different. Prestidigitation literally means nimble (from French word *preste*) and finger (from Latin *digitus*). It is more about the art of sleight of hand.

Vernon spent countless hours working his nimble fingers. He considered every moment he wasn't practicing squandered. "I'm seventy-eight years old, and I've been studying magic for seventy-two years," he told a reporter. "I wasted the first six years of my life." The hours he spent perfecting his technique and developing wonderful new magical ideas were bliss. While Houdini was happiest on a stage, Vernon was his truest self in the back rooms, with other magicians, inventing, creating, and teaching magic.

"Sometimes time doesn't mean anything to me," Vernon told two of his many biographers, Bruce and Keith Burns. "There are times when I intend to go to bed, get ready, put on my pajamas, and suddenly decide to work on some kind of card trick. It's kind of frightening. I look out the window, and the sun is coming up, and I say to myself, 'I've only been here for an hour and a half.'"

Houdini's and Vernon's magic were not only different; they actually clashed. Houdini's magic was big and bold and larger than life. He believed that magic was about the performer more than the performance, and the bigger, gaudier, more dangerous, more thrilling, the better.

Vernon hated all that stuff. His idea of magic was pure simplicity.

"Anything mysterious is magic, something people can't explain," he said. "Something weird happens. Something strange. There's nothing strange about a guy getting out of a straitjacket. He wiggles around and tries to get the thing or whatever. Houdini didn't do any magic. He did escapes and put his name across. He couldn't do magic."

"What sort of magic do you do?" a fellow magician named Cliff Green asked Vernon when they were both young. Vernon artfully shuffled a deck of cards and put them down.

"Name a card," Vernon said.

"Three of diamonds," Green replied.

Vernon cut the cards directly to the three of diamonds.

"That," Vernon said, "is the kind of magic I do."

Vernon cared deeply about the smallest details of the magic trick. His longtime friend Howard Hamburg—a beloved card magician in his own right in Los Angeles—tells a story. He was doing one of the classics of magic, the sponge ball illusion. There were two sponge balls on the table. Hamburg would pick one up and put it in the hand of a volunteer—almost always a woman. He would take the other sponge ball and place it in his own pocket, and then he turned to the woman and said, "How many sponge balls are in your hand?" She said one, he would nod, and ask her to open her hand. Two sponge balls appeared.

"I noticed," Hamburg says, "that the effect was never as spectacular as I liked. That should be a wow moment, and it was good, but it was never as good as I thought it should be. So, I asked the Professor (everyone called Vernon "the Professor"), and he had me go through the trick exactly as I did it, and he heard me ask 'How many sponge balls are in your hand?' He stopped me. And he said, 'You're missing a word.'

"I said, 'missing a word?' And he said, 'Yeah, it should be 'How many sponge balls are in your hand, stupid.'

"And I got it. That was the genius of the Professor. I was making her feel stupid, like she had done something wrong, like she should have known better. And then he told me that the right way to say it is: 'How many sponge balls *should be* in your hand.' It was those two words, 'should be,' that made all the difference."

None of this parsing would have appealed to Houdini. He did not play for small moments. He thrashed and smashed and bet his life that he would get out and then he would. Houdini and Vernon saw the world so differently. As fate would have it, Vernon outlived Houdini by sixty-six years. And he spent many of them chipping away at Houdini's legend.

"Houdini wasn't a magician," Vernon said. "He was an ambulance chaser."

Statements like these—and Dai Vernon made dozens of them—have made him something of a villain in Houdini World. On the other hand, Houdini is often considered a hack in Vernon World. It is, in many ways, magic's great rivalry, the two sides of the magical coin.

The rivalry began in that room in 1922 with a battle of wits. Houdini took great pride in his abilities as a card magician. He did, after all, call himself the King of Cards and Cardo, and while he failed to win over many audiences as a card magician, he never doubted his own greatness. Houdini did gain some notice for the dramatic way he cut cards and for doing various fancy flourishes with them. In the "King of Cards" poster, he holds his arms out, as if asking for a hug, and playing cards are spread across both arms. Another shows his hands as he does some fancy one-handed shuffling.

But most of the great sleight-of-hand artists will tell you the essence of card magic—the puzzling and mystifying part—eluded Harry Houdini.

"He probably had some technical skill," Joshua Jay says. "There are a few movie shorts that show him making cards disappear, and so you could see some skill there. But there really is no evidence that shows he was a great or good or even average card magician. But he was Houdini. If you asked a layman, 'Do you think Houdini was a great card magician?' they would almost certainly say yes. But if you ask magicians who have studied Houdini, 'Do you think Houdini was a great card magician?' you will get a very different answer."

Houdini was so sure of his own brilliance as a card magician, he issued a standing challenge to all magicians everywhere: "Show me a card trick three times, and I will know its secret."

This was pure Houdini. Everything to him was a

challenge. He had a hundred different challenges going at all times. He had a standing detective story challenge: "Read a few paragraphs from different sections of the book, and I will tell you the killer." He challenged people to hold their breath as long as he could. He challenged people to match biceps with him. He challenged people to figure out how he escaped. He might have challenged people to hit him in the stomach.

But the card challenge was a particular favorite. Numerous magicians took the card challenge. John Scarne, who would go on to become a prolific author of books on card games as well as magic, was just a boy when he showed Houdini a marvelous trick. He had Houdini choose a card and place it back in the deck. The card somehow appeared inside Scarne's wallet.

"You caught me napping that time," Houdini told Scarne, and he began to smile. "I didn't even see you take the wallet out of your pocket."

For Scarne, fooling Houdini was one of the great memories of his life. He adored Houdini so much he refused to even tell his mother about his card trick success. "I had too much respect for Houdini to ever tell Mother that I'd fooled him," he said. "And, furthermore, if I did, I thought she wouldn't believe it."

Vernon, as we know, was not a Houdini fan, so when he challenged Houdini, there was a different sort of tension surrounding it. Vernon did not have Houdini choose a card. Instead, he pulled the ace of clubs from the deck and asked Houdini to sign it. Houdini was a bit puzzled by the tactic—Vernon was one of the first to have volunteers sign cards—but he wrote "H.H." on the front of the card as instructed. Vernon blew on the ink to dry it while Houdini looked on curiously.

Vernon put the ace facedown on top of the deck, and, very deliberately, so the action could not be missed, placed another card on top of it. He made sure that Houdini was watching closely. Vernon then gently riffled the deck with his thumb and showed that the ace of clubs had popped up to the top.

"Do it again," Houdini said.

The second time, Vernon slipped the ace of clubs into the second position; he tipped the deck so Houdini could see his card below the top card. He again riffled the cards with his thumb, gave them a quick shake and showed that the ace again rose to the top.

"You have two aces of clubs," Houdini guessed.

"Both with your initials on it?" Vernon asked.

"Do it again," Houdini said.

Vernon did the trick again, precisely as before, putting the ace underneath the top card and then, with a shake, bringing it to the top. At this point, Vernon had done the trick three times—the terms of the challenge, and Houdini was still baffled, but he refused to accept defeat. He called for Bess to come over and see the trick, a cunning but hardly subtle way of forcing Vernon to do the trick a fourth time. Vernon did it again, delighting Bess.

She asked him to do it yet again, a fifth time. Vernon repeated the trick.

Houdini still could not figure out how it was done.

"Again," he commanded. The other magicians in the room teased Houdini, asking him to give in. Houdini did not like being teased. And Houdini did not give in.

"Again," Houdini said again.

"This is it, the last time," Vernon said. He put the ace under the top card. He riffled the cards with his thumb. The ace was on top again. Houdini, without saying a word, left the room.

Dai Vernon's utter scorn for Houdini's card magic talents was basically unlimited.

"He couldn't even shuffle a pack without bending and breaking them," Vernon said.

"He couldn't do card magic any better than you could," Vernon said.

"He was not the king of anything when it came to cards," Vernon said.

Vernon's judgment of Houdini's ability as a card magician has become gospel among magicians.

"As a card magician," the magic historian Mike Caveney says, "Houdini was a butcher."

"He was certainly not a great card magician," David Copperfield says.

"You grow up looking at that poster," Jen Kramer says, "and then somewhere along the way you learn that he really wasn't very good as a card magician."

"He was a showman," Joshua Jay says. "But there is little evidence to suggest he was well versed with playing cards, and the things that we know 'fooled' him wouldn't fool someone who spent hundreds of hours holding a deck of cards."

So why does the "King of Cards" poster still adorn the childhood walls of so many? Why does it inspire so many young people?

The answer was in that room. Vernon may have had no respect at all for Houdini's card magic, but he performed that same card trick the rest of his life. He came up with a wonderful name for it: the Ambitious Card. But he called it something else too: the Trick That Fooled Houdini. That's why it became legend.

"In the end, it doesn't matter one bit that Houdini wasn't a great card magician," Jen Kramer says. "What matters is: he's Houdini. When I looked up at that poster, I didn't care if he was a great card magician. And I still don't really care.

"It comes down to wonder. It comes down to

communicate to people that what's seemingly impossible might not really be impossible. That's what I think about with Houdini. That's what everybody thinks about Houdini. He was magical. Everything he touched became magical."

MAGIC MADE EASY

If you want anything in illusions,
card tricks, or secrets write:
Harry Houdini's
School of Magic
INVENTOR ORIGINATOR AND
Manufacturing Magician.
221 East 69th Street
New York City
Send Money In Any Safe Way.
—*From Professor Harry Houdini,*
"Magic Made Easy"

In 1898, Houdini realized that time had run out. Time after time, through the years, he had given himself a deadline to become a sensation. "If I cannot make a name for myself in one year," he had told Bess so many times, "I will give it up and get some sort of steady work." They had tried to make it as magicians, as actors, as comedians, as spiritualists. He had called himself Harry Houdini, Harry Raynor, Professor Murat, Cardo, the Wizard of Shackles, the King of Cards, and Projea, the Wild Man of Mexico. Together, they fell through every trap door. Finally, in desperation, Houdini wrote to some of the great magicians of the time—Harry Kellar, Herrmann

159

the Great, Nevil Maskelyne—and begged for the chance to be an assistant. Kellar and Maskelyne wrote back that they had no openings. Herrmann did not respond at all.

"Things got so bad," Harry wrote many years later, "that I contemplated quitting the show business and retiring to private life, meaning to work the day at one of my trades (being really proficient in several) and open a school of magic, which with entertainments would occupy my evenings."

Houdini was twenty-four years old, and he saw himself following his father's dark path. Finally, with nowhere to turn, Houdini and Bess moved in with Cecilia. Harry's brother-in-law secured him a steady job at the Yale Lock factory.

Harry did open what he called a School of Magic; it eerily echoed Mayer Samuel's attempts to start a school of Jewish studies. Houdini promised to teach "all branches of Spiritualism, Slate Writing and Sleight of Hand." And as part of the school, he published a pamphlet called "Magic Made Easy."

Much of the pamphlet is stock magic dealer fluff; Houdini offered for sale marked decks, expanding flowers, and a magnetic magic wand no thicker than your finger. He offered many different kinds of books, including the *Dictionary of Dreams*, for "people who take pleasure in remembering and analyzing their dreams."

Then there were Houdini's personal touches. For fifty cents, he promised to teach anyone how to make a word appear on his or her arm as if written in blood. For a dollar, he would show a customer how to hypnotize animals ("This is very easy to do," he assured). He also offered a few free secrets in "Magic Made Easy," including methods for a few self-working card bits and some corny tricks such as how to pull a string through your neck and how to change a glass of ink into water. He also gave out a few free lessons for amateur magicians:

First practice, second practice, and
  practice before a mirror.
Never repeat your tricks to the same
  audience the same evening.
Don't tell them what you're going to do,
  as the effect of tricks become greater
  when they are unexpected.
Don't expose your tricks as they lose
  their value when too common.
Borrow all the coin you can and forget
  to return it. That's one way of making
  money. But there are others.

Houdini was not being entirely honest here; he had run out of ideas for making money. The dirty secret of "Magic Made Easy" was that Houdini had capitulated. He offered secrets, all of his secrets, including the Hindoo Needle Trick—"You swallow 40 to 50 sewing needles," he explained, "then a bunch of thread. And bring them up all threaded. One of the best and easiest tricks to do"—which would become one of Houdini's most famous and influential tricks. Magicians, including Penn and Teller, still perform the Hindoo Needle Trick.

Houdini offered it for five bucks.

He offered to teach anyone his entire handcuff act, which was still very much in its early stages. "You defy the police authorities and sheriffs to place handcuffs or leg shackles on you," he wrote, "and you can easily escape."

For a negotiated price, he even offered up Metamorphosis. He had given up.

But he caught a break, though it hardly seemed like one at the time: As far as anybody knows, nobody at all responded to "Magic Made Easy." The Houdini School of Magic closed before it opened. Houdini went on the road to fulfill a few lingering contracts, and in what he expected to be his last time on the road as a magician, he shared the stage with the Champion Lady Swimmers, Wertz and Adair's head-to-head balancing act, and the world's tiniest triplets.

As the year turned to 1899, Houdini performed in Chicago. He put forth a fifty-dollar challenge to anyone who could produce handcuffs that could hold him. An Evanston police officer named James Waldron came up on stage and locked a pair of handcuffs on Houdini's wrists. Houdini wrestled with them for twenty minutes before finally, shamefully admitting defeat. He soon learned that the game had been rigged; Waldron had removed the springs of the cuffs and put in a slug so that they were not possible to open. Houdini was outraged but defeated. This was the low point.

"I'm finished," he told Bess, as they planned their return to New York and a new life without magic.

Within the year, Harry Houdini was one of the biggest stars in America.

ESCAPE

And when Herod would have brought him forth; the same night Peter was sleeping between two soldiers, bound with two chains: and the keepers before the door kept the prison. And behold, the angel of the Lord came upon him, and a light shined in the prison; and he smote Peter on the side, and raised him up, saying, Arise up quickly. And his chains fell from his hands.

—Acts of the Apostles,
chapter 12, verse 7

It has always been one of my boasts— and who doesn't like to boast now and again when we forget that the hoodoo is in hiding—that I went St. Peter one better. He broke prison, but he had the assistance of an angel. I've broken numberless prisons single-handed.

—Harry Houdini, *Collier's*, 1925

BECK

We don't know the first time Houdini escaped from handcuffs, but we do know that in November of 1895, he first challenged audience members to lock him in their personal handcuffs. Few people had their own set of handcuffs—it was a gimmick more than anything—but it was an effective gimmick, and the audience seemed to like it. He added it to the act.

A few days later in Gloucester, a small town on Massachusetts's North Shore, Houdini had a real moment of inspiration: he walked into the local police station and challenged the officers to lock him in handcuffs. They did it, he escaped, and the whole thing got a brief mention in the newspaper. That told Houdini he was on to something; he generally measured his success by newspaper ink. A couple of days later, he went into a police station in Woonsocket, Rhode Island, and escaped from handcuffs in eighteen seconds. He received a full story this time. Then he did it in Worcester, Massachusetts.

"He unlocks them all with as much ease as if they were strings around his wrists," the local paper reported.

Then it was off to Holyoke, where he received eerily similar praise: "It makes no difference with Mr. Houdini what kind of handcuffs are produced," the reporter wrote. "He unlocks them all with as much ease as if they were strings around his wrists."

Why do both stories sound alike? Because Houdini wrote them. He wrote all the stories that appeared in newspapers in the early days. This wasn't exactly uncommon—other entertainers wrote their own billings—but nobody has as much enthusiasm for the activities of self-promotion as Houdini has. He once told a friendly reporter, "I have written for more newspapers than anyone in history."

Houdini continued to show up at police stations in the hopes of getting attention (and writing ever more magnificent stories he hoped the papers would pick up), but he rarely did. Bess dutifully clipped newspaper articles they did get, even the smallest ones, and she sent them off to all the big booking agents, but nothing broke through until one odd day in January of 1899. Houdini halfheartedly showed up at a police station in Chicago, and the *Chicago Journal* wrote the story:

Harry Houdini, the strolling magician, surprised the detectives at police head-quarters last night by his ability to remove handcuffs, leg-irons and other articles of police jewelry without unlocking them.

For an hour or more, the policemen tried to bind him with handcuffs, ropes, and cords, but each time he went behind the curtain of the cabinet he had constructed in the squad room and appeared in a few seconds carrying them in his hand. Houdini laughed at the amazement he caused but refused to tell the policemen how he accomplished his feats.

It's an odd story. Houdini generally stopped in at police stations to promote a show, but he did not have a show to promote then. The story referred to him as "the strolling magician."

But this was the story, the one that broke through.

Because it's almost certain that a man named Martin Beck read it.

Like Houdini, Martin Beck was a secret-keeper. Beck would not tell anyone where or when he was born. At different times, he was said to come from Austria, Germany, and Slovakia. Whatever his past life, he came to America to be an actor, and when he failed, he found himself working as a waiter in a beer garden in Chicago. Then he went to San Francisco with a vaudeville company.

There he met Morris Meyerfeld, Jr., a dry-goods store owner who, through some business deal, found himself a co-owner of the Orpheum

Theater in San Francisco. He didn't know what to do with the Orpheum, but Beck had big ideas and encouraged Meyerfeld to acquire more theaters. Together they created the Orpheum Circuit, which became the biggest vaudeville circuit in the western part of the United States. In time, Beck would become the most prominent man in all the industry, building the Palace Theater in New York, vaudeville's ultimate showplace.

Beck had many gifts, but perhaps the greatest of those was his pitch-perfect sense of talent. He brought Charlie Chaplin to the American stage. He hired Will Rogers and the Marx Brothers; introduced Fanny Brice and Sophie Tucker. And, most famously, he discovered Houdini. Beck and a few other theater owners went to catch Houdini's act in St. Paul, Minnesota, in 1899. Before the show, Beck—"perhaps more in a joke than sincerity," Houdini wrote—challenged him to escape from some handcuffs he had brought along.

Houdini did what he always did. He escaped. And Beck was impressed. He invited Houdini and Bess for a dinner, where Beck offered his blunt assessment. Bess never forgot the moment.

"I think you're a rotten showman," she recalled Beck saying to Houdini. "Why don't you cut out the little magical stuff—it only distracts the audience—and just give a couple of big thrillers, like the handcuffs and the trunk trick. There are plenty of good magicians doing the stock stuff, and doing it well, at forty per. You have two big stunts at which nobody can touch you. Those are the big things to cash in on."

Houdini had been so many different things that perhaps he had lost a sense of himself. What was he, after eight years in show business? A stage magician? A card magician? A spiritualist? A comedian? He had been all of that and more, whatever put the next meal on the table, but now here was someone (and not just anyone: this was the powerful Martin Beck) telling him to stop pretending to be something else.

Beck was telling Houdini to become an escape artist. Only in 1899, as Jim Steinmeyer says, there was no such phrase and no such thing. "The role simply did not exist," Steinmeyer says. "There was no such thing as an 'escape artist' before Houdini."

At first, Houdini didn't know what to make of this. He still saw himself as the heir to Robert-Houdin. But if Martin Beck thought that escape was his ticket, he wasn't going to argue.

On March 14, 1899, Beck sent Houdini a telegram.

HOUDINI, PALMGARDEN . . . ST. PAUL, MINN.
YOU CAN OPEN OMAHA MARCH TWENTY-SIXTH, SIXTY DOLLARS,

WILL SEE ACT, PROBABLY MAKE YOU
PROPOSITION FOR ALL NEXT SEASON.
M. BECK

Below this telegram, Houdini wrote:

The first wire Beck sent me, next I was
working at a joint in Omaha, Neb. but
was talk of the town. This wire changed
my whole Life's journey.
—H. Houdini

NAKED AMBITION

If modern magic has a voice, it's the somewhat gruff Chicago voice of Jim Steinmeyer. He has done everything imaginable in the art form—performed, written, created, invented, philosophized, everything. We met in the basement of the Magic Castle, a magical clubhouse in the heart of Los Angeles. He looked exactly as I imagined; professorial with a neatly trimmed gray and white beard.

"You know," he began, "I'm really done with Houdini."

This was not how I expected this to go.

"I'm bored with Houdini," he continued. "And I'm bored with those guys who idolize Houdini. Whenever you try to say something, anything, that they think is even the slightest bit negative about Houdini, they kick you in the teeth. I don't want to say it's a cult because that's goofy. But it's a surprisingly active movement, all these people still defending this guy. It's slightly weird."

This was not a promising start for an interview about Houdini.

Steinmeyer's story is legend. His brother was the magician first, a regular at the Mazda Magic Shop in Oak Park, Illinois. When he lost interest,

Jim got the magic collection, and it captivated him. He liked working tricks again and again. He liked thinking about why they worked, not just from a technical standpoint but from a magical one. He wanted to invent his own tricks that sparked wonder in people.

One day, on a lark, he sent a few of his best illusions to the biggest magician of the time, Doug Henning, who liked them so much that he hired Steinmeyer on the spot.

In the years since, he has consulted the greatest magicians of the age from Henning to Orson Welles to David Copperfield. He has worked with numerous Broadway shows—he's the guy who made the magic carpet fly in *Aladdin* on Broadway—and has invented countless tricks including two of the classic illusions of the last half century. One, I will save for later. But the other is called Origami.

You've probably seen some version of Origami on television or on a stage somewhere. Steinmeyer invented it for Henning, but it has since been performed by just about every stage magician for more than a quarter century. It begins when the magician places a small box, about twelve by twelve, on a table. A mirror is put behind it so that the audience can see the back of the box, which is fastened by two ivory skewers and a wooden pole.

The magician begins to unfold the box—

Origami!—until it transforms into a much bigger box, roughly four times bigger than the original one. An assistant steps into the box, the top is folded down, and—as you no doubt expected—the box is folded back into its original tiny shape.

Steinmeyer invented the trick for Doug Henning, who would recite a poem as the box was broken down.

> A little box proved otherwise
> The world at large, made small in size

Once the box is small, the skewers and wooden pole are put back. There's applause. The magician removes the skewers and pole and starts unfolding the box again.

Henning recites the rest of his poem:

> And as they gazed, the wonder grew
> The more they saw, the less they knew
> Each fold and crease had not explained
> All wonders of the world contained

At last, the small box has become big again, and the assistant steps out wearing an entirely different outfit and a mask. This is Origami. It has been copied, borrowed, and outright stolen so often, that Steinmeyer has stopped trying to keep up.

Origami is the quintessential illusion because

it's timeless. It would have thrilled people in Houdini's time, and it still thrills people today. Steinmeyer believes deeply that magic should be timeless, and in that spirit, he has dedicated much of his life to studying and writing about its history.

Which is how—and why—he grew sick and tired of Houdini.

"There is one thing about Houdini that interests me," he said, a promising turn in the conversation. "It is . . . well, first, let me do this. I don't even know where I'm going with it, but let me say it. No one's interesting to me unless they're flawed. You can't write a book about the great man who is without flaws, without something you can connect with.

"And the fascinating thing about Houdini is his limitations, and how those limitations created this guy, this wonder. You see people go back and rewrite those limitations out of him because they don't want to be critical, and they want Houdini to be a superhero, and I don't care. I have no interest in superheroes. That's why Houdini bores me."

"So, tell me about Houdini's flaws," I said.

"For one thing," Steinmeyer said, "he was ruthless."

Houdini did three surprising things in 1899 after Martin Beck gave him a break.

The first thing he did was get top billing.

Becoming the star of the show seemed a long shot for a guy escaping from handcuffs and boxes when he came to San Francisco to perform in Beck's beloved first theater. Top billing went to a male impersonator named Johnstone Bennett. She was already a big star, an actress and singer who would disappear into her characters. She played multiple roles in a farce called *A Quiet Evening at Home.*

The advertisements called the show "Johnstone Bennett's Vaudeville Celebrities with Orpheum Stars."

And below that in smaller type, it read:

Assisted by the Mysterious!
The Mystifying!
HOUDINI
And MLLE BEATRICE HOUDINI

It was clear who was the headliner. Until the reviews started coming in.

"Houdini did a number of the smoothest card tricks that ancient or modern history mentions," the *San Francisco Call* wrote after opening night. "To try and describe such tricks is worse than relating the flavor of a perfect fruit. They cannot be described adequately. They must be seen to be believed. And even then, believing does not always follow sight. One finds it is not easy to accept the apparently miraculous in this age. And Houdini does the miraculous to all seeing."

Do these seem like over-the-top compliments for a magician who barely six months before was ready to quit and get a job in a factory? Could Houdini have been so good (with card tricks, no less) that he left the reporter so breathless?

And what did the reporter think of Johnstone Bennett? It's fair to say that he wasn't quite as impressed.

"The difference between Houdini's and Johnstone Bennett's engagements—one a huge success, the other not as huge—illuminates very nicely how expectation affects an artist's reputation."

Another *San Francisco Call* critic was equally critical of Bennett but found Houdini to be first rate. And this became a trend for all the critics: raves for Houdini, rotten tomatoes for Johnstone Bennett. Was it just a case of Houdini finally coming into his own as a performer while Bennett found herself at the end of her career? It's possible.

It's also possible—more than possible—that Houdini planted the stories himself.

A week or so later, Houdini was quoted in the *Los Angeles Times* sounding offended because of a Johnstone Bennett quote about San Francisco.

"You can say for me if you will," he said, "that I do not agree with Johnstone Bennett at all in her expression of opinion that San Francisco is a jay town, and the coast not appreciative. I have been treated splendidly and have nothing but good opinions to offer about the people."

A "jay" town meant "filled with bumpkins." It's unclear that Bennett ever said that. But within a couple of weeks, Harry Houdini grabbed top billing of the Orpheum Circuit. Johnstone Bennett was working elsewhere.

The first surprising thing Houdini did in 1899 was somehow get top billing on one of the biggest shows on vaudeville. The second was get into a public fight with an enigmatic bearded weirdo who called himself Professor Alfred Benzon. He was some kind of character. For a time, Benzon called himself the "King of Cards," which so infuriated Houdini that he clipped the advertisement for his scrapbook and scribbled "NOT" in big letters in front of it. Benzon, by all accounts, though, was a gifted card manipulator. He could take a thoroughly shuffled deck and, with his eyes closed, mix the cards and deal each person at the table a predetermined poker hand.

"He was one of the greats," Dai Vernon said. "He had a $250,000 insurance policy on his hands."

Benzon started the fight with Houdini by writing a long and detailed story in the *San Francisco Examiner* titled "Houdini's Tricks

179

Exposed." Benzon didn't just reveal what he claimed were Houdini's secrets for getting out of handcuffs.

"If you want to have a little amusement at the expense of Houdini," he wrote, and he offered specific tips for humiliating the "professor of trickery." He said the key was the to bring a "pair with a newfangled lock and key." He mocked Houdini at length.

Beck told Houdini to ignore such nonsense. "The more he writes and tries to expose you," he wrote Houdini, "the more he is advertising you."

But Houdini could not ignore Benzon. All his life, he could not ignore anyone who insulted him or challenged him or performed too similar an act or just set him off, whether intentionally or unintentionally. So, yes, he went after Benzon and went after him hard.

"This man, Benzon, makes himself ridiculous," Houdini replied in the next day's paper. "He pretends to describe the handcuff trick but instead gives an imaginary narration of an alleged performance and proceeds to explain how simple it all is . . . I do nothing of the sort.

"Benzon has exposed nothing. I will wager him any amount of money, from $1,000 upward, that I do all this I have described, and he cannot do any part of it nor explain it . . . He's a puzzle salesman and copied his alleged expose from an old book of magic. The book sells for 10 cents.

And as suckers are born every minute, it is still in print."

Back and forth they went, and the hotter it became between them, the more interesting the act became. Steinmeyer had it right from the start: It isn't the *how* that makes magic work. It is the *why*. And Professor Benzon's determination to embarrass and discredit him crystallized the *why* for Harry Houdini.

"If you think about the so-called escape artist," Steinmeyer says, "what is it? What does it even mean? It's one of those weird acts where if you describe it to people, just cold, they will say, 'I'm sorry, I'm supposed to watch what?' The whole thing, there's nothing happening. You're going to watch a cabinet, and the guy is going to get out of something, and you don't even know why he's locked up in the first place? You would go, 'I'm not quite sure what this act is.' "

Benzon gave the act authority. Houdini was going to prove Professor Benzon wrong, prove that he didn't need cheap tricks to get out of these handcuffs. He was going to show people that even though many wanted to keep him down, they could not.

"People needed to have a hero," says David Copperfield, the most famous magician in the world. "They wanted to see a person who could do what they wanted to do: escape! That was a powerful idea. Nobody has ever aspired to pull a dove out of a silk handkerchief. But to get out of a handcuff or a straitjacket, that was real."

In his efforts to expose Houdini, Professor Benzon had freed him instead.

And here's the best part of all: in quintessential Houdini style, Professor Benzon was almost certainly a plant. The two had worked together behind the scenes to create the feud.

And that feud, in addition to giving Houdini's act purpose, also led directly to the third surprising choice of 1899.

"Benzon says I use a key in my mouth," Houdini wrote. "What do I do with that key when I am cuffed with my hands behind my back, as I always am in my exhibitions? Why, I can do the trick stripped naked."

And within days, he began to do his escapes in the nude.

"All right, let me tell you the other thing I find interesting," Steinmeyer says. "Houdini is a very nice Jewish boy who is raised on the East Side and is from a very respectable family. His father is a rabbi. His mother dotes on him.

"And yet a part of him is drawn to edginess. He writes a book called *The Right Way to Do Wrong*, which is all about rubbing elbows with criminals. Astonishing! Who did that then? People just weren't thinking like that. And then his first bills say he's the only magician who performs stark naked. That would be somewhat risqué now. Back then it was unthinkable. You see people who want to clean up Houdini's image, and I want to tell them: This is a man who performed in the nude in 1899! He knew exactly what he was doing."

On July 13, 1899—just a few days after his newspaper feud with Professor Benzon—Harry Houdini showed up at a San Francisco police station. He stripped in front of a dozen detectives. He let them thoroughly examine him for keys or wire or anything that might help him escape. A detective then taped his mouth shut. They then put five handcuffs on his wrists, five more on his ankles, and used one pair of handcuffs to connect the wrist and ankle cuffs. Detectives then carried him into a room and left him on the floor.

Five minutes later, Houdini returned, still naked, the tape still on his mouth and the handcuffs off his body and reconnected in a long daisy chain.

That began the nude escapes. The irony was that Houdini was a known prude. Later, he even refused to kiss his actress love interests when he was making silent movies. He once lost his mind when Bess, as a joke, sat on another man's lap.

Yet he happily and regularly stripped naked for handcuff escapes. He knew that these naked escapes were commercial gold, that he was taking advantage of his handsome features and athletic body. He even commissioned Frederick Bushnell's studio photography company to take photos of him in the nude as he reenacted the San Francisco escape. Those photographs—and others Houdini would have taken later—appeared in newspapers and magazines all over the world throughout his life and for many years after his death.

For the next few months, Houdini performed naked or near-naked escapes again and again in police stations across America. The *St. Louis Post-Dispatch* wrote, "He performed for the St. Louis police in a costume so brief, he had no place to conceal keys or wires," and published a series of near-naked Houdini sketches. In Buffalo, he wore nothing at all as he worked his way out of a rusty old pair of English cuffs. In Philadelphia, he performed his needles trick while "in charming and total dishabille."

It's astonishing how willingly police officers let him strip naked in their stations. Only once, in New York, did anyone stop him. "That don't go," the officer said when Houdini began to disrobe. "You've got to keep your clothes on."

By the end of 1899, Houdini was a star. He was pulling in as much as $400 a week—almost six million dollars a year by 2019 dollars. He was drawing huge crowds and getting prominent newspaper notices in every town he visited. It seemed like he had achieved everything he ever wanted.

And that's when Houdini did the craziest thing of all. He threw it all away and went overseas to start all over again in England.

SCOTLAND YARD

Houdini felt cheated. Yes, Martin Beck had helped him break through. Yes, he was making more money than ever before, enough to allow his mother to live like a queen. Yes, people knew his name all over America. But success couldn't satisfy Houdini. He started to complain that Beck's 20 percent cut was outrageous. He believed that theaters were using him and his name to enrich themselves. A friend called him "the cheapest headliner in the business," and Houdini shared his frustration with Beck.

"No manager would believe your act was fit for vaudeville," Beck barked back. "They all considered it a museum act."

A break was inevitable. And, Houdini's friend T. Nelson Downs showed the way.

Thomas Nelson Downs was something else. I knew nothing at all about him before starting all this, but he might be my favorite minor character in Houdini's story. Downs was about seven years older than Houdini, born on a farm in Marshalltown, Iowa, in 1867. Downs's father died when he was very young, which meant Thomas had to go to work to help support the family. He was desperately lonely, and to fill the void, he began to perform small magic tricks. He sometimes would go to the grocery store in town, crack eggs, and have coins come out. It was an auspicious beginning for someone who would become known as "The King of Koins."

Downs had a charming and whimsical quality as a magician. There's a gorgeous publicity poster of him as "The World's Unequaled Palmist and Prestidigitateur," a boast that you imagine was not excessively challenged. On the bottom of the poster, there is a series of six small vignettes featuring Downs in action. And even though these are simple paintings, simple moments frozen in time, they seem to animate when you look at them. You can't help but smile. There was just a way about him.

He would take the stage like no other magician. He would walk onto the stage, bow, and smile. Then he would take one step, bow, and smile, another step, bow, and smile, and so on until he finally reached his place in the center.

"As done by Downs," the magician Stanley Collins wrote, "this made a dignified and arresting entrance, one which I am sure only he could have made without appearing ridiculous."

He was a genius at coin magic. He was twenty-nine years old in 1896 when he introduced his masterpiece: the Miser's Dream. In the trick, Downs would pluck dozens of coins out of midair and drop them in a top hat. In his religious book, *When Bad Things Happen to Good People*,

Harold Kushner wrote, "It has been said that just as every actor yearns to play Hamlet, every Bible student yearns to write a commentary on the Book of Job." Well, every sleight-of-hand magician wants to take a shot at the Miser's Dream. It's more or less the perfect illusion because it's funny and baffling and thrilling to see someone pull money out of thin air. Even Houdini performed it late in his career under the title of Money for Nothing.

But those who saw Downs perform Miser's Dream said that no one will ever achieve the combination of grace and absurdity of the creator's performance. Downs's deftness was unmatched; he could palm forty half dollars in each hand, making them invisible to the audience's eye. He walked into the audience and pulled a seemingly endless supply of coins out of people's ears, noses, and, especially, their beards.

When asked how he did it, Downs smiled.

"It's simple," he said. "You've just got to get the money out of their whiskers."

Downs and Houdini first met in 1893 at the Chicago World's Fair, back when both were struggling to make a name for themselves. Downs admired Houdini's grit and determination—"He had to fight every inch of the way," Downs once said—and Houdini delighted in Downs's charm: "He was one of the historical lights of magic."

In the spring of 1899, Downs went to Europe.

He had been observing the successes that other performers had overseas and believed that there was a big and untapped market for magic. He planned his trip very carefully. He wrote repeatedly to theater owners, particularly in London. He managed to secure a spot at the Palace Theatre in London. Houdini watched closely and jealously from across the ocean. He griped to friends that Downs was making "the salary of an ambassador."

"Come over," Downs wrote to him in one of the many letters they exchanged.

That sounded good to Houdini. The United States was still a young country at the turn of the century. And, for once, Houdini and Martin Beck were on the same page; Beck told Houdini that success in England, Germany, and France would "boom you to the top notch."

It's also possible that Beck wanted Houdini to go as far away as possible.

But Houdini did not prepare for his trip the way Downs had. He didn't do any prep work. Instead, Beck said he would have his theater man in Europe, Richard Pitriot, set up some bookings.

Harry and Bess set sail for London on May 30, 1900, on the SS *Kensington*. The trip was a nightmare for Houdini. He was deathly seasick, an ailment that would haunt him all his life, and at one point he was so violently ill that he threatened to jump off the ship; Bess had to tie him to the bedpost with sheets. This scene seems unlikely but funny; imagine the most celebrated escape artist the world has ever known to be unable to escape sheets his wife tied around him.

Seasickness was only the start of the nightmare. When they got to London, they found that Pitriot—who was supposed to travel with them but had begged out at the last second—had not set up any contracts or secured any bookings. "A damn liar," Houdini wrote to Beck. And it only got worse when Houdini realized that nobody in England had any idea who he was. He passed around press clippings, but these left theater owners cold. Who couldn't escape from those flimsy American jails?

So, Houdini went to escape from Scotland Yard.

My favorite version of the story goes like this: Houdini kicked around England for days or even weeks. Only a man named C. Dundas Slater showed even the slightest interest in him. Slater managed the Alhambra Theatre, and he had a weakness for novelty acts. Just two weeks earlier, he had offered an audition to a handcuff magician named Cirnoc (who bombed). Slater sensed that Houdini had something Cirnoc lacked.

"If you can escape from the handcuffs at Scotland Yard," Slater told Houdini, "I'll sign you."

"Can you go with me now?" Houdini replied.

They went together to the famed police headquarters and met with William Melville, the superintendent of Scotland Yard's Special Branch. Melville was dismissive of Houdini but decided it might be amusing to play along. He had Houdini wrap his arms around a pillar. Melville clamped on a pair of English handcuffs (they were known as darbies) with Houdini's face pressed up against the pillar.

"Here's how we fasten the Yankee criminals who come over here and get into trouble," Melville said. "We'll be back for you."

"Wait," Houdini replied instantly. "I'll go with you." He promptly dropped the handcuffs on the floor.

"This trip to Scotland Yard," Downs wrote, "convinced Mr. Slater that here was a man of unusual ability as he dumbfounded the Scotland Yard police by escaping from all their locks which they supposed would hold the cleverest and most hardened criminals."

Slater put Houdini on the bill at the Alhambra for two weeks and then kept him on for another six. Houdini was an instant smash. "The Sensation of London," it said on the posters hanging all over town. There was even a quote from Superintendent Melville himself calling Houdini "Absolutely a Miracle."

This being Houdini, we must ask: Is the Scotland Yard story true? "I'm not a big fan of challenging popular Houdini stories, but . . ." our intrepid Houdini truth-finder John Cox says. But he must point out that there is little evidence backing up the story. Scotland Yard's curator in 1982 stated, "There is no record of any conversation between Supt. Melville and Houdini, nor is there any record of the escape from a pair of handcuffs taking place."

John spilled his doubts to Patrick Culliton, who shook his head sadly at his friend's lack of faith.

"It happened," Culliton said.

Either way, Houdini's instincts about Europe were exactly right. He quickly became one of the biggest stars in the world. The more famous he became, the more relentless he became. He slept five hours a night. He traveled from country to country and played to packed theaters. He took on all challenges, escaped from at least fifty prisons, and along the way gave more interviews, posed for more photos, and appeared in more newspapers than any entertainer ever had before. He became the toast of Paris. He defeated the German police. He escaped from an impenetrable Russian prison on wheels. He became a legend in his own time, but even this was not enough. Houdini intended to live forever.

NOT A LOVE MATCH

Nobody has neutral feelings about Harry Houdini. His personality does not inspire mild emotions; no one has ever said, "I'm ambivalent about the guy." Many people along this journey adore Houdini for his ambition, his ingenuity, his relentlessness, and for the way he became larger than life. But there are also people who can't stand him. Mike Caveney is one of them.

You wouldn't expect it from Mike. He might be the world's leading authority on magic history, but he would never say that about himself. He's much too modest. He's a delight, really. He's a kind person, always happy, always helpful, and a splendid and quirky performer. His signature illusion revolves around toilet paper. He takes out a long piece of toilet paper, tears apart dozens of squares, and hands them out to people in the crowd. After a while, people hand the squares back, and he shows that they have reattached to form one long piece again. It's one of those illusions that sounds so silly and pointless, but when he does it live, it leaves everyone howling with laughter. Mike calls himself "The Assassin of Gloom."

The Assassin of Gloom loathes Houdini.

It didn't start that way. Caveney's first magical memory was when his third-grade teacher read *The Great Houdini* to his class. The other kids liked it, but Mike, well, he wasn't just smitten. He was altered. "I just about fell out of my chair," he says.

When class ended, he couldn't get Houdini out of his head. He thought himself a fully formed kid: he already loved sports, comic books, television, movies. Houdini, though, scrambled his brain. As soon as school ended, he called over his friends and said, "Tie me to a ladder." Being third-grade boys, they didn't need to be asked twice. They tied up Caveney as tightly as they could. As Mike struggled to get out of those ropes (spoiler alert: he didn't get out; they had to untie him, which took longer than anyone expected), he knew that this was his destiny, that he would spend his life doing magical things.

"Half the kids, they get a magic book, maybe they fool around with it a little, then they go back to playing baseball, or they discover girls," he says. "They have no need to do this. What is it about the one kid in ten thousand? What is it about our minds? Why does magic unlock something inside our brains? I don't know. I only know that it's all I ever wanted to do. Even now, it's all I ever want to do or think about."

The more Mike learned about magic, the more he wanted to know. He didn't just want to learn the trick's secrets. He wanted to learn about old magicians and uncover old illusions. "Mike is the greatest magic historian in the world," Joshua Jay says, "because there's no limit to his curiosity. He wants to know everything. He loves to go back and find the most obscure magicians, the most forgotten illusions, and then bring them back to life."

So, what happened? How did Mike develop this disdain for Houdini?

"Look, there's no denying that Houdini is the biggest thing going in magic," he says. "He's probably more famous today than he was even at his height. But the more I read about him, the more I talked to people about him, the more I realized: Houdini was a pretty miserable guy. This gets me in some trouble with the Houdini crowd. But let's face it: the guy was an ass."

He begins to tell a few stories about how Houdini was an ass. And let's be clear: there is no shortage of such stories.

"There's a story about Servais Le Roy that I think is pretty typical of Houdini," Caveney says.

Le Roy was a beloved magician—Caveney calls him ten times the magician Houdini ever was—and one year the Society of American Magicians (SAM) honored him with a dinner. Houdini, president of SAM, made the presentation.

"Le Roy was going to say a few words," Mike

said. "Houdini gave him the cup and told him, 'Just take it and sit down.' That's how he was. He didn't want anyone taking the spotlight off of him. There are too many stories like that to ignore. Nobody can deny his genius for self-promotion and his incredible energy. But he was a bully, and he was out for number one, and he was limited as a magician.

"In fact," he said with a little laughter, "I'm wondering why you're so fascinated by him."

Well, Caveney is not wrong about the details. Houdini had a big ego, a rough nature, and he ruthlessly went about destroying imposters and critics and people he perceived as competitors. He was a handful for friends and an insatiable enemy. Then again, I could counter by saying that he had his charms, too. Houdini loved kids and animals, he was often extremely generous, he cared nothing about creature comforts, he dedicated his life to his mother, he worked very hard to keep alive the memories of magicians who had been forgotten.

All of this made him Houdini. I could not blame Mike for despising him any more than I could blame John Cox for loving him. Houdini contained multitudes.

But there is something else. The writer Richard Ben Cramer once wrote of the great hitter Ted Williams, "Few men try for best ever, and Ted Williams is one of those."

Harry Houdini too was one of those. He grasped for the stars. He sought immortality. And he would not yield, not ever. This is the part of Houdini that echoes through the years. And it was never more in focus than in his epic and astonishing battle with a man named William Hope Hodgson.

William Hope Hodgson was a bodybuilder, a teacher, a photographer, a soldier, a poet, a novelist, and a sailor. He ran away from home to be a sailor when he was thirteen: he once earned a medal from the Royal Humane Society for diving into shark-infested waters to rescue a crew member. After his days at sea, he opened up a School of Physical Culture, sort of an early-twentieth-century Gold's Gym, in his hometown of Blackburn in northern England. He also wrote poetry and science fiction; his writing was good enough that it influenced such acclaimed authors as H. P. Lovecraft and Terry Pratchett.

Hodgson and Houdini met on October 24, 1902. At the time, Houdini was reaching new heights virtually every week. In 1901 alone, he had been a raging success in England, Germany, Czechoslovakia, and Denmark before winning over Paris. And one of the most compelling parts of his act was that he held an open challenge to anyone who dared bring along handcuffs to test the Great Houdini.

Hodgson dared. He wrote a letter to Houdini spelling out his dare:

Sir,

Being interested in your apparently anatomically impossible handcuff feat, I have decided to take up your challenge tonight on the following conditions:

1st—I bring and use my own irons (so look out).

2nd—I iron you myself.

3rd—If you are unable to free yourself, the forfeit to be given to the Blackburn infirmary.

Should you succeed, I shall be the first one to offer congratulations. If not, then the infirmary will benefit.

W. Hope Hodgson

The trap was set, and Houdini—who normally had an instinct for such things—simply accepted the challenge like he always had. Most of them were lighthearted affairs; the challenger usually was doing it for a laugh and, in the end, fully expected that Houdini would figure out a way to escape. Hodgson had a different idea.

At ten o'clock in the evening, at the end of Houdini's final performance of the day. Hodgson and a friend brought numerous handcuffs and chains to the stage. Houdini looked at them dubiously and said, "These have been tampered with."

Hodgson interrupted to remind Houdini that he was allowed to bring his own irons. And perhaps this was the moment that Houdini saw the emerging trap; he was reluctant to go on. But the crowd's cheers overwhelmed him, as they always did.

"I shall do my best to free myself," Houdini sang out to the audience, "provided that you allow me a little extra time in which to deal with these unusual difficulties."

Houdini might have been worried only about the cuffs. But Hodgson's multilayered plan involved more than that. He had spent years studying the human anatomy, and so he knew a lot about pressure points. He and a bulky friend got on either side of Houdini and snapped a cuff around Houdini's right bicep, pulled its chain tight behind his back, and clamped the other cuff on Houdini's left bicep. They did this again, roughly pinning Houdini's elbows against his hip—so roughly that at one point Houdini shouted out in pain that there was nothing in the challenge about his arms being broken. He demanded that Hodgson's friend leave the stage.

"The challenge was that you and you alone would iron me," Houdini said. Hodgson, realizing that Houdini would win that point with the crowd, nodded and sent his friend away.

But Hodgson was plenty strong himself. He snapped two more cuffs around Houdini's wrists and again pulled them behind his back. Houdini was put into a kneeling position as chains were pushed through the handcuffs and connected to a pair of leg cuffs around his ankles before one more pair of leg cuffs was clamped on.

Houdini could not move without feeling agonizing pain. A small tent was placed over Houdini—Houdini performed all his escapes in a tent, out of the eye of the audience—and the orchestra began to play. The challenge had begun.

After fifteen minutes, at Houdini's request, the tent was lifted. The crowd roared in anticipation, but Houdini had not moved. He seemed broken. He quietly asked if he could be elevated to his knees. His brother Hardeen brought out a glass of water. The canopy dropped again.

Another fifteen or twenty minutes passed, and the little tent rose again. Again, the crowd rose to their feet and shouted. Again, Houdini was entirely immobilized; he had made no progress at all. Houdini quietly asked that the shackles be removed just for a moment because he had lost all feeling in his arms. Hodgson declined the request even as the crowd booed him.

"This is a contest, not a love match," Hodgson shouted at the crowd.

A doctor was called to the stage, and after a quick look at Houdini's blue arms, he announced that it was cruel to keep this contest going. Hodgson was unmoved.

"If Houdini is beaten," he said, "then let him give in."

He really thought Houdini would. An ordinary escape artist—an ordinary person—would have given up. But if Houdini had underestimated Hodgson at the start, now Hodgson under-estimated him. The canopy dropped once more. The orchestra again began to play.

After another fifteen minutes, Houdini shouted: "My hands are free!" People in the audience stood and applauded, some of the loudest cheers Houdini would hear in his life. But the escape was not complete, and Houdini went back to work on the other handcuffs.

Hodgson was outraged. He later claimed to have seen a key placed in one of the locks and suspected collusion between Houdini and his brother. But in the moment, he also knew without a doubt that he had lost. Once Houdini's hands were free, it was only a matter of time until he escaped the other locks. The crowd was getting feverish. Houdini had them on his side. Hodgson left the building.

A few minutes past midnight, Houdini leapt from underneath the canopy. His clothes were torn, his arms bloodied, and he could barely speak. But the chains were all off. The crowd's awe and wonder were overwhelming.

"I have performed for fourteen years," Houdini told the newspapers. "And I have never been treated so brutally." One reporter described his arms "as though some tiger had clawed him." Houdini insisted the handcuffs had been plugged and that Hodgson had cheated.

"With six pairs of handcuffs in that strained position for an hour!" Houdini told a San Francisco reporter five years later. "My God! I suffered the tortures of hell. I sweat blood!"

Houdini never stopped attacking Hodgson's character, calling him "no gentleman." Hodgson feebly tried to fight back. "It was obviously against the rules of fair play that Mr. Houdini's brother and wife should have been allowed to go near him at any time during the contest," he wrote to the Blackburn newspapers. Hodgson also made the case that he had done nothing to hurt Houdini; the pain was caused entirely by his efforts to escape.

But now, Hodgson was trying to win on Houdini's turf. Nobody beat Harry Houdini in a newspaper war.

"I'm sometimes called a Houdini hater," Mike Caveney says, "but that isn't it. I just see Houdini for who he was. There were greater magicians. There were many more generous magicians.

But I readily admit, Houdini was willing to do whatever was necessary to be the most famous magician."

Yes. That's exactly it. That's why so many cherish Houdini, despite his many faults and limitations and quirks. Few men try for best ever, and Harry Houdini was one of those. William Hope Hodgson did everything right in his effort to defeat Houdini. He shamed Houdini into taking the challenge. He used cuffs that were all but impossible to pick. He fastened them securely and violently. It should have worked. He made one mistake, though: he thought Houdini would surrender.

Houdini never surrendered. That was what made him Houdini.

THE FIGHT OF COLOGNE

Houdini's favorite escape was not an escape at all. It was a fight for honor. The odds really were against him, and skills he had perfected as an escape artist were of little use to him. But he won just the same, and Houdini never tired of telling the story of how he beat the feared German police.

Houdini arrived to perform in Germany in 1902, just as Kaiser Wilhelm II's government cracked down on fraud in entertainment. The police went after acts of fraud of all kinds including, improbably, a famed horse named Kluger Hans (Clever Hans, in English) who seemed to have the ability to add numbers and tell time. The German board of education formed a thirteen-member committee to investigate Kluger Hans; they eventually ruled that no fraud or tricks were used. Kluger Hans was officially declared a clever horse.

Anna Rothe was not so lucky. She was a renowned medium of the day; Sherlock Holmes author Arthur Conan Doyle said that she "had such powers in a high degree." In 1902, Rothe was on stage in Berlin pulling hyacinth and narcissus flowers out of the air when two German police officers rushed the stage and wrestled her to the ground. They found that Rothe had hidden 157 flowers and various fruits under her coat. She was taken to jail to await trial.

That trial was a sensation; Houdini himself paid ten marks to get a standing-room spot in the courtroom. Rothe was found guilty and sentenced to eighteen months in prison. The warning had been declared: Kaiser Wilhelm's government would not tolerate fraud, even in what might seem like harmless entertainment.

"Every singer and vaudeville comedian must submit his entire act, in typewritten form, to the police fourteen days before date of opening," Houdini complained in the *Daily Mirror*. "The police look the matter over, and if there is anything about it they don't like, such material is promptly cut out."

Houdini was doubly troubled because Kaiser Wilhelm was known to be a rabid anti-Semite. Another Jewish magician would have skipped Germany entirely. But Houdini was Houdini; in such things, he was entirely fearless. When he got to Germany, he immediately arranged an exclusive escape for more than three hundred German police officers. He stripped naked, had a bandage placed over his mouth, and allowed himself to be bound by numerous handcuffs, leg irons, finger-locks, and thumbscrews. He escaped in less than ten minutes.

"At this time," the police wrote in a statement,

"we are unable to explain the way in which the locks are opened."

The statement might seem tepid, but Houdini never let the details stand in the way of a good story. He declared himself "The only artist in the history of Europe to whom the German police have given the Imperial certificates." (As far as anyone knows, there never was any such thing as an Imperial certificate.)

German audiences loved Houdini. He performed using the shaky German he had spoken as a child, and everyone appreciated the effort. But above all else, there was something about the way he escaped, something about one man defying his bonders and breaking free, that spoke to the German spirit. Houdini performed for sellout crowds throughout the country, particularly at his beloved Wintergarten Theater in Berlin.

Which is why he was as surprised as anyone when a newspaper in Cologne, *Rheinische Zeitung*, ran a story with the headline "Die Entlarvung Houdinis" (The Unmasking of Houdini).

The newspaper's charge was confusing. They wrote that Houdini had attempted to bribe one police officer to help with an escape and actually bribed another police employee to get him out of a different predicament. Both bribes were alleged by the same person, a patrolman named Werner Graff, who would become Houdini's favorite enemy.

Graff was perfectly suited for the role of cartoonish villain in Houdini's story. Graff, a humorless man who never seemed able to read a situation, told the paper that he owned a particularly complicated lock and key, and that Houdini had offered twenty marks to borrow it for a demonstration before the police. Graff said Houdini told him exactly how he would perform the trick (hiding the key in his anus) and that "we could both make a lot of money."

Graff said he refused the money and was so incensed by Houdini's insolence that days later he took the stage and challenged Houdini to escape from that same lock. According to Graff's complaint, Houdini pleaded with a second police employee named Lott—"I will be ruined!" Houdini shouted—and bribed him to get a duplicate lock. Houdini then filed through Graff's lock to escape and switched it with Lott's duplicate lock for the eyes of the crowd.

To this day, no one knows if Graff's charges were true (they're hard even to understand). In his epic biography, Ken Silverman leaned toward Graff's version because the various methods described—shouting about how he would be ruined if he failed, using a few dollars to convince a police officer to help—sounded very much like Houdini's style

"Yes, more likely than no," he concluded.

This all went to trial, where Houdini, of course,

told an entirely different story. He fully denied the initial bribe and said that Graff made up the whole thing. As for the incident on stage, Houdini's denial was shakier. He admitted breaking Graff's lock but said it was because Graff sneakily had given him a busted lock that could not be opened. In one of the more dramatic moments of the trial, Houdini emotionally recounted how Bess had seen Graff switch the locks and then shouted out, "This officer is a common liar! He has changed the locks!" Houdini was fined three marks for publicly insulting an officer, but it was well worth it. Graff's credibility was in tatters.

Whoever was right, whoever was lying, Houdini easily won. In what must be one of the stranger moments in judicial record, the judge asked Houdini how he could get out of Graff's lock without using a pick. Houdini took the lock (which Graff had been forced to bring to court) and banged the bolt against a metal plate he kept hidden below his knee. In time, the mechanism weakened, and the lock opened. Houdini then gave the judge a private show as he picked his way through various locks and chains.

"I knew in order to win my lawsuit, I would have to open any lock that was placed before me," he later wrote. The judge ordered Graff to pay two hundred marks and the newspaper to pay fifty.

Graff couldn't see that he was defeated. He appealed the case to a higher court and lost. He appealed a second time and lost again. In one of the trials, Houdini was he asked to open a safe, and this turned out to be easy because the judge forgot to lock it. Good fortune was on his side throughout.

Graff was ordered to pay all court costs, which included travel expenses for the numerous witnesses Houdini had brought to speak on his behalf. For the rest of his life, Houdini used a fake but real-sounding "newspaper account" in his publicity material:

> In the highest court, Police Officer Werner Graff was found guilty of slandering Houdini, heavily fined, he must pay all costs and insert an advertisement in all of the Cologne newspapers, proclaiming his punishment, at the same time "IN THE NAME OF THE KING" openly apologize to Houdini for insulting him.
>
> This open apology is the severest punishment that can be given to a royal official, and as the lawsuit has been running over a year, the costs will run into thousands of dollars.

All of this was exaggerated in typical Houdini style, but the victory was real. Houdini sometimes would say that defeating Werner Graff was "the greatest thing I ever did in my life."

MIRRORS

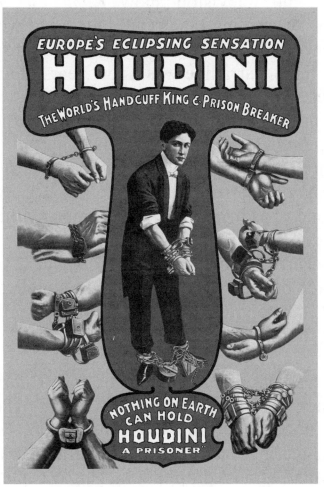

remain desperate to connect with Patrick Culliton. I spend quite a lot of time surfing the internet to find a copy of his book *Houdini: The Key*. So far, it has led nowhere, but I have learned some things about Patrick. For instance, I have learned that he was close friends with the actor, musician, artist, and martial artist David Carradine.

You probably remember Carradine: He starred in the old television show *Kung Fu*, among others. Carradine and Culliton both went to Hollywood High School, though not quite at the same time. Carradine was a few years older than Patrick.

I came across all this while reading Carradine's book, *Endless Highway*, which is partly a story of Carradine's troubled life and partly a story of the many celebrities he came to know. Carradine was one of Hollywood's most famous wild men; he was nearly court-martialed when in the army, he was arrested multiple times, he once assaulted a police officer. He was also a drug addict. This small adventure from the book can probably stand for the rest:

> I was passing the bottle of Jose Cuervo back and forth with Bob Dylan when I noticed a drunken Indian who was staggering around with a little Martin guitar, almost dropping it. This was Gene Clark, of the Byrds . . . Gene followed me. He started talking to Dylan in a loud voice, saying Bob was a no-talent wimp, and he'd be nobody if the Byrds hadn't

recorded his song, "Mr. Tambourine Man." (I think Gene had it backwards; it was the other way around.) . . . Suddenly with a sort of it's-a-good-day-to-die, blood-curdling cry, he came at Dylan, brandishing a pool cue. Dylan jumped, almost dropping the Jose Cuervo. I leaned in between them. Gene stopped and stared at me . . . I turned back to Bob, but he had split.

Carradine writes quite a bit in the book about Patrick Culliton, but the story wasn't what I expected.

"Patrick was a shell-shocked Vietnam vet and half-crazed a lot of time," he wrote.

I didn't know about Patrick being a Vietnam veteran. Most of what I had read about him or from him involved his Houdini theories. If you go to any website with a lively Houdini discussion before 2016, you inevitably will find a Patrick Culliton comment. And in those comments, he comes across as a funny, kind, somewhat obsessed person who loves Houdini and wants to share what he has learned about him. This is also how he is described to me by numerous people. "Patrick's weird," one told me, "but harmless."

Carradine's book, however, paints a darker portrait. At one point well into their friendship, Patrick got engaged to Carradine's daughter

Calista. When their engagement fell through, Patrick went wild.

"With Calista gone, Patrick started drinking a lot," Carradine wrote. "We mourned our loss together. One night he got completely out of hand and physically attacked me. He came at me with a maniacal, crazed Vietnam vet grin . . . I sidestepped his lunge, and he went right into the balcony rail. He almost took it out and had a flying lesson. I caught him before he plunged to his death."

And now, I wonder more than ever: how did Houdini come into Patrick Culliton's life?

THE MIRROR CUFFS

Five days before St. Patrick's Day, March 12, 1904, Harry Houdini performed at the Hippodrome, a new theater on Charing Cross Road in London. It was a Saturday night, and the crowd was lively and tipsy. To get to the stage, a performer had to walk through a saloon that opened up to a large auditorium. Houdini called it the most beautiful stage in the world.

"Ladies and gentlemen!" Houdini said to the crowd, as he announced every night, "I will now invite forward anyone who would bring handcuffs to challenge Houdini!"

Music began to play, and as usual, several people took to the stage. One of them was a nondescript man named Will A. Bennet. He held a pair of handcuffs in his right hand.

These were no ordinary handcuffs, and Bennet was no ordinary challenger. He was a reporter for the *Daily Mirror*, and he was after a story. He had approached his editor with what he called a gag: he wanted to defeat Houdini by finding a pair of inescapable handcuffs. The editor was dubious that such handcuffs existed or that Bennet could succeed.

"He agreed," Bennet later wrote, "in much the same way as he might have done had I suggested

215

it would be a good gag if I could get his Majesty King Edward VII to give me an interview."

With tentative permission, Bennet traveled to Birmingham, "where, if anywhere, I reckoned I should find the handcuffs capable of holding Houdini." He spent the day running in and out of locksmith shops until he found a police officer who said he knew a man. They walked to the shop of Nathaniel Hart, who had spent five years perfecting a lock that no man could escape.

Hart was proud to show Bennet his unusual cuffs. They were gorgeous, made of a single piece of metal, rigid, shaped like a figure eight or a pair of eyeglasses. The wrist openings were side by side, but the cuffs were formed so that the hands of the prisoner would be slightly angled away from each other. The singular feature of the cuffs was a long thick cylinder that ran across the top. That was the feature that made the cuffs unbreakable; to open them, you needed to push a long key into the side of the cylinder and turn it delicately several times in opposite directions. No one could turn the key at precisely the right tension while locked inside them.

"The mechanism was too complicated for me to follow," Bennet would say, "and no wonder, considering that it had taken five years to perfect, but I understood enough to know that if there was a pair of handcuffs in the world capable of holding Houdini, I had them in my grasp."

Bennet immediately offered to buy the cuffs from Hart.

"No, no sir," Hart replied. "They are not for sale. I wouldn't sell them for their weight in gold twice over."

Bennet explained that he hoped to use the cuffs to confine Harry Houdini. Hart was intrigued and agreed to lend him the cuffs for two weeks. The next night, Bennet showed up on the Hippodrome stage with what would become known as the Mirror Cuffs.

Houdini looked them over carefully and doubtfully. He had learned a key lesson from his hellish duel with William Hope Hodgson in Blackburn: don't take a challenge you can't win.

"These are not regulation handcuffs," Houdini said, and he handed them back and headed toward some of the other challengers. The orchestra began to play music again; Bennet asked them to stop.

"On behalf of the *Daily Illustrated Mirror*," he shouted, "I have just challenged Mr. Houdini to permit me to fasten these handcuffs on his wrists. Mr. Houdini declines."

It turns out Will Bennet knew a little something about public relations and was not about to let Houdini escape so easily.

"In the course of my journalistic duties this week," he continued, "I interviewed a blacksmith at Birmingham who has spent five years of his life perfecting a lock which he alleges no mortal man can pick. The handcuff I wish to fasten upon Mr. Houdini has such a lock. It is made of the finest British steel, by a British workman and, being the property of the *Daily Illustrated Mirror*, has been bought with British gold. It is all British in fact."

The crowd began to buzz.

"I think I am right in saying that Mr. Houdini is an American," Bennet continued. "Americans are fond of saying that they have nothing to fear from anything British. Mr. Houdini is, evidently, afraid of British-made handcuffs, for he will not put on this pair."

Now the audience was fully charged. Houdini shouted out again that these were not regulation cuffs and tried to go on, racing over to other challengers. In quick succession, he put on three different handcuffs, easily escaping from each.

"Mr. Houdini, you claim to be the 'Handcuff King,'" Bennet said. "Everywhere I see huge posters depicting how you have escaped from formidable Russian and German fetters and prisons . . . If you again refuse to put on these handcuffs, my contention is that you are no longer entitled to use the words, 'Handcuff King.'"

Houdini was stopped cold. He walked back over to Bennet and looked at the cuffs again. People in the crowd began to chant, "Make a match! Make a match!" Houdini was trapped.

"I cannot possibly accept this gentleman's challenge tonight," Houdini said, "because I am restricted as to time. His handcuffs, he admits, have taken an artificer five years to make. I know, therefore, I can't get out of them in five minutes."

Houdini suggested a unique special challenge on St. Patrick's Day. Bennet accepted. For the next five days, the London papers (particularly the *Daily Mirror*) were crowded with stories about how Harry Houdini would try to break free from the unbreakable Mirror Cuffs. Houdini was unusually reserved before the challenge. He was known for his boasts, but now he seemed shockingly reticent about the whole thing.

"Although I have never failed to open any handcuff or manacle in days gone by," Houdini wrote in the *Daily Mirror* the next day, "I am not quite confident as to opening this one. Should I fail to undo the handcuff, I will be the first to acknowledge it; but rest assured I will not fail to entertain and please my audience, whatever the ultimate result may be."

At midafternoon on St. Patrick's Day, Houdini took the stage. More than four thousand people jammed into the Hippodrome, including one hundred Fleet Street journalists. The Mirror Cuffs were the talk of London. The crowd impatiently waited through the six opening acts, then went wild when Houdini took the stage. The Mirror reported the opening cheer as "one of the finest ovations mortal man has ever received."

"I am ready," Houdini said. Without delay, Bennet stepped forward and clamped closed the Mirror Cuffs on Houdini's wrists. It was 3:15 p.m. precisely.

"I am now locked in a handcuff that has taken a British mechanic five years to make," Houdini said to the crowd. "I do not know whether I am going to get out of it or not, but I can assure you I am going to do my best."

Enormous roars engulfed Houdini as he stepped into his tent—the "ghost house," as he had come to call it—and the orchestra began to play. One of the great ironies of the Mirror Cuffs and so many of Houdini's other great escapes: nobody could see him, except in their own minds.

"Could you imagine audiences now just sitting there with nothing happening on the stage?" John Cox asks. "It's crazy to think about, right? We are in a time where if there is even a moment of dead air on television, everybody goes crazy. But if you think about it, Houdini's gift was his ability to create tension. People didn't need to see him. They could picture him behind the tent struggling with the Mirror Cuffs. And the longer it went on, the more exciting it became."

After twenty-two minutes, Houdini emerged— the crowd let out an enormous cheer thinking he was free—but everyone quickly noticed that the cuffs were still on Houdini's wrists. Houdini explained that he had come out so he could get a closer look at the lock under the electric lights.

Thirteen minutes after that, at 3:50 p.m., Houdini again came out from the tent—in Bennet's memory he was "now showing signs of defeat in his crumpled shirt and streaming face."

"My knees hurt," Houdini said. "But I am not done yet."

At this, Bennet—no William Hope Hodgson—gracefully consented: "The *Mirror* has no desire to submit Mr. Houdini to a torture test. And if Mr. Houdini will permit me, I shall have great pleasure in offering him the use of my cushion."

Houdini accepted and was brought a cup of water. He returned to his tent.

What was the atmosphere like? The *Mirror* reported that "Ladies trembled with suppressed excitement, and despite the weary wait, not a yawn was to be noticed throughout the vast audience." Houdini was in the tent for twenty more minutes, and at 4:10 p.m.—almost a full hour since the challenge began—Houdini emerged once more. The cuffs were still locked tight on his wrists. He looked so battered and beaten that Bess left the theater in near-hysterics; she could take no more.

"Will you remove the cuffs for a moment,"

Houdini asked Bennet, "in order that I may take my coat off?"

Bennet shook his head no, and the crowd began to hiss and yell menacingly in disapproval. Bennet raised a hand and said in as calm a voice as he could manage, "Ladies and gentlemen, I only ask for fair play between Mr. Houdini and myself. I do not wish to take any unfair advantage of him, but in justice to my paper, I must see that he takes no unfair advantage of me. Mr. Houdini has seen me lock the handcuffs. If he were now to see me unlock them, he would have a valuable clue to the secret of their mechanism. I respectfully submit that Mr. Houdini's request is unreasonable and for that reason, I decline to grant it."

The crowd then turned to Houdini, to see how he would take this rejection.

He shrugged as if he expected the refusal. Then he somehow grabbed a small penknife from his pocket. He pulled it open with his teeth. And in a series of sudden and wild movements, he ripped apart his jacket so that it fell from his body.

The extraordinary sounds of glee and laughter and encouragement and pure joy, Houdini, and Bennet would both say, exceeded anything they could have imagined. Houdini went back into the ghost house for the final time. Ten minutes later, he returned. And this time he held the unlocked Mirror Cuffs in his hand.

People rushed the stage. They pulled Houdini upon their shoulders and carried him around the theater. Houdini was so overcome that he began to sob.

"I entered this ring feeling like a doomed man," he said to the crowd. "There were times when I thought I could not get out of those handcuffs. But your applause gave me courage, and I determined to do or die. I have never seen such handcuffs, locks within locks. I have thought this was my Waterloo, after nineteen years of work. I have not slept for nights. But I will do so tonight."

For the rest of his life, Harry Houdini happily explained most of his escapes to close friends and left behind detailed notes that magicians have repeatedly studied. But he never explained how he escaped the Mirror Cuffs. More than one hundred years have gone by, and countless people have claimed to uncover the secret. But here's the truth: we don't know, even now.

This is what makes the Mirror Cuffs, for me, Houdini's most fascinating escape.

HOW HE DID IT
(THEORY ONE)

We start with Will Goldston's guess. Houdini's life—and the world of magic in his time—spilled over with charming rogues, honest liars, reformed con men, and such. Will Goldston was a character all his own. He performed as a magician, though he never made much of a name for himself on the stage and was mostly known for being an English magic dealer and book publisher. Goldston's trade, in large part, was stealing magicians' secrets and putting them into print. How did he get the secrets? While Goldston put on the airs of a proper and modest English gentleman, he was an astute politician who knew how to find people's pressure points.

"In retrospect," Jim Steinmeyer wrote in *The Glamorous Deception*, about the life of magician Chung Ling Soo, "it seems that magicians often befriended Goldston because they were afraid of him—like offering food to a wild wolf so he wouldn't bite. If Goldston didn't like someone, he could inflict a great deal of damage."

Goldston brilliantly played Houdini, feeding the man's ego relentlessly and transparently. "A great artiste and a great man," he wrote of Houdini. While Houdini was perpetually suspicious and ready for a fight, he was helpless against such praise. The men exchanged once-a-week letters for the last twenty years of Houdini's life. Goldston waited only three years after Houdini's death to write *Sensational Tales of Mystery Men*, where he took repeated cheap shots at his old friend.

"Houdini was a man of moods, sometimes sweet and kind, but just as often the reverse," Goldston wrote. "His childishness, his irritability, his quick temper often overshadowed the rest."

We'll let one Goldston story in the book stand for all of them: Goldston wrote that he once showed Houdini a prized painting he had purchased. Houdini took one look at the painting and insisted that it was actually his. Goldston was mortified and offered to show Houdini the receipt. But Houdini waved his hand and said that it did not matter if Goldston had actually purchased it. The painting had been promised to Houdini and, as such, belonged to Houdini.

"Harry," Goldston said (or at least wrote), "your friendship is worth more to me than that picture. Don't let's have words over it."

"No," Houdini replied. "Don't let's. I'll take it."

And Houdini took the painting off the wall.

Houdini could be like that; there are stories of him claiming possession of books and magical apparatus that he simply believed should be in

225

his collection. But it should be said that Goldston may have had reasons for portraying Houdini in a negative light. He was a devoted spiritualist who held a powerful grudge against Houdini for unmasking fraudulent mediums and attacking spiritualism. Goldston was also a jealous man; you can almost feel the envy bubbling over as he writes of Houdini, the magician.

"He was generally acknowledged as a great performer," Goldston wrote in his book. "This he certainly was. He was also described as a magical manager. This he was not. He was a clever conjurer and nothing more."

Whatever jealousy or bitterness lingered inside Goldston, he did know Houdini well. So, when he offered his theory about how Houdini escaped from the Mirror Cuffs in *Sensational Tales*, it caused quite a bit of commotion in the magic community.

Goldston wrote his theory as a short story called "Did Houdini Fail?"

"A man whose sources of information were usually correct," he wrote, "told me that Houdini never escaped from the handcuffs."

Goldston's theory was that the Mirror Cuffs defeated Houdini. Yes, Houdini had expressed public worry about the challenge, but Goldston believed Houdini did not take the affair seriously in private. He was, after all, Harry Houdini, and he had escaped handcuffs all over the world. In

Goldston's retelling, Houdini was cocky and unconcerned.

After only a few minutes of working on the cuffs, Goldston wrote, Houdini realized he was overmatched. The locks-inside-locks brilliance of the Mirror Cuffs could not be picked, and he began to panic. This was why he kept coming out of the tent, Goldston believed. He was stalling. He was hoping that someone in his family would save the day.

Finally, Houdini caught Bess's eye and—perhaps through the coded body language they had worked on together as spiritualists—let her know that she had to get the key. Bess sensed his desperation; nobody knew Houdini's doubts and fears better than she did.

Now comes the crux of Goldston's theory: he wrote that Bess approached Bennet, the *Daily Mirror* reporter, and pleaded with him to give her the key. She explained that while the Mirror Cuffs was a publicity play for the newspaper, it was life and death for Harry Houdini. She talked about how failure could end his career. In later versions of the theory, Bess sobbed helplessly. Bennet being a gentleman, naturally gave her the key. She somehow passed the key to Houdini when she brought him a glass of water.

In the most romantic version, she slipped it to him through a kiss.

"When Houdini came to see me two days later,"

Goldston wrote, "I put the question to him point-blank. 'Say, Harry,' I said, 'they're telling me you unlocked the handcuffs with the journalist's key. Is that true?'

" 'Who's been saying that?' he demanded.

" 'Never mind who. Is it true?'

" 'Since you know so much, Will, you had better find out the rest,' he said."

Goldston's theory does have some support from the *Daily Mirror* story that ran the next day. In the middle of it—rather abruptly and for no obvious reason—there's an unexpected celebration of Bess Houdini:

> Mr. Houdini calls his charming wife his mascot. "Eleven years ago, she brought me luck," says the handcuff marvel, "and it has been with me ever since. I never had any before I married her." Mrs. Houdini is a fair, cultured, beautiful American lady, petite, fascinating and clever.

A celebration of Bess's culture, beauty, and cleverness seems a little out of place in a story about Houdini's handcuff escape; it might lend some credence to Goldston's notion that she played a role in his escape.

But, alas, there are significant problems with Goldston's theory. First, by all newspaper accounts, it wasn't Bess who brought Houdini the glass of water on stage—it was the Hippodrome theater manager. The Mirror Cuffs escape was one of the most thoroughly covered events in the history of magic, and not one story has Bess approaching Houdini at any point before the cuffs are off.

Second, it only takes a quick glance at the Mirror Cuffs key—a cylindrical key, six to eight inches long—to eliminate the possibility that you could hide it in a glass of water or pass it with a kiss.

But the third and most significant logical problem with Goldston's theory was his notion that Houdini would have come into the Mirror Cuffs challenge underprepared and overconfident. No one who has taken even a fleeting look at Houdini's life at all could believe such a thing. Houdini was unflagging in his preparation for every challenge. Houdini was a fear-based animal; he worried constantly about how the slightest slipup could end his career. As such, he blunted any possibility of failure by always—always—stacking the odds in his favor. This was a large part of what made him Houdini.

The very notion that Houdini walked blindly into the Mirror Cuffs challenge is so ridiculous that it makes you wonder how well Goldston really knew his old friend.

"I'm afraid we shall never know what actually happened," Goldston wrote. "But you can take it from me that Houdini had the greatest shock of his life. He afterward told me that he would sooner face death a dozen times than live through that ordeal again."

Will Goldston spent countless hours conversing with, questioning, and learning from Harry Houdini. But in the end, he fell for the trick just like anyone else.

HOW HE DID IT
(THEORY TWO)

Our second guess about how Harry escaped comes from a mystery man named Joseph P. Wilson. Nobody knows who he was; it's possible that he was the same Joseph P. Wilson who edited the much-missed *Salesology* magazine ("devoted to increased efficiency in sales") but probably not. It's also possible that Joseph P. Wilson was a pseudonym. Either way, in 1920—before Houdini's death—Joseph P. Wilson wrote a story in *Illustrated World* magazine called "Uncrowning the Handcuff King."

"The January *Illustrated World* goes out of its way to publish an expose of escape acts under the caption of 'Uncrowning the Handcuff King,'" A. M. Wilson wrote in his magic magazine *The Sphinx*. "One Joseph P. Wilson contributes the article. I presume he has a grudge against Houdini."

Wilson undoubtedly did have a grudge against Houdini, but he cleverly never mentioned his name in this article. Wilson referred to his subject pejoratively as the "handcuff king" or "king," or something less flattering.

"Opinions are many as to how the handcuff king actually makes his escape from irons, chains,

231

and locks," he began. "Many believe that this is a pure gift—that King Pickum was brought into this world to amuse and mystify the good folks at the expense of His Majesty, the Law. Others claim that small bones and 'soft' bones enable the gifted one to shake the shackles."

You get the tone right away: Wilson had come to put the handcuff king in his place. He wrote that to be a handcuff king, you don't need special skills. You don't need extreme flexibility, great strength, a deep understanding of locks, or a supernatural ability.

What you need, he wrote plainly, is a key.

And that's it. He wrote that unless handcuffs are gaffed—made in such a way that they will open with some particular lever or gesture—they will not open without a key. He wrote that no one, not even the handcuff king, has ever escaped real handcuffs without a key.

He then offered his Mirror Cuffs theory: The whole thing, every bit of it, was an act. He wrote that Houdini had pretended to be stuck in the cuffs and that he knew how to get out of them the whole time. He wrote that the locksmith was a fraud. He wrote that Houdini had made the handcuffs himself:

Wilson summed it up like so: "All of which proves that if you can hide a key and hire help, you can king away to your heart's content."

Joseph P. Wilson, whoever he was, did not get

it right. His claim was built around the premise that the Mirror Cuffs were gaffed. But we know they were not. The original cuffs (along with a duplicate silver set given to Houdini as a gift) are featured in David Copperfield's private museum, and they have been studied at length by Copperfield himself, along with numerous other magicians and experts. They are not tricked up. They do not open on command.

Bill Liles, a lock expert, has closely studied the Mirror Cuffs and said that not only would it have been impossible for Houdini to pick the lock in the seventy minutes; it's not entirely clear how he could have opened such a complicated lock even with the key. If there is some secret way to open them, no one has discovered it in more than one hundred years of trying. The Mirror Cuffs are exactly what Bennet claimed them to be.

Houdini was so confident in the invulnerability of the Mirror Cuffs that after his escape he put the following letter in the *Mirror*:

To Whom It May Concern!

Since my success in mastering the celebrated Daily Mirror Handcuff it has come to my knowledge that certain disappointed, skeptical persons have made use of most unjust remarks against the result of last Thursday's contest.

In particular, one person has had the

brazen audacity to proclaim himself able to open the Mirror Handcuff in two minutes.

Such being the case, I hereby challenge any mortal being to open the Mirror Handcuff in the same space of time that I did. I will allow him the use of both hands, also any instrument or instruments, barring the actual key. The cuff must not be broken or spoilt. Should he succeed, I will forfeit 100 guineas.

Furthermore, it has reached my ears that people are saying that at the contest I slipped one hand before undoing the Mirror Handcuff. I now agree to forfeit a further sum of 25 guineas to anyone who can pick the handcuff within twenty-four consecutive hours with one hand locked in the manacle.

Harry Houdini

Many people wrote in to say that they could break free of the Mirror Cuffs, and a few days later one was given the chance. He was a "reed thin 23-year-old" named Bruce Beaumont; the instant Houdini saw him, he knew that Beaumont could slip his wrists through the cuffs.

Houdini was nobody's fool; he promptly locked the cuffs and just handed them to Beaumont. "Open them now," Houdini said. Beaumont was incensed and shouted that Houdini had changed the rules of the contest. Nobody in the crowd was much interested; they booed Beaumont until he threw the Mirror Cuffs down in disgust. Management approached the stage and asked the crowd if they would like to see Bruce Beaumont thrown out. They did. He was.

So, no, Joseph P. Wilson did not get it right. But was he on to something? Was the Mirror Cuffs escape a setup? Let's go to the next set of theories.

HOW HE DID IT
(THEORIES GALORE)

Doug Henning, the biggest magician in the world during the 1970s, thought that the lesson of the Mirror Cuffs was that the secret didn't really matter.

"While it is unthinkable that a canny showman like Houdini would ever have accepted such a publicized challenge without knowing exactly how he would meet it," he wrote, "the incident graphically illustrates how through his showmanship, he was able to transcend the puzzle of how his escapes were done and move audiences to near hysteria over the fact that he was able to do them."

He added: "While there has been great conjecture among magicians, no one knows how Houdini escaped from the Mirror Cuffs."

The Amazing Randi came to the same conclusion. Randi has spent a lifetime studying and following in the footsteps of his hero Houdini. In his long life, he has performed just about every Houdini escape. He, like Houdini, dedicated much of his life to the world of skepticism.

"I can personally think of many subterfuges that Harry could have employed to escape, and I'm sure that some of these have already occurred to my readers," he wrote. "I must add that the handcuffs were in perfect working order when Houdini had forced himself from them. There were no marks or signs of them having been forced in any way by the master escape artist.

"How he did achieve the escape from the Mirror Handcuffs is not known."

In the end, this is good enough for many. We don't know. We'll never know. But while such uncertainties might suit some, they do not play well in Houdini World. There are always people who want to know, who need to know, everything there is to know about Harry Houdini. The Mirror Cuffs escape is one of the most exciting puzzles of Houdini's life. None of these people are going to just let "We'll never know" stand as an answer.

Joe Notaro is one of the leading explorers of Houdini World. His obsession with Houdini—like John Cox's obsession or mine—began with the Tony Curtis movie. Notaro had been given a magic set earlier that year, but it was the movie—specifically the way Curtis portrayed the ambitious, likable, and moody Houdini—that unlocked the handcuffs in Notaro's brain. He says that from then on, he did all his book reports and school projects on Houdini.

When Notaro got out of school, he generally moved on his with his life but still kept in touch with his Houdini side. He took his family to Appleton to see the Houdini childhood home.

He taught a few magic classes, made Houdini presentations at conventions, and collected Houdini memorabilia.

Then in 2011, he started the website Houdini Circumstantial Evidence. The name, like the site, was dedicated to true Houdini insiders: *Circumstantial Evidence* was the alternate title for Houdini's silent movie, *The Grim Game*. The website freed up Notaro in the same way that Wild About Harry freed up John Cox. Now, he had an excuse to do what he really wanted to do: spend a lot of time and effort investigating Harry Houdini.

Notaro's first big break was directly connected to the Mirror Cuffs when he solved one of the challenge's biggest mysteries: he found the name of the *Daily Mirror* reporter who challenged Houdini, Will A. Bennet.

There were no bylines in newspapers in the early twentieth century. Bennet's name was not mentioned in any of the stories surrounding the challenge. One day, Notaro was looking at an Australian newspaper, and he ran across an April 1910 story in the *Sydney Evening News*—this was years after the challenge—and Will A. Bennet recounted how he challenged and almost defeated Harry Houdini as a reporter for the *Daily Mirror*. It might not have won Notaro the Pulitzer, but among fellow Houdini obsessives, it was a landmark discovery.

Questions immediately were asked. Was Will A. Bennet a real person or a pseudonym? Paul Davies, a regular contributor at Handcuffs.org, found evidence that proved Will A. Bennet was the man's real name.

Okay, but was he the *Daily Mirror* reporter? A Houdini researcher named Narinder Chadda took his daughter to the British Library to find the source of the Will A. Bennet story, which appeared in a relatively obscure periodical called *Pearson's Weekly*. That article had Bennet's signature, which they matched to a 1913 photo that Davies found of Bennet referring to the Mirror Cuffs challenge. So now they definitively knew what Bennet looked like.

All that was left to do was find the 1904 picture taken after the Mirror Cuffs escape and look at the previously unidentified man standing next to Houdini. It was unmistakable. He was Will A. Bennet.

You might wonder: Why would so many people go to so much effort to find out something seemingly so small and unimportant about an escape from more than a century ago? But that's the fun: the chase, the willingness to go beyond what anyone outside of your world would find excessive.

If you're from another group, you might wonder something else: What about the locksmith who supposedly spent five years building the Mirror

Cuffs, Nathaniel Hart? Didn't someone from Houdini World try to find out about him?

Of course. You will want to hear from Mick Hanzlik.

Mick Hanzlik was a supremely likable second-generation locksmith from Northampton in England's East Midlands. His father, Josef, opened Hanzlik Locksmiths on Lutterworth Road, and Mick took it over. He was a jovial man and a bit of a local legend. In addition to his locksmith duties, he interviewed celebrities and other local characters on his own show for a small Northampton radio station.

Hanzlik became smitten by Houdini when he was eleven or twelve—that seems to be the magical age. His entry wasn't a movie but instead William Lindsay Gresham's book, *The Man Who Walked Through Walls*. He never tired of reading about Houdini; he ended up building what he and others called the largest Houdini library north of London.

His interest in Nathaniel Hart comes from the most obvious place: as a locksmith who was the son of a locksmith, Hanzlik was utterly fascinated by the man who supposedly had spent years building the Mirror Cuffs. Mick was relentless in his pursuit. Long after most people in Houdini World had reached the seemingly obvious conclusion that Hart was a fictional character invented by Bennet to give the whole thing some drama, Hanzlik kept on going. He searched birth certificates. He scanned Birmingham business directories. He refused to accept the possibility that Nathaniel Hart was make-believe.

Even now, if you scan the comment boards on handcuff and lock websites—there are many more than you might expect—you are almost certain to find a comment like this one Mick posted on a site called Antique Locks:

> Hello - first timer!
>
> I am looking for any information on Birmingham Locksmith Nathaniel Hart, whom I think was still active in 1904.
>
> I also would like contact details of any living relatives.
>
> This is for research I am doing on a possible link with Harry Houdini.
>
> Many thanks
> Mick Hanzlik,
> Master Locksmith,
> Northampton

After he came up empty, Hanzlik devised alternate theories. For a time, he thought Hart might just be a pseudonym for Houdini's beloved locksmith Thomas Froggatt. That was probably right—most Houdini students think that Froggatt was Hart—but Mick couldn't bear to think of a world without Nathaniel Hart, and he walked back his own theory.

"If Nathaniel Hart existed—and I still think he did—I think it would be inevitable that he and Tom would meet up," he wrote. "Originally thought that Tom and Nathaniel were the same person. But now I'd like to think that they knew each other."

Mick would not give up the chase. In order to get closer to Hart, he even made his own set of Mirror Cuffs, spending more years building them than Hart himself had spent. He finally finished the Hanzlik Mirror Cuffs in 2014, and they were gorgeous, the talk of Houdini World.

Mick Hanzlik died of cancer just a few months later. Mick never found Nathaniel Hart. But he never stopped believing in him.

While the Amazing Randi believes we'll never know for sure, he leans toward Goldston's theory that Houdini must have found a way to get the key. Ken Silverman agreed. "The bringing onstage a glass of water for Houdini to drink," he wrote, "does figure in several of his most phenomenal escapes."

Jim Steinmeyer, meanwhile, thinks the precise opposite. "Having seen the Mirror Cuffs and how they work," he says, "the one thing I can tell you for sure is that there's no way he could have opened them with a key."

Will A. Bennet offered a fascinating and mysterious clue.

"Everything ended happily, except, perhaps, for my locksmith, who was brokenhearted when he first heard the news," Bennet wrote. "But, at all events, he had the satisfaction of knowing that he had done more than any other of his craft had ever been able to accomplish; and further, although I must not betray trade secrets, that it was only a peculiar physical defect that enabled Houdini to defeat his beautiful mechanism."

A peculiar physical defect? Silverman did find a clipping somewhere—he could not identify the source—that quoted Nathaniel Hart himself saying Houdini escaped because he had a malformed hand that allowed him to contort his bones.

"My own theory, if you are interested," John Cox says, "is that the Mirror Cuffs Challenge was a creation of Houdini. I think the cuffs were made to Houdini's specifications, and one loop was slightly enlarged. That is what allowed him to slip out of one side. You can see that the loops are irregular. He then used the key to open them and release the other hand. I feel it was necessary to slip one side because of the way he was cuffed; it would not have been possible to work the key in the lock."

So many theories.

Joshua Jay thinks the whole thing was probably set up from the start.

"As a piece of living history that remains unsolved, it's a lovely anecdote," he says. "And while my scholarship in that area is limited, from what I know of Houdini, it would have all been a stitch-up.

"But here's the key thing everybody gets wrong about Houdini: I don't fault him for things like this. Orchestrating moments like this was his genius. People hear about them, and they might be disappointed, the same way laymen are often disappointed by the methods of magic tricks. But they're necessary to create lasting moments. We shouldn't avoid that. We should celebrate it. This was how Houdini wrote himself into history."

MY GUESS

He switched the cuffs. Yeah, I know, I just quoted Josh saying that the method doesn't matter, that it is the magic that endures, but let's face it: you can't write several chapters about the Mirror Cuffs and not at least try to guess the secret. My guess is that he switched the cuffs. I base my theory on a hint I got from Joe Notaro, and I think it's the most elegant of all the possibilities.

There are three known sets of Mirror Cuffs. One is the original; the second is a duplicate given to him as a gift. Both are owned by David Copperfield. But there is a third set—Notaro found a photograph of what was called "The Special Pair of Handcuffs" in *The Tatler* magazine. They look identical to the Mirror Cuffs, but there is a key difference: these cuffs were not opened with the long and thin Bramah-style key that would have been impossible to use once locked in the cuffs. Instead, these open with a small key that would be both easy to hide and easy to use to escape the cuffs.

This is what Notaro (and I) believe happened: Everyone was shown the real Mirror Cuffs in the days before the escape. In publicity photographs, Houdini was seen wearing the real ones, and after the escape was done, Houdini walked onstage holding them.

But when Will A. Bennet locked the cuffs on Houdini's wrists, he did not use the real Mirror Cuffs. He instead used the *Tatler* cuffs that were easy for Houdini to escape.

"I don't buy into theories where a key is concealed in the glass of water or in Bess's mouth when she gives him a kiss," Notaro says. "I also don't buy into the theory that he slipped one hand (although capable) to use a key. All of these things divert attention from the real secret."

Notaro concedes that we can't know if our guess is right. He and others have studied the photographs of Houdini while onstage at the Hippodrome, but the cuffs are so similar there is simply no way to tell which ones Houdini was wearing.

Look, this theory has as many problems as all the rest. But I like it.

In the end: what is magic? One of the loveliest definitions comes from the writer Ken Kesey. He was writing about how Deadheads—those Grateful Dead fans—traveled in the band not for the music or the drugs but for a sliver of magic. And every now and again, they found it.

"When you see something like that," he wrote, "there's a crack in your mind, and you know it's a trick, but you can't figure it out. The crack lets in all the light. It opens up all the possibilities."

That is what the Mirror Cuffs escape does: it opens up all the possibilities. Did Bess plead with the reporter for the key and then somehow—either through water or a kiss—pass that key to Houdini? Unlikely, but maybe.

Did Houdini merely pull his hand out from the Mirror Cuffs and then use the key or a pick to get out of them? Unlikely, but maybe.

Did Houdini work with the *Daily Mirror* from beginning to end? Did he coordinate with Will A. Bennet? Did he create the stunning handcuffs with the help of his locksmith Thomas Froggatt? Did he invent the stubbornly artistic locksmith Nathaniel Hart to create marvelous mythology?

The crack that lets in all the light is this: we'll never know.

I think he switched the cuffs, though.

A few weeks after Harry Houdini died, Bess showed the locksmith Charles Courtney the Mirror Cuffs. They were locked. Courtney asked Bess if he could open them. She shook her head.

"I must never let anyone touch that lock," Bess said. "These handcuffs—he promised me that if he can pierce the veil of death, he will unlock them. Then I will know that he has returned to me."

MIRACLES

On a cold winter day in Columbus, Ohio, I watched an extraordinary magician named Eric Mead describe a miracle for more than an hour. The trick, invented by magician Chris Kenner, is called Three Fly.

If you go on to the internet, you can find a

dozen tutorials to teach you how to do Three Fly. It's really the most basic of tricks. You have three silver dollars in your left hand and none in the right hand. Instantly and invisibly, one of the coins flies to the right hand. This happens so quickly that it's hard for the mind to process what happened. The magician waits for your mind to recalibrate and then does it again, this time with two coins in the left hand, one coin in the right. One coin flies invisibly from left hand to right. Finally, the third coin goes over.

In most of our hands, it is little more than a birthday party illusion.

But it is a miracle for Eric Mead. He does it with such audacity. He shows us one particular move that is so bold and brazen that you simply cannot believe he gets away with it. But he does, and in his hands Three Fly becomes something so much more.

"I wish I could be you right now," he tells the audience, "and see this for the first time."

Eric began in magic the same way most magicians do: when he was six, he received a book on Houdini. Wonder has been Eric's North Star ever since. These days he's one of the most sought-after magical speakers in the United States. He set a record for doing the most TED Talks, the influential video series dedicated to new ideas, and has worked with just about every major company.

But Eric has spent most of his life as a working magician—emphasis on working—which meant countless hours in clubs, on cruises, on the streets, in living rooms, at banquets, in restaurants, at conventions, wherever people would pay to see little miracles. He has faced every kind of audience, which has meant all his life he has dealt with skepticism, with cynicism, with people trying to figure out the trick.

Once, a middle-aged man came up to him and said, "There comes a time when you must put childish things away." Eric is not the sort to let what anyone says affect him or bother him; he long before had put away such sensitivities. But there was something about the man's appearance (this was at a convention for physicists, and the man had a slide rule in his pocket) and the way he said it caused Eric to think hard about what magic means.

"For me," he wrote in his book *Tangled Web*, "it begins with the recognition that at its heart, performance magic is a search. It's a search for the secret place hiding inside the viewer where there is no understanding, no control, and everything is a swirling, meaningless dance. Wonder. Astonishment. Awe. We spend so much of our time and energy denying and suppressing this part of ourselves that some of us become convinced that it doesn't exist.

"Good magic sneaks up on you and finds the

secret passage to the part of you that knows this is bullshit. It sweeps your mental supports out from under you for a moment and reminds you that the essential nature of life is mystery."

THE NEEDLES

I'm sitting in the second row, and Houdini is doing a trick. He would take some needles and put them in his mouth, and a spool of thread, and then he would thread the needles. So, he asked for a volunteer out of the audience, and who do you think went up on stage? And he opened his mouth wide. "I wanna prove that there is no trickery to this trick. What do you see in there?" And I said, "Pyorrhea!" And left the stage.

—Groucho Marx

A confession: I never got the Needles. It is this crazy, legendary thing, perhaps the most copied Houdini trick of them all. Teller was performing the Needles the first time his longtime partner Penn Jillette saw him. Chloé Crawford did the Needles for *The Illusionists* on Broadway (but with razor blades instead of needles). It's Joshua Jay's favorite Houdini trick—so much so, that Josh bought Houdini's original needles and keeps them in a place of honor in his New York apartment.

"It's this perfect little mystery," he says to me as I hold the box with the needles.

"The only mystery to me," I say, "is why anybody likes it."

"Oh, you've got to be kidding," he says. "It's the greatest."

Houdini sure loved it. He performed every chance he could. He performed it in small parlors for presidents and kings and on huge stages, even though it was ludicrous.

"In this trick," Houdini explained, "I swallow—if one's eyes are to be trusted—anywhere from fifty to a hundred and fifty needles and from to ten to thirty yards of thread; then after a few seconds I bring up the needles all threaded."

First of all: gross. But more to the point, imagine how that looked from the audience's perspective. If you were sitting past the third row, you couldn't even see the needles and you sure as heck couldn't see the thread.

"They knew there were needles," vaudeville star the Great Leon said of the audience, "because Houdini told them so."

You might remember that Houdini offered to sell the trick's secret for five bucks back when he was down on his luck. Back then, he said the Needles (which he called the Hindoo Needle Trick) "was taught to me by a Hindoo at World's Fair in 1893." He might have picked it up that year, but it was almost certainly from a well-known sideshow performer called Maxey the Needle King. Maxey, according to the *Detroit*

Free Press that same year of 1893, would "fill his mouth with needles and thread and brings the former out all threaded."

And Maxey didn't invent the trick either. The Needles goes back at least to 1879 when an author who called himself Professor Lorento put its secret in his book *Amateur Amusements.* "Be careful not to swallow the needles," Professor Lorento warned his readers. A useful tip. In other words, the Needles was a well-known party trick by the time Houdini started performing it.

And yet: Houdini somehow turned it into a timeless classic of magic.

"What was Houdini about?" Joshua Jay says. "Danger and impossibility. That was his unbeatable combination. That's why I love the Needles so much; it's like Houdini in miniature. It's a perfect little blend of danger and impossibility, the danger as the needles went down, and impossibility when they came back up threaded."

I understood what Josh was saying. Still, I didn't get it at all.

And then I was lucky enough to meet Juan Tamariz.

Spain's Juan Tamariz hides his genius in plain sight. When he performs his sleight-of-hand act—always wearing his iconic purple top hat and black vest with a rose pinned on it—he appears to be a wonderful, bumbling, and lovable grandfather who never seems entirely sure he can actually pull off the trick he's trying.

"Will the card come to the top?" he asks his volunteers in his thick Spanish accent. "Will it? Yes? Yes? No. No, it will not work. No, we do not have enough magic. We must try again tomorrow. No, it will not . . . WAIT! [Tamariz's "WAIT" comes out so loud and suddenly that half the audience jumps at the word.] . . . Yes, something is happening. Yes, the card is moving up to the sixth position! Now to the fifth position! It is moving up, yes, yes, yes, no. No, it has stopped. It cannot go any higher. No, we must admit defeat and . . . WAIT!"

And when the card does reach the top and the impossible magic happens, he smiles and credits the magic of the people around him and plays an invisible violin and sings, "Ya, da da, da da!"

If you see Tamariz perform, you will smile. You will laugh. You will get caught up in the emotion of the moment. You might feel your head spin a little bit. But there's a good chance that you will not fully appreciate that you are watching the most admired magician on earth.

"The greatest magician," Joshua Jay says.

"The greatest," magician David Blaine says.

"The greatest magician in the world," magician and writer Jamy Ian Swiss says.

"The Maestro," magician and children's author Adam Rubin says.

"Maybe the greatest magician ever," Eric Mead says.

Everyone inside magic understands his brilliance. Aspiring card magicians travel to Madrid to study with him. Some of the most famous magicians on earth hope only to be invited to one of his after-show gatherings, where a choice few magicians and friends huddle together just to see what kind of freeform magic Tamariz can come up with.

"It happens anywhere from two a.m. to six a.m., after a late-night dinner and lots of booze," the mentalist Asi Wind said in a wonderful movie called *Our Magic*. "And then he takes his mat out and his cards, and he says, 'Ah, maybe, perhaps, something crazy will happen. Shuffle!' And then he goes into this half an hour or hour of magic, and he blows your mind. I think every person who gets to be there, at least once in his lifetime, is lucky."

"Everyone," Joshua Jay says, "has tried to copy his energy, his approach, his connection to the audience."

Tamariz has a wonderful thought about the power of magic, and it is the thing that made me, for the first time, fully understand and appreciate why Houdini survives and why the Needles lasts. He has an entire lecture called "The Magic Way," where he breaks down his thoughts on what a magician should do with every part of his body—

his eyes, his voice, his hands, his feet. He can talk for hours just about the feet, exactly how you should stand (feet at forty-five-degree angle, spread a little bit apart), how you should step, how you should walk on the stage and so on.

He says that magic can become art only if you use it to express what he calls your "interior world."

"For me, you must use magic to express love, to express passion, to express your feelings about life," he says. "If you do not express your interior world, if your interior world is not rich and interesting, you can still be a great showman. You can be a great communicator. You can be a great performer. But, for me, you cannot be a great artist."

And him saying that made me realize: the Needles—both literally and figuratively—perfectly expresses Houdini's interior world. Houdini's grand ambition was to show that he was different, invincible, courageous, immortal. He could escape from anything. He could survive anything. He could eat needles and then pull them from inside with a piece of thread.

"What do we do as artists?" Tamariz asks. "We take a dream, our dream, yes, and we put it into other people. We show them what is in our dream. At the same time, we make them say, 'No! This is impossible! Cannot be done! Perhaps I am dreaming now!' This is two things,

258

the intellectual, 'Oh, this is what I am seeing.' And the emotional, 'No, this is impossible!' "

And with that, the Needles opened up for me. I understood. The Needles is a strange dream brought to life by Harry Houdini. He didn't invent it. He didn't add much to it. But it is his dream.

THE CHALLENGES

What was it that kept Houdini going? It's a mysterious question. For others, the motivation, the inspiration, it's obvious. Love keeps Juan Tamariz going. Love is what gives him energy, what brings him focus, what makes him excited to perform for people even when he's exhausted. He doesn't just love the magic. He loves the audience. He loves the volunteers he brings on the stage. He loves the little moments of connection he feels when he looks out into the audience—he says it is like being attached to them by a piece of thread. He talks about the seven veils of mystery, the seven things that come through in great magic, though nobody quite understands why.

First, there is the mystery of the love. The more you love magic, the more the audience can feel it. "How do they know?" he asks, and he shrugs, for this is the mystery. "They know."

Second is the mystery of knowledge. The more you know about the trick—even seemingly trivial things such as who invented it, the history of how it evolved over the years, what other tricks are like it—the better it works. "How do they feel this?" Tamariz asks. "I don't know. It's a mystery."

Third is the mystery of work—the better the work you put in to prepare, the richer the experience for the audience. Fourth is the mystery of energy—the more energy you feel inside, the more passion you feel as you perform, the richer the experience. Again, how can the audience possibly know? They just do.

Fifth is something Tamariz calls the mystery of the truth. Magicians lie, as we know. They tell you that there's nothing there when there's something there. They tell you that this is a normal deck of cards or a normal set of handcuffs or a normal packing trunk, and it might not be anything at all. But Tamariz says, "The more truth that is in the thing, the more people believe it to be true. People feel this, and I don't know how they feel this."

Sixth is the mystery of the interior world; as you know Tamariz believes that true art is about expressing a person's deepest feelings about what it is to be alive.

And the last, the seventh veil of mystery, is the same as the first, the mystery of love.

There is no misunderstanding what it is that makes Tamariz go. He is awed and fascinated by every aspect of magic and is driven by love.

"It must be more than applause," he says. "It must be more than fame."

Harry Houdini was a different sort of man.

• • •

Houdini often said that his drive came from the promise he made to Mayer Samuel, the promise to take care of his mother. And there is no question that protecting and supporting Cecilia was a driving force in his life. He would recall how, in London in 1901, he came upon a window display of a gorgeous dress made for Queen Victoria, who had died just months earlier. Houdini burst into the shop in his typically dramatic way.

"I am Houdini," he pronounced. "And I would like to purchase the Queen's dress for my mother."

The conservative English shopkeeper looked appalled and slightly frightened; it was unseemly to sell a dress made for the Queen of England. But Houdini proved surprisingly persuasive by offering fifty pounds, more than the average English household made in a year, and the shop-keeper accepted on the condition that the dress never be worn in Great Britain.

Houdini promptly sent for his mother and met her for his performance in Hamburg. They went together back to Budapest, Houdini's birthplace, and Houdini held a grand reception in her honor. Cecilia wore Queen Victoria's dress. "Mother and I were awake all night talking over the affair," Houdini said, "and if happiness ever entered my life to its fullest, it was in sharing Mother's wonderful enjoyment at playing a queen for a day."

The story might be exaggerated—this is Houdini, after all—but the point is that he cared for Cecilia. He spoiled her. "I have kept the promise I made to my father that Mother would never want for anything," he wrote. "What more could any man want?"

But Houdini did want more, and he wanted it with white-hot intensity that lasted until the day he died.

What was it? Was it money? He never stopped demanding more money. He was Houdini, after all, and as such he deserved to be the highest-paid performer in the world. Nobody fought theater owners harder. He lost friends over it. Once, when he was approached to play in a silent film version of *20,000 Leagues Under the Sea*, he demanded $40,000 ($1 million in 2019 dollars), a fee so fantastic that even he conceded, "I'm afraid I want too much." But he would not back down. Houdini never backed down.

But he seemed more driven by the idea of money than money itself. He had simple tastes in food, clothing, luxury. He didn't crave creature comforts. He lived with his mother, and he wore tattered old clothes and famously wore them haphazardly; more than one person through the years wrote about Houdini in the streets looking like a bum. Bess used to tell people that she had to quietly buy new underwear for Houdini and take the old ones out of circulation without him knowing it.

He spent money on two things: first was magic books and paraphernalia. He spent almost all of his free time in whatever city he happened to be in wandering through old bookstores and adding to what would become the largest magic library in the world.

The second thing: fame. When it came to self-promotion, Houdini spent like a sailor. He wined and dined reporters—probably bribing a few along the way—and hired brilliantly talented ghostwriters, including the now renowned horror novelist H. P. Lovecraft, to tell exaggerated tales about him or write short stories under the Houdini name. He had posters plastered all over every town where he performed. He set up hundreds of public displays—bridge jumps, straitjacket escapes, jailbreaks—to encourage people to come to the shows.

Even Houdini's most famous critic, Dai Vernon, conceded that Houdini was a genius when it came to publicity. "If he had been a butcher, a cobbler, an architect, or a lawyer, he would have been known all over the world. He was obsessed with one thing: to make his name a household word."

"Houdini is completely modern in his sensibility," Steinmeyer said. "One would say it's admirable, but it's also genuinely freakish. He had a modern view of fame, something that runs entirely counter to his own time."

And in the end, fame was the guiding light for Houdini. And nothing better demonstrates this than the challenge phase of Houdini's career. In the years after he became the Great Houdini but before he became possessed by death, Houdini took on challenges. Day after day after day, at the height of his career, Houdini would ask people to dig deep into their own experiences and try to come up with a trap that could hold him. And he would always escape.

"We the undersigned," a challenge in London began, "do hereby challenge you to allow us to come on the stage and tie you to a chair, and we will guarantee to tie you so that it will be impossible for you to make your escape."

"We are skeptical," began another one in New York, "as to your ability to escape from a complete, regulation straitjacket such as used on the murderous insane at Blackwell's Island."

"We the Hogan Envelope Company believe a giant Envelope can be made by which will enclose Houdini and successfully prevent his escape," read a third.

The challenges kept coming, one after another after another, each progressively more devious and trying and grueling. The American Chicle Company challenged him to get out of the packing cases they used to send Black Jack gum to soldiers in France. The Pennsylvania Steel Company challenged Houdini to free himself after they lashed him to an eight-foot plank using ropes and sailor's knots. The suffragettes of England challenged Houdini to escape after being tied down to a mattress with sheets and bandages.

In Glasgow, he sat on a coffee-table-sized piece of wood and waited while nine carpenters built a crate around him in front of the audience. They then put chains all around it and tied it tight with rope. The curtain fell. Houdini escaped in fifteen minutes.

"Mobs waited for me," Houdini said after that one. "They took me shoulder high and carried me home."

Houdini always escaped. He had no choice. People locked him in caskets and baskets, boxes and crates and glass cases. They bound him in chains and ropes, handcuffs and straitjackets. They put him in envelopes. The University of Pennsylvania football team put him inside a giant football. Houdini was out in thirty-four minutes.

Another time, five Chinese sailors chained, strapped, and tied Houdini to a device they called a Sanguaw, which was just a large isosceles triangle made of wood. Houdini struggled with that one but eventually managed to get his legs free. He then somehow pulled himself to the top of the contraption and used his teeth to untie the knots. After that escape, he openly questioned the wisdom of accepting that challenge.

But he kept on accepting almost every challenge; his only demand was that he be given twenty-four hours with the challenge to work out his escape plan. The daily strain was immense. The physical grind was overwhelming. Houdini believed that every challenge was potentially career-ending for him; it would only take one failure and people would say, "Ah, that Houdini is washed up."

He had countless ways to escape. He carried every kind of pick imaginable. He tricked up some of the challenge boxes by replacing long nails with short ones (that way he could just bang his way out). He also was small and an athletic marvel with surpassing dexterity; he could pull himself up from any position, bend himself into any shape, overpower any weakness in the contraptions.

And, when he couldn't manipulate or will his way free, he found other ways. "If I find a lock or a jail I can't spiritualize," Houdini once told his friend T. Nelson Downs, "I must fix or arrange a way out."

On those rare occasions when he had exhausted all of his ideas, when his inventive assistants Jim Collins or Franz Kukol could not come up with a way out, he relied on his motivating force: he wanted out more than anyone wanted to keep him in.

STRAITJACKETS

THE WORLD FAMOUS
HOUDINI
THE FIRST HUMAN BEING TO
SUCCESSFULLY ESCAPE FROM A
REGULATION STRAIT JACKET AS USED
ON THE MURDEROUS INSANE
—Advertisement for Houdini

Look," Lee Terbosic is saying. "The straitjacket has been done to death. I mean it has been done to death. You've seen it how many times? Everyone has seen it how many times? You cannot go in front of an audience now and just get out of a straitjacket and expect anyone to care. They cared when Houdini did it because he was the first one to do it. Now? Now, you need something else."

Lee Terbosic is not an escape artist. He is, instead, a friendly young card magician in Pittsburgh, much more from the tradition of Dai Vernon and Juan Tamariz than Houdini. He always has a deck of cards in his hands. On weekends, he does a show called 52 Up Close, where he tells stories and jokes through various first-rate card tricks. In fact, as we sit in a hotel lobby, he casually pulls out a deck of cards and shows me a trick. He has me pick a card. I take the three of hearts. He then shuffles but instead of pulling out my card, he holds the deck up, just so, and I can see the side of the cards.

It reads, "THREE OF HEARTS."

This has become something of a trademark trick for Lee, though it is not his favorite. That honor belongs to a complicated and extended card trick that allows him to tell the entire history of his beloved Pittsburgh Steelers football team. Lee is a Pittsburgh guy, through and through, which, oddly enough, is exactly why I'm talking with him about Houdini.

In 1916, Houdini performed a straitjacket escape while dangling upside down high above downtown Pittsburgh.

One hundred years later, to the minute, Terbosic has decided he will perform the same escape in exactly the same place.

I ask him if he's ever done this before.

"No," he says. "I do a straitjacket escape, but I don't do it like that. When Houdini escaped from a straitjacket, it was different. It was new. It was dangerous. He played up the danger. He talked all the time about how these were the same jackets they used to restrain people in the insane asylum. And he flopped around like he was fighting death right there in front of your eyes."

He shrugs.

"I can't do it that way," he says. "Nobody would believe it."

Jim Steinmeyer believes that Houdini was not just the first escape artist, he was also the last. Sure, there have been many others who performed escapes since Houdini, but he says that's different because they are not really performing as escape artists.

They are performing as Houdini.

"You'll be very hard-pressed to find an escape artist even today who does the act without even *saying* Houdini twenty times during the act," he says. "It's always like, 'Allow me to do my homage to Houdini,' or 'Houdini would do this escape a certain way, but I will do it a different way,' or 'this was the escape that Houdini himself said was blah blah blah.' The act doesn't even make sense without Houdini."

This is most true when it comes to the straitjacket. When Houdini came up with the idea to escape from a straitjacket, it was so new that almost nobody even knew what he was talking about. This was long before he became famous. In late 1895, Houdini was traveling with a doomed magic show near St. John, in Canada, when he was given a tour of a psychiatric hospital (he called it a place of "violent maniacs"). At one point, he saw one man fighting to get out of this garment of straps and hooks.

"Entranced," Houdini wrote, "I watched the efforts of this man, whose struggles caused the beads of perspiration to fall off from him . . . It left so vivid an impression on my mind that I hardly slept that night, and in such moments as I slept, I saw nothing but straitjackets, maniacs, and padded cells! In the wakeful part of the night, I wondered what the effect would be to an audience to see a man placed in a straitjacket and watch him force himself free."

As it turns out, the effects were, at first, minimal. When he first performed it—probably in San Francisco in 1899—the audience was more puzzled than thrilled. Houdini couldn't figure it out; he had long relied on his instincts, and he just *knew* that the straitjacket escape would leave the audience breathless. It was such an exciting escape. Nobody else was doing it, so why didn't anybody care?

The simple answer is the overall story made no sense. Houdini told them about the psychiatric hospital, and the madmen wrapped up in strait-jackets, and how impossible it was to get out of one of these crazy things, but few got it. What was this thing again? How hard was it to escape? Houdini was asking them to suspend disbelief, but that doesn't really work in magic.

"The classic example is of Peter Pan," the magician Eric Mead says. "You go to the show, and you see the wires while Peter flies around the stage. And because you're caught up in the theatrical experience of the show, you pretend not to see them; you imagine that the wires are not there. That's a suspension of disbelief. This can't work in a magic show. If you watch a magician make someone float on stage, and you can see the wires, that's just a lousy magic show."

How could Houdini make people understand the difficulty, the near impossibility, of slipping out of a straitjacket? As it turns out, his brother Hardeen unlocked the mystery. Houdini had performed the straitjacket, like he performed all his escapes, behind a curtain. He came out of the tent sweating profusely, often bruised and sometimes bleeding, his clothes torn. But nobody saw him escape. They assumed there was some trick to it.

But Hardeen realized something: there isn't a trick to escaping the straitjacket. There are no gimmicks, no trap doors, no secret keys. That was its power. David Blaine likes to say that the secret to performing the famous bullet catch illusion is this: "You have to catch the bullet." The secret to escaping a straitjacket is to escape the straitjacket. Hardeen performed the escape in full public view so that everyone could see exactly how he did it. And once people saw, they understood.

From that point on, Houdini performed the straitjacket escape for everyone to see, and he performed the heck out of it. He made it look even harder than it is, pulling and fighting and sweating and rolling around on the ground, looking all the while, as one journalist wrote, "like a cat in a bag."

"I always wanted to perform the straitjacket escape the way Houdini did, you know, with all the flopping around," Dorothy Dietrich says. "I think that was the right way to do it, full of energy and flair and excitement. Houdini would flop around, and it looked like he was fighting for his life. It was exciting. I see other magicians work the straitjacket, and they just stand there, and I am shouting out, 'What are you doing? Get on the floor! Show them how much you are fighting for your freedom!'

"I feel very strongly that it was the way Houdini performed the straitjacket escape that made it legendary. I always wanted to do it the same way, but unfortunately, as a woman, I couldn't get away with doing that. I couldn't just fall on the floor and do all those gyrations. I had to escape in what you might call a more ladylike way, and it bothered me."

The more Houdini performed the straitjacket, the more legends built around it. Many still believe Houdini escaped the jacket by dislocating his shoulder and then popping it back into place after he was done. Not true. Houdini loved that theory so much he began promoting himself as the man who dislocated his shoulder.

The upside-down straitjacket escape came later and from an unusual source, the mind of an imaginative teenager in Sheffield, England, named Randolph Douglas. Randolph met Houdini when he was a child. He instantly became a ferocious and loyal Houdini fan, so much so that for a short while he performed as Randini (Houdini didn't mind at all; he liked Randolph and saw him as a rare protégé).

Houdini came to visit Randolph and his mother, Kitty, after a show in 1914. Randolph was nineteen and a blossoming master locksmith; Houdini wanted to discuss a few technical things, but first Randolph had a surprise. After tea, they went to the attic, where Randolph put on a straitjacket. Houdini was amused and he settled in to watch his young fan emulate his escape.

Instead, Kitty tied ropes around Randolph's legs. And then, to Houdini's astonishment, she hoisted the ropes until her son was hanging upside down a foot or two above the ground. Houdini watched Randolph escape while hanging upside down—it's a little bit easier that way, actually, because gravity helps pull off the jacket—and immediately saw possibilities. For years after that, Houdini would promote his shows by going to the center of town, getting pulled up several stories, and performing the Randolph Douglas upside-down straitjacket escape for everyone to see.

In 1916, Houdini performed next to the *Post-Sun* newspaper office (he almost always did these escapes next to newspaper buildings). First, though, he promoted like only Houdini could promote.

From the *Pittsburgh Daily Post*:

> About the most interested spectator in the thousands who will gather in front of the *Post-Sun* building at 12:30 today to watch Houdini attempt to escape from a straitjacket while suspended in the air will be Mrs. Houdini, wife of the "Handcuff King." Houdini has proven himself a wizard at escaping from straitjackets hundreds of times in full view of theater audiences, but today will be the first time he has ever attempted to free himself while suspended in the air.

And this, which ran the next day:

> In the presence of a crowd which filled surrounding streets, Harry Houdini, "handcuff king," yesterday afternoon freed himself from a canvas leather reinforced straightjacket *while hanging head downward, 50 feet above the sidewalk in*

front of the Post-Sun building. The feat was accomplished by the "wizard" in a fraction of a second more than three minutes, and he was lowered to the street amid the cheers of the assembled crowd . . . *Yesterday was the first time he had attempted the feat.*

It was always the first time for Houdini. In fact, Houdini had done the escape numerous times—beginning in Kansas City in 1915—but you could get away with those sorts of boasts in those days before radio and television and camera phones. A few weeks before the Pittsburgh escape, he told the *Boston Post* that he had only just come up with the idea because a local construction foreman, after seeing Houdini escape from a straitjacket, had idly wondered if "Suspended in the air, Houdini would be helpless."

The escapes were sensations. Countless more people saw Houdini hanging from the air in a straitjacket than ever saw him on a stage. In Washington, he escaped in front of what the *Washington Post* called "the biggest crowd ever assembled in Washington at one place except for the inauguration of a president." In Baltimore, downtown traffic came to a complete standstill for an entire afternoon. In Salt Lake City, the blocks surrounding the Walker bank building were "a solid mass of humanity." In Atlantic City, he escaped in a bathing suit while thousands of people on the beach and boardwalk stared into the sky to see.

"I do escape a straitjacket," Lee Terbosic says. "But I play it for laughs. That's really the only way I can make it fit into my act, the only way it works for me. I have someone come on stage and tie the straitjacket as tight as they can. I always say to them, 'tighter. No, tighter . . . No, okay, looser.' That usually works.

"Then some music starts playing, and I'm working to get out of it. All of a sudden, the music stops, and I seem to stop. I turn to the person and say, 'Well, you did a really good job with this thing.' Then when I'm trying to get it over my head, the music stops again, and I'm like, 'You did a REALLY good job.' Or I will say I have an itch. Sometimes I get people to scratch my nose."

Terbosic shrugs.

"It has to be comedy," he says. "I have a line I use. I say: 'This is what being born feels like.' "

Terbosic instinctively understood what Steinmeyer was saying: if you try to escape from a straitjacket, you are trying to be Houdini. "And nobody can be Houdini," Terbosic says. "He's bigger than life. No matter what anyone ever does, he will always be the greatest magician of all time."

When Terbosic came across the Houdini 1916 escape, he came up with an idea, a way to do the straitjacket more seriously, more like how Houdini did it. And as he began putting the whole thing together, he came to fully appreciate Houdini's genius: Nothing about doing a straitjacket escape in downtown Pittsburgh is easy. Nothing. He needed a crane. He required permits. He needed police for crowd control. He needed to convince the city to help. He needed publicity. He needed more publicity. He needed even more publicity. He had to convince dozens of people to let him do it.

Oh, and then he actually had to teach himself how to do the escape. He had never done it upside down before. "Being upside down for an extended period of time, there's a chance of blackout," he says. "That wouldn't be good."

To avoid that, Lee would spend a period of time every day just hanging upside down. He read books upside down. He checked Twitter upside down.

"Do you think you will feel a little bit like Houdini felt?" I ask him.

"I don't know," he says. "I hope so."

On the day of the escape, Lee Terbosic brought his mother along to watch. This was an homage to Houdini, who so deeply loved his mother and who brought Bess with him to the Pittsburgh straitjacket escape to, in the words of the *Pittsburgh Post-Gazette*, "provide emotional support."

"I'm nervous," Kathy Terbosic told the newspaper. "But he knows what he's doing."

Lee did know what he was doing. The crowd was not quite the same size as the one that saw Houdini, but more than a thousand people showed up. Lee escaped the jacket in about half the time it took Houdini and then added a special treat for the crowd. He pulled out a Terrible Towel—a yellow towel that Steelers fans spin during games—and twirled it for the screaming crowd.

Did he feel like Houdini? He isn't sure. But a few months later, Terbosic began hosting a television show called *Houdini's Last Secrets*. In it, he traveled the world with Houdini's great-nephew George Hardeen and performed many of Houdini's greatest escapes and messed around with many of Houdini's locks and keys.

"I think once you try to be Houdini," he says, "you never want to stop."

THE BELLS
OF THE KREMLIN

I'd like to tell you my favorite story about
Houdini. It had to do with his visit to the
Kremlin, the night he rang the bells in the
Kremlin.

This was in a private performance for
the royal family, the Czar and the royal
family, with Rasputin in the background
gnashing his teeth with jealous rage. And
Houdini had asked for the various people
in this small audience to write on slips of
paper some impossible thing they would
like to have performed. One of them had
written, "Ring the bells in the Kremlin."

Houdini had arranged it that this would
be chosen apparently by free choice. And
to ring the bells in the Kremlin may not
sound like much, but as a matter of fact,
at that time no ropes were connecting
the bells, and for a century at least, they
had been silent. So, after this command,
Houdini moved to the window, raised
his arm. It was a snowy night, moments,
very dramatic pause. Then over the snow-
covered square, it could be heard, first
very dimly and finally in full chorus, the

bells of the Kremlin. You could imagine the effect of that, particularly on Rasputin.

Now, ordinarily I don't explain how tricks are done. No magician—amateur or professional—likes to do that. But in this particular case, I think I can tell you that, since it's unlikely that anyone will be doing this particular trick again, as Houdini raised his hand, his wife, who was standing at a window in a hotel on the other side of the square which was right near the bell tower, his wife received the signal and with an air gun shot the bells. Bing, boom, boom, boom. It always struck me as a particularly ingenious miracle.

—Orson Welles on
BBC's *Sketchbook*, 1955

One fun thing about Houdini myths is that they have continued to emerge in the many decades since Houdini died. The above story is one of those myths. Best anyone can tell, it was wholly invented by the great director Orson Welles.

The Bells of the Kremlin is one of my favorite Houdini stories, even though it is both untrue and entirely implausible. Houdini did tour Russia in 1903, but he certainly did not perform for Czar Nicholas II, a virulent anti-Semite who intensified pogroms against Russian Jews.

Nicholas once refused to allow an orchestra to play in Yalta because a few of the musicians were Jewish—he certainly did not invite a Jew, no matter how famous, to do a private performance in the Kremlin.

He also did not begin to fall under the spell of Rasputin until two years after Houdini left Russia.

Most importantly, nobody is sure what bells Welles was talking about.

Nobody should believe this story, and yet many do. We want to believe. It has appeared in numerous Houdini books, movies, and a mini-series about Houdini's life. Sometimes, when I mentioned the book to friends, they would ask about that time Houdini made the Kremlin bells ring. They definitively do not want to hear that it never happened. I apologize to them all.

Orson Welles would not apologize, however. He was a born magician and a born liar; he happily admitted guilty on both counts. From the moment he picked up a Mysto Magic kit for kids, he knew his destiny.

"I discovered at the age of six," he said, "that almost everything in this world was phony, worked with mirrors. Since then, I've always wanted to be a magician."

That year, Welles went to see his first great magic show. He sat mesmerized as Howard Thurston, Houdini's greatest rival, performed his classic Levitation of the Princess Karnak. While the princess floated, Thurston stepped away and implored the audience to be perfectly silent, for even the tiniest sound could wake the princess and put her very life in jeopardy.

"We all knew he was lying," Welles later wrote. "We knew we could cough our heads off and whatever machinery was holding up the Princess wouldn't budge. But we couldn't see the machinery—Thurston had shown us it couldn't be there, so we gave up. It wasn't a puzzle anymore—it was magic. In the precise meaning of the word, it was marvelous and wonderful. Nobody made a sound."

Welles took his love of magic (and lying) and brought it to the theater and to the movies. Whether in a magic show, on the stage or screen, Welles believed that truth and fiction were meant to swirl together, as if in a windstorm. He first smashed through the American consciousness with his famous 1938 *War of the Worlds* radio broadcast, in which he and his Mercury players retold H. G. Wells's classic story in the form of several news reports, and inspired panic among listeners who did not realize that it was a fictional account.

"It was a magic trick," Welles said.

His career crescendo, the movie *Citizen Kane*, had a similar revolutionary impact, incorporating dozens of filming techniques that had never been used before to guide moviegoers through glass and time. "I took what I knew from the theater," he explained, "and from magic."

Welles's love of Houdini was something strange. He did not think of Houdini as a great magician. In fact, like Dai Vernon and many others, he didn't think of Houdini as a magician at all.

"He was not an illusionist, he was a challenger," he told one interviewer. "He challenged the audience. He didn't seduce them. He set up a kind of Olympic game and then won it at the end . . . he had a kind of contempt for illusionists."

And yet, when he came up with the story of the Bells of the Kremlin, he made Houdini the hero. Why, when he preferred Thurston? Many current magicians lament how Houdini has blotted out the superior sunlight of magicians such as Max Malini or Nevil Maskelyne or Harry Blackstone or Harry Kellar or Chung Ling Soo, but they cannot deny a simple truth: the story does not work with Thurston or any of the rest.

By the early 1950s, when Welles told the story for the first time, Thurston was already all but gone from collective memory, as was vaudeville. Silent film had all but disappeared, and even radio, that modern invention that first brought Welles to the attention of America, was fading against the power of television. There was only one man with enough enduring legend to make the Bells of the Kremlin work as a story, and that was Harry Houdini.

Welles met Houdini twice in his childhood. The first time, Houdini taught him a trick—maybe it was a particular way to false shuffle, maybe it was a trick with a red handkerchief (Welles remembered it different ways through the years). But he clearly remembered wanting to go out and perform the trick he had learned right away without perfecting it. Houdini told him, "You must practice a trick, Orson, a thousand times before you perform it."

You never perform a trick until you practice it a thousand times. Welles believed it. But his second interaction with Houdini—probably around 1925, when Houdini was near the end— was in the dressing room when a representative of the prolific magic manufacturer Carl Brayer knocked on the door.

"Hello, Harry," the man said, "I've just got a new vanishing lamp. Here it is. New principle."

And did Houdini practice with the lamp a thousand times? No.

"Fine," he said without even looking at the new lamp. "I'll put it in the show tonight."

Welles said that was the day he decided never again to take advice from elders.

There is a true story about Houdini in Russia that I think is even better than the Bells of the

Kremlin. Houdini did perform in Russia for months, and all the while he was conscious of the country's rampant anti-Semitism. It was a struggle just to get into the country to perform; nobody is entirely sure how he pulled that off. Some theorize that he claimed to be Catholic, like his wife Bess, but Houdini vehemently denied ever hiding his Jewishness. He was secular, yes, and his favorite holiday was Christmas— every year he and Bess had beautiful, personal Christmas cards made—but Houdini boldly never pretended to be anything other than the son of Rabbi Mayer Samuel Weiss.

"Despite the nature of his vocation," wrote Rabbi Bernard Drachman, who would give Houdini's eulogy and also claimed to have officiated his bar mitzvah, "he had a profound reverence for the Jewish father and deep-seated filial affection for his parents and reverence for their memory."

Or as Houdini wrote to his friend Dr. Joseph Wiatt, a Boston dentist: "I never was ashamed to acknowledge I was a Jew and never will be."

Houdini probably wouldn't have gotten away with trying to feign Catholicism anyway. He boldly and publicly wrote about Russia's anti-Semitism even while he was there. "It has even gone so far that they will not allow a Jew to turn Christian," he wrote in his monthly *Daily Mirror* column. "This is a fearful country to be in."

He was haunted by the anti-Semitism he encountered and wrote angrily about the government shutting down the only synagogue in Moscow and about a Jewish delegation hoping to reopen it being denied an audience with the czar. He went out of his way to visit two cities devastated by pogroms.

"At the present time," he wrote after he left the country, "the Russian censor is very busy making heavy ink blots on a great many of the newspapers that are sent into Russia, as they have too true an account of what happened in Glischnick, where so many Jews were slaughtered. There is an awful state of affairs in some of the cities, but it has been like this for years."

Despite it all, Houdini was a smash in Russia. Audiences loved him as much in Moscow as they did in Berlin or Paris or London or New York. Houdini spoke no Russian, and few spoke English then, but he found that the language of escape was universal.

After a while, Houdini wanted to challenge the Russian police like he had police all over the world. At first, they refused every request, but Houdini was not easily discouraged. There are numerous theories about how he finally got them to accept, but my favorite is the one that portrays Houdini wandering out to a deserted race track and shouting to no one in particular, "I defy the police departments of the world to handcuff me!" The unnerved police arrest him, and at the station he asks for permission to escape from a cell in the infamous Butyrskaya prison, where revolutionaries had been held for a half century. The chief, a man Houdini called Lebedeff, refuses but does offer to let Houdini try to escape from one of the horse-drawn transports that the Russian government used to take prisoners to Siberia, called the Russian Carette. Houdini was thrilled and accepted immediately, even without fully understanding what it was.

The Russian Carette was no ordinary jail cell. The lock demanded two different keys, one to lock, the other to unlock. The positioning of the lock was problematic; it was roughly three feet outside the cell, and there seemed no way to reach it even if you had the right key. Houdini seemed to lose before he began.

He also was not allowed to bring reporters or witnesses to the escape. When he arrived, he was thoroughly strip searched and was told that he was being offered a great opportunity, but that if he failed, he would have to go to Siberia like any other prisoner. Houdini agreed. And he escaped.

"Moscow has had its share of sensations during the past few months," Houdini wrote about himself in the *Dramatic Mirror* that same year of 1903. "First came the escape from the 'Siberian Cell' by Little Houdini."

He said it took him a full forty-five minutes

(in later retellings, the time was shortened significantly). How did he do it? Nobody knows. The only surviving accounts of the escape come from Houdini and his trusted assistant Franz Kukol, but speculation ranges from the absurd (he sawed his way through the floor) to the mysterious (he managed to hide both a pick and an extension device that allowed him to open the lock from inside the cell) to the cynical and most likely (he simply bribed the Russian police to give him the key and a way out).

There's no way to know, for sure. The escape from the Russian Carette was never reported in any Russian newspapers. The Russian police refused even to acknowledge that Houdini had escaped, perhaps out of embarrassment. (Houdini always regretted that they did not give him the police certificate they had promised.) In the end, it was up to Houdini to spread the word, which he joyfully did for the rest of his life.

LIFE AND DEATH

It can get repetitive hearing people say that they were introduced to magic through Harry Houdini. Almost all of them were, after all. They read a Houdini book or saw a Houdini movie or heard some Houdini story and fell in love with the art. He is omnipresent in magic; it would be almost impossible for anyone to get into magic without Houdini appearing somewhere in the story.

A child anywhere in the world shows a flickering interest in a magic trick. What's the first thing the parent thinks? *Oh, look at my little Houdini.* What the first thing the child asks for? A Houdini book to read or a Houdini movie to watch. He is everywhere in magic, everywhere in life, around every corner, constantly in the news, Houdini, Houdini, Houdini.

"There's a thing—I've written about this for magicians—there's a thing in magic called 'black art,' " Jim Steinmeyer says. "Black art is a really old type of stagecraft where you are using levels of black onstage to hide things in the shadows. One of the elements of black art, one of the formulas of black art, is called a 'dazzler.' It is a very bright light that's onstage, and it's basically in your eyes. A photographer would say that it makes your eyes stop down. It crushes all the blacks. If there's something dark near the dazzler, you can't see it.

"Houdini is a dazzler. His light is so bright that nobody, not even his hero Robert-Houdin, can be seen."

Paul Cosentino didn't care about magic as a boy growing up in Australia—he didn't care much about anything. He felt lost much of the time. His mother was a school principal, his father an engineer. Education surrounded him, yet Cosentino couldn't read. Doctors suspected he was dyslexic, but tests revealed there was something more at play. He remembers now: there were so many tests: eye tests, IQ tests, comprehension tests. He so deeply hated taking those tests, but he took them just the same, and none of them explained why he couldn't do what it seemed like every other boy and girl in the world could with such ease.

"I was this kid who sits in the back of the room," he says. "Nobody notices him. I was scared and lonely and maybe a little bit angry too. I just didn't fit in the world at all."

Then came that day. His class went to the school library, and each child was told to go find a special book to read. He wandered the aisles of books aimlessly; the letters on the books were nothing but a blur to him. Then he saw one. It was big and bright with a colorful cover. Cosentino liked colorful pictures. He liked comic books. He liked superheroes.

He brought the book back to the small library and opened it up. It was filled with gorgeous magic posters. He didn't know any of the magicians, but he liked the posters.

"I remember just turning the pages, looking through it; they're very attractive," he says. "I'm not really sure what I was looking for, to be honest with you. It had posters of Carter the Great and Thurston and guys like that, not that I knew who any of them were then. My mother was the principal of the school, and she saw me looking at this book. I am sure she thought, *Hallelujah, at least the book is open.*

"I kept on turning the pages. But I couldn't read any of the words. They meant nothing to me."

Cosentino stops with the dramatic pause of the performer he has become.

"And then," he says, "I saw Houdini."

He did not know it was Houdini; he had not yet heard of him. But the poster was of a muscular man stripped almost naked, draped in chains, and Cosentino was starstruck. Houdini stared directly at Cosentino with this commanding look, like he was the one in control even though he was the one in chains.

"I just remember that intense gaze," he says. "It was like nothing I had ever seen before. I think he even had eyeliner on. I know it's corny to say or whatever, but I felt something. My mother saw my face. She came over to see what I was looking at. Below Houdini, there was this tagline, this message. I asked her to read it to me.

"And she said, 'Nothing on earth can hold Houdini prisoner.' "

That did it. Those words—*Nothing on earth can hold Houdini prisoner*—and that gaze, all of it: they changed Paul Cosentino's life. He had not yet heard a Houdini story. He had not yet seen Houdini escape. He was not entirely sure what Houdini even did. But he saw that famous poster with that famous slogan, and something flipped inside him.

"As a kid struggling with the world, that is a pretty powerful message, you know?" he says. "Nobody can hold you. Nobody. You can get out of any jail. You can escape from any box. You can escape from death. It was really quite mystical."

That was the day he began practicing magic. That very day. His first successful trick was a simple French drop, which is used to make a coin disappear.

"My father, he's a genius," Cosentino says. "He's a structural engineer—I mean, to a twelve-year-old boy, how can you get more genius than that? I performed my coin trick on him. The coin vanishes, but it was bad, it was sloppy sleight of hand, I was just a kid starting out. Only for the first time, my father looked at me, and he had this look on his face. He didn't know. He said, 'How did you do that?' That's a huge transfer of power, to do something that my father didn't know.

"Power. That is why I wanted to be like Houdini, right? For me, it's all about power. I had felt so powerless as a child. I wanted to be able to do things no one else can do. Instead, I couldn't do anything that everybody else could do. I was not engaged. I had learning disabilities. I was dyslexic. I was told when to go to bed, when to eat. But now, for just a minute, I had control."

What was it about Houdini that could shake an eight-year-old boy in Australia to his core? For Cosentino, that power was about danger. Houdini was dangerous. He knew that sooner or later, people would tire of seeing him escape. He prolonged it as long as he could by attempting different kinds of escapes every day, by taking on different challenges and reaching unimaginable heights of fame. But he lived with the constant fear that tomorrow everyone would forget him.

Fame is a bee
It has a song—
It has a sting—
Ah, too, it has a wing
—Emily Dickinson

Houdini never worried about the sting of fame. But he desperately feared the wing, desperately feared that one day it would fly away. He had been in show business long enough to know: people are fickle. He often told the story of Mattie Lee Price, a small young woman from Georgia who had performed extraordinary feats of strength in the dime museums on the dark edges of vaudeville. They called her the Georgia Wonder (actually one of several Georgia Wonders through the years). She would lift three men in a chair or pull a stick out of the hands of a man much bigger than her.

"For a time," Houdini said, "she was a sensation of the highest order."

But then, he watched as people tired of the Georgia Wonder. There was no reason for it, necessarily. The act was as good as it had ever been. But you can only do the same thing for so long before people move on, and Houdini could not bear the same happening to him.

He guarded his fame with fury, and he struck down with great vengeance against anyone he believed was trying to imitate him, undercut him, or steal from him.

"To anyone who seemed likely to filch a share of his limelight," Will Goldston wrote, "Houdini was a tyrant."

Take Kleppini. He was a German magician who called himself an escape artist. This alone would have set off Houdini, who believed himself to be the only one. Kleppini, though, went further. His name was an obvious attempt to cash in on Houdini's, and beyond that, he bragged in promotional material that he escaped from Houdini's very own cuffs.

When Houdini saw the advertisement, he blew up. He was performing in Holland at the time, but he immediately went to management to demand four days off.

Two days later as Kleppini performed his usual batch of handcuff escapes and gave his usual spiel about the handcuffs of the Great Houdini, an old man with tinted glasses and a mustache stood up in the crowd.

"*Nicht Wahr! Nicht Wahr!*" the man shouted. "Not true! Not true!"

Kleppini saw this and scoffed. "How could you know the truth?"

And with the grace of a lifelong performer, the man tore off his mustache and glasses and leaped down to the center of the stage.

"You say I am not telling the truth!" he cried out. "Well look! I am Houdini!"

The crowd was dumbfounded. An immediate challenge was issued for the following night. Behind the scenes, Houdini met with Kleppini's manager and, acting as if he wanted to work together, sneakily planted the idea that the challenge would involve combination French cuffs that opened with the five-letter word *CLEFS*, French for keys. The next night, Houdini offered multiple handcuffs for the challenge but, as he expected, Kleppini eagerly took the French cuffs and went into his cabinet. With the trap set, Houdini turned dramatically to the audience.

"Ladies and gentlemen!" he said. "You can all go home. I do not lock a cuff on a man merely to let him escape."

Kleppini stayed in the cabinet for the rest of the night. He could not get out of the cuffs. The stage manager was so incensed by the whole thing that he had the whole cabinet thrown off the stage with Kleppini still in it. Houdini refused to open the cuffs until after one in the morning, and only after he brought several reporters with him to witness it. Houdini smiled when he saw that Kleppini had tried to get out by spelling "C-L-E-F-S." He reached over and put in the actual combination.

He spelled out the word "F-R-A-U-D."

Houdini revenge stories are our oldest daughter's favorite. She has no use at all for Houdini, and often talks about how convinced she is that the ghost of Houdini lives in our house among the collectibles and posters that I keep. But she does love the revenge stories.

Hilmar the Uncuffable was a minor German escape artist, barely scratching out a living. But no imposter was too insignificant for Houdini to squash. Through the years he went after such luminaries as Mourdini and Hougini and Kleppini and Rudini and Coutini and the Great Cirnoc.

The destruction of Hilmar, though, brought special joy to Houdini's heart. Hilmar would take the tiny stages and shout out that he could make escapes no American could even dream of. He was, of course, referring to Houdini, who was well known throughout Europe not just for being an escape artist but also for being an American. He took pride in that; being American meant everything to Houdini.

"He was the ultimate American, cocky and ready for a fight, raw," Mike Caveney says. "You couldn't hold him down. 'Don't Tread on Me.' That became his identity, and I'm not sure if he could have pulled it off the same way in America. The irony is that in some ways, Houdini needed to go to Europe to become an American."

It's not clear how Houdini heard about such a small-timer as Hilmar, but he had a particularly sensitive antenna for imposters. Houdini showed up at a Hilmar performance with what he called a "common pair of German cuffs." The challenge was issued, and Houdini snapped them on Hilmar's wrists. Hilmar was only in his cabinet for a few minutes before asking Houdini to release him.

Houdini wrote a giddy private account of what happened next:

I grabbed him by the arm, took him to the footlights and said, "Now, tell the audience you could not get out of the cuffs."

He refused to do so, so I said, "All right, you need not, but I will not unlock you. Take the cuffs as a souvenir of Houdini and go. Go to a locksmith, as I refuse to unlock you."

He then showed his cur spirit and cried like a babe.

Houdini kept trying new stunts to keep people's attention. He got a lot of press in 1906, when he escaped from what he called "murderers' row" at the United States Jail in Washington. This was not an especially difficult escape—it was not much different from other jails in other cities—but it drew attention because it had been the pre-execution cell of Charles Guiteau, the assassin of President James Garfield, twenty-five years earlier. Houdini escaped, and then he freed the other prisoners and moved them to different cells. The whole thing took twenty-one minutes. It was quite a smash. Two months later, he got some notices for making the same escape at the Boston Tombs.

But there were only so many famous jails to escape, so many kinds of handcuffs to slip, so many challenges to win. As he turned thirty-five, he felt his star fading. In 1908, he performed in St. Louis to a small and unenthusiastic crowd. He wrote this in his diary:

> Manager Tate informs me, "You are not worth five dollars to me." I told him, "I hope you're wrong." We shall see.

Six weeks later, he appeared at the Keith's Theater in Cleveland and found that he was not even the headliner for the show.

> Arrived in Cleveland, seven o'clock. Am not featured. Is this week the first step toward oblivion? No attention paid to me.

Houdini grew frantic. He needed something new. And then, he came up with it.

He would no longer just escape chains.

He could escape death itself.

"Breaking out of prison cells and freeing myself from handcuffs couldn't go on forever," Houdini wrote in a magazine story in 1919. "And being a good showman—which I insist I am—I sought for other means of entertaining the public. I knew, as everyone knows, that the easiest way to attract a crowd is to let it be known that at a given time and a given place someone is going to attempt something that in the event of failure will mean sudden death."

There had always been an element of danger

in magic. But mostly it was illusion. The magic shows with decapitations, guns, knives, swords, sawing of people in half were thrilling, but no one thought they were real. People were utterly shocked when Houdini's friend Chung Ling Soo—real name William Robinson—died performing the bullet catch.

Magic wasn't supposed to be about danger. That was for the sideshow performers; they were the daredevils who would do anything. Ivan Chabert, for instance, called himself the Fire King and, in his most famous act, he would go into an oven while holding a steak. "He emerged tartar," the late Ricky Jay said, "and the steak was cooked to perfection."

Houdini wanted to bring real danger—or at least the appearance of real danger—to magic.

"That fear is what attracts us to the man who paints the flagstaff on the tall building, or to the 'human fly,' who scales the walls of the same building," Houdini wrote. "If we knew there was no possibility of either one of them falling or, if they did fall, that they wouldn't injure themselves in any way, we wouldn't pay any more attention to them than we do a nursemaid wheeling a baby carriage.

"Therefore, I said to myself, 'Why not give the public a real thrill?' "

And so, he began to do dangerous things. In 1908, he came up with his first death-defying escape: the Milk Can. Before he ever did it, he had posters splattered all over St. Louis reading, "Failure Means A Drowning Death!" A giant milk can was filled with water. After Houdini stepped inside and some of the water spilled out, more water was poured in on top of his head. The lid was slammed shut and locked.

The audience watched spellbound.

The water was the secret. Without the water, this was just another Houdini escape. But the water put an entirely different image into people's minds, and Houdini amplified that image by daring people to hold their breath along with him. Audience members would start to hold their breaths as the escape began and, every few seconds, you would hear more people start to cough and exhale. Houdini had made them ultra-aware of what was happening: *He was drowning in that can! Nobody can hold their breath for that long!* And if anyone missed the hints, a man with an ax stood by the can as a warning that this might be the audience to see Houdini die.

Houdini's great rival Howard Thurston took the audience members into a dream world and left them spellbound. Houdini instead wanted people clinging to each other and silently praying.

Death, ironically, gave Houdini a second life.

Houdini didn't just feel invulnerable on the stage. He was utterly fearless as can be seen in his brief but fascinating fling with aviation. Cosentino says that in Australia, people connect Houdini as much to flying as they do to magic. This is because Houdini grew obsessed by the idea of becoming the first man to ever fly a plane in Australia.

Remember how Houdini advised Orson Welles to practice a trick a thousand times but did not keep that counsel himself? Houdini bought a French Voisin biplane for five thousand dollars, made one semi-successful flight in Germany, and immediately had the plane shipped to Australia. When his mind was set on something, he was not the practicing kind.

Houdini tried for weeks to have the first successful Australian flight. He truly could have died in the attempt. Those early days of aviation were wild and impossibly dangerous, even more so in the unpredictable Australian winds. Houdini knew almost nothing about the physics of flight, the limitations of his equipment, or what to do in an emergency, but he had what had always carried him through: limitless courage, street smarts, and an intense ambition to get into the papers.

On March 18, 1910, just north of Melbourne, Houdini attempted three flights. Two of them were deemed "successful," one lasting a full three minutes and covering two miles. He believed that he had become the first person to fly in Australia.

Many years later, there was an Australian postage stamp that commemorated the event.

But you already know, I'm sure, that it's never that simple with Houdini. Was he really the first to fly? Well, it depends on your definition of flying. There had been countless hot-air balloon flights in Australia before Houdini, and various flying machines had been invented by Australian Lawrence Hargrave, an early pioneer of flight.

Though it doesn't sound nearly as romantic, the proper way to describe Houdini's achievement is to say he was the first to fly a controlled-power aircraft. But even that probably isn't true. When the Australian Post Office issued its flight stamps, it credited Colin Defries for making the first flight, three months before Houdini.

Still, as Cosentino says, even in Australia, most people still think Houdini was first.

Because he was Houdini.

You can't talk about Houdini and life and death without talking about the "Under the Ice" story. Everybody, it seems, has heard the "Under the Ice" story. It has been told and retold in books and magazines and comic books and movies, including in Tony Curtis's *Houdini*.

John Cox, our intrepid Houdini fact-checker, is groaning even now. The "Under the Ice" story drives him even crazier than the "Acid on the Dress" story.

"No, stop, you're not going to tell that, right?" John asks.

Of course, we are.

In late November 1906, Houdini planned to do a bridge jump escape on a frigid day in Detroit, but temperatures dropped, and the Detroit River froze over. Everyone told Houdini he would have to postpone the escape. Houdini shook his head.

"No matter," he said. "Cut a hole in the ice, and I shall dive into it."

Nobody thought this was an especially good idea, but Houdini did as Houdini wanted. He jumped into the water, but when he looked up, he realized that he could not find the hole. He went to the surface and felt his way around, and even though he could hold his breath longer than any man alive, he was running out of air. Luckily, he found that if he pressed his lips up to the tiny gap between the ice and water, he could get enough oxygen to go on.

All the while, people outside waited in a panic for Houdini to emerge. Minutes went by. More minutes. Soon, people began to accept the terrible truth: Houdini was dead. In the most fanciful version of "Under the Ice"—the one told in Harold Kellock's original Houdini biography—newspaper boys outside of Bess's hotel room began hawking their papers by shouting "Extra! Extra! Read all about it! Houdini Dead! Read all about it!"

In time, Houdini found the opening, emerged from the ice, and showed up at the hotel to give a grand embrace to a shell-shocked Bess.

"Under the Ice," is not just a myth. It's a landmark myth, a story that Houdini fans like John Cox and Patrick Culliton and others can disprove in dozens of ways. The river wasn't frozen over when Houdini did his bridge jump in Detroit. Nobody thought he was dead. Et cetera.

But, as usual with Houdini, truth is beside the point.

"Yes, of course, the 'Under the Ice' story is a total invention," writer and magician Jamy Ian Swiss says. "It's a total, deliberate invention. And you know what? I love that. The idea that anybody would miss the point on that, I don't get it at all. What is Houdini's job? The job is to fool people. The job is to inspire people. He escaped death. What could be more inspirational than that?"

So, yes, it is not hard to see what the young Cosentino saw when he looked into the eyes of Houdini. He could feel danger radiating from the book, and he was drawn to that. He wanted to be dangerous himself.

And these days, Cosentino is the most famous magician in Australia. He plays out to sold-out audiences across the country. He does television specials. He's a star.

"Would it have happened had I not seen that book?" he asks. "I don't see how."

To be clear: a typical Cosentino show looks nothing like a Houdini show; he offers a high-energy fusion of magic and music, big illusions and choreography and flashing lights. He wears a fedora—"I try to be some combination of Michael Jackson, Gene Kelly, and Indiana Jones," he explains. He makes assistants appear and disappear in a rapid flurry, then he dances, then he reads someone's mind, he dances, does a card trick, dances again, and that's the show.

Still, if you look closely, you still see the Houdini inside. For a television special, Cosentino decided to do the ultimate Houdini tribute. He and his brother built what they called the Crazy Cell. Cosentino started by being put in a straitjacket. Then he was chained with leg irons. Then he was put in a cage locked from the outside. Three Houdini classics—straitjackets, cuffs, and jails—in one illusion.

Then he added his own Cosentino twist: The ceiling of the cell had giant sharp spikes sticking out. It was secured by a rope. And the rope was set on fire.

Cosentino calculated that the fire would burn through the ropes in one minute and fifty-five seconds, giving him that much time to escape before the ceiling of spikes crashed down on him. He admitted to the audience that the timing wasn't precise; fire is unpredictable that way. In rehearsal, he said, the rope had burned in just one minute and forty-five seconds.

"The first time we did this," Cosentino's brother John explained to the audience, "it was so close, I can't tell you. We wanted to pull it from the show. We swore we'd never do it again."

Houdini would have loved that part. Death was in the air. Danger was everywhere. The crowd held their breath. Cosentino worked himself out of the straitjacket by flopping around; it took him more than a minute to get out. Time ticked away. He began working on the chains and finally got them off with nine seconds left on the clock. The smoke was rising, and he still needed to pick the outside lock of the cell. He shouted out, "Come on!" And with that, Cosentino picked the lock and leaped from the cage just as the ceiling of spikes crashed to the ground.

He had done it. He had escaped like Houdini.

"I don't know what Houdini would have thought," he says. "I think we know he didn't like people he thought were imitators. That's pretty clear, right? But I guess I'd tell him that he saved my life. Little boys like me, we need Houdini, you know? He's a symbol of hope."

"Hope for what?" I ask.

"Escape, mate," he says. "We all want to escape."

Cosentino pauses. There's something else to say.

"It began with Houdini," he says. "That was the turning point, but if I'm being honest with myself, after a while, I moved on from Houdini. I became obsessed with someone else. A different magician. I saw a show in a big stadium, oh my gosh, he was like a rock star. This wasn't a theater show. There were pyrotechnics, bells, and whistles; he was dating supermodels. And Houdini, I never forgot him, you know, but he sort of went away. The new magician became my hero. He's the one who I patterned myself after."

"Who was that?" I ask.

He laughs. We both know exactly who he is talking about.

"David Copperfield, mate."

COPPERFIELD

EPIC RAP BATTLE I

[Harry Houdini]

You've never seen a body quite the same
as that of Houdini
Slippery like linguine, sneaking out of
teeny weeny

Little spaces small enough to fit your
   talent, David
You're not a challenge, David
Your biggest endowment's your bank
   account balances, baby

[David Copperfield]

When I was a child, you were a god to me
I had to do what you do
But now you're like a Chinese wall to me
Bitch, I'll walk right through you
This ain't magic that you're used to
I float a rose, hands free, like it's
   Bluetooth
My grand illusions make your parlor
   tricks irrelevant
The foot of Lady Liberty is stomping on
   your elephant
      — Peter Shukoff and Lloyd Ahlquist,
          Epic Rap Battles of History:
  "David Copperfield vs. Harry Houdini"

KORBY'S CLOTHING STORE

There's an overwhelming mystery about David Copperfield—a puzzle that defies a solution, a lock without a key. And this is too bad because I feel sure that if you could unlock it, if you could pierce through the fog and mist and solve this riddle, then you would have a direct route not only to the heart of David Copperfield but, yes, to the heart of Houdini too.

They are nothing alike.

And they are everything alike.

On a dark and quiet street, there's a haberdashery that never opens. Inside, mannequins wear 1960s suits. Ties are folded precisely and glow red and green under glass, like pearls and diamonds in a jewelry store. Fedoras and homburgs, derbies and porkpies, hats of all kinds sit on shelves above folded shirts. A gold cash register with MasterCard and VISA stickers stands behind bottles of cologne. In the register window, $5.00 is perpetually rung up.

In a corner, a 1960s television set, a 13-inch screen with VHF and UHF plays an old television show called *The Man from U.N.C.L.E.*

This was their favorite show together, father and son.

On the wall, every wall, are photographs. Hyman Kotkin is in one, dashing and young in his army uniform. Hyman was handsome; at one point, he had aspirations of becoming an actor. In another photograph, he is older, white hair, as he stands with his wife, Rebecca, and their young son. We seem to be standing in Hyman Kotkin's store, Korby's, For Town & Country, Men & Boys. We seem to be on Main Street in Metuchen, New Jersey, and though the air is still and there are no customers and we are not in New Jersey, you can't help but think that Hyman himself will come out with a piece of tailor's chalk in his hand and a vinyl tape measure dangling from his back pocket, and he will eye you and smile and say, "Let's try a forty-two regular, I think that's the one."

But we are not in New Jersey.

We are in Las Vegas, in a nondescript and unmarked warehouse.

We are in David Copperfield's world.

"The lie was never a lie for me," Copperfield says. "I never thought of it as something that's not true. I think of our need to dream. I think of our need to be transported. I think of the need to have hope. This is part of what it is to be human."

They are nothing alike. They are everything alike. On the surface, how can you look at David Copperfield and Harry Houdini and not see mirror images? They are two Jewish boys who fell in love with magic at a young age, changed their names to follow their dreams, and became the most famous magicians of their respective times. They each collected books and magical objects. They each worked tirelessly—obsessively, even. They both became larger than life.

But beneath the surface, as Copperfield says, they are entirely different men with entirely different motivations. In ways large and small, Copperfield long ago surpassed Houdini—and every other magician before him. He has made more money than any magician. He has been seen more than any magician. He has sold more tickets, done more television specials, received more awards, and left more audiences awestruck. He owns islands in the Caribbean—this is not directly connected to the rest but, let's face it, it's pretty mind-blowing. He has performed on Broadway, earned a star on the Hollywood Walk of Fame, and set eleven Guinness World Records. He has had his face on postage stamps in six different countries.

And yet, there is something about Houdini that always challenges him.

At the back of this mirror of Korby's haberdashery there is what looks like a wall. But nothing here is as it appears, and when a switch is flipped—sometimes it requires the pulling of a necktie, sometimes the pressing of a number on the register—the wall slides open.

This is how you get into David Copperfield's private museum.

Is it a museum? Copperfield and the people who work for him call it the Warehouse. Others see it as a wonderland, a dizzying maze of stairs and doors and small rooms and big rooms, each leading to treasures more marvelous and mystifying than the ones before. It's hard to even keep your balance. The first room you walk up to contains the world's greatest collection of ventriloquist dummies. Edgar Bergen's Charlie McCarthy is here as is Shari Lewis's Lamb Chop and the world's largest collection of the props used by ventriloquist Paul Winchell. This is a personal room for Copperfield. But, as you will see, they're all personal rooms for Copperfield.

Walk up some stairs and through a hallway and you find an enormous room filled with statues and Hollywood sets and marquees and pieces from various plays and movies. Copperfield has the statues from the film *Citizen Kane* here, the Black Pearl figurehead from *Pirates of the Caribbean*, and the flying machine from *Hudson Hawk*. There are posters and stage props from hundreds of shows and movies.

The Hollywood stuff is so over the top that something crazy happened at the end of the tour. David's producer, a marvelous sleight-of-hand magician named Chris Kenner, took me to a small room, a closet, really. Inside the closet were boxes filled with dozens and dozens of letters written by Houdini, a treasure trove of insights into the man. As I looked excitedly at all this Houdini stuff, Chris suddenly said: "Hey, I want to show you something."

With that, he reached behind an old lamp on a corner coffee table. He pulled out a little gold statue. He handed it to me to hold. It was an Academy Award.

"Feel how heavy this is," he said.

"Is this an actual Academy Award?" I asked.

"I think so," he said. "Isn't it amazing how heavy that thing is?" Chris was just amazed by the weight of the statue; he has worked with Copperfield for so long, that the things that would leave the rest of us breathless—such as, I don't know, the fact that there's an Oscar just lying around on a table in a backroom closet—don't impress him much these days. Such wonders come with the job. As Chris put it back ("Heavy, right?" he said) I asked him, "Whose Oscar is that?"

He seemed surprised by the question; he had no idea. He never even thought to look. He pulled the statue back out and showed me what the inscription said.

"Academy First Award to Michael Curtiz For the Direction of 'Casablanca.' "

This is the sort of place Copperfield's museum is, a place where an Oscar from perhaps the greatest film ever made sits behind a lamp. Was it real or a copy? I don't know. The papers did later report that Copperfield sold Curtiz's Oscar for two million dollars.

More stairs, more doors, and you find yourself in Tannen's backroom. Tannen's is the most famous magic shop and in New York, this room is the most wonderful storeroom in the world, a breathtaking workshop that looks as if it came directly out of the imagination of a ten-year-old who dreams of magic all day. There are containers and bottles and jugs, teapots and crystals and shiny shards of glass, tiny boxes that demand to be opened. There are polished knives that bend and fake guns that smell like firecrackers, and chattering teeth and little clocks and coins of every color, playing cards and flowers that lean toward you, wands and small drums and lightbulbs that glow though they are not plugged in. Here you see every gag, every trick, every device, every gadget, every toy you could ever imagine and many you would never imagine. Each one has a price tag on them though none is for sale.

"This isn't what the backroom at Tannen's looks like at all," Copperfield explains. "This is just how I have pictured it in my mind."

You will want to stay forever in the backroom

of Tannen's, but there is so much more to see. You must see the gorgeous clocks handcrafted by Jean Eugène Robert-Houdin himself, and you must see the rifle that killed Chung Ling Soo in the 1918 bullet catch that went wrong. There is Alexander's turban, Dante the Magician's cane, and the great magician Max Malini's dog-eared personal copy of *The Expert at the Card Table*, the book many in the art call the Bible. Every magician of any renown is represented in Copperfield's Wonderland—you can see posters and pictures and magic tricks of Dai Vernon, Carter the Great, the two Harry Blackstones, Kellar, Thurston. My favorite piece is a giant music box. Wind it up and you watch a young woman teach a bird how to sing.

And finally, most importantly, most dramatically, there is Houdini. No magician in American history—probably no celebrity in American history—has left behind more memorabilia, collectibles, autographs, museum pieces than he did, and the best of it is here. The milk can is here. A refurbished water torture cell is here. You can see a thousand Houdini keys, and a thousand more locks, a Houdini straitjacket, and one of his early magic wands.

"If Houdini was standing right where you're standing," Copperfield told Oprah Winfrey, "he would see his entire life surrounding him."

Is this a museum? No. This is David

Copperfield. This is his life. As you look around, that's what you come to understand. Copperfield began as a ventriloquist; Paul Winchell was his idol. He longed to perform, to sing and dance on the Broadway stage, to act in the movies. He found magic the first time he walked into Tannen's Magic Shop. And then he sought to take magic to a higher place, the highest place, the stratosphere above even Kellar and Thurston and Vernon. He has sought to challenge—and even surpass—Houdini himself.

"David Copperfield, to the best of my observations, has used Houdini as a benchmark," one magician says. "And in all measurable ways, he has surpassed Houdini. He's more successful, more famous, more popular. And I should add, this is not an un-Houdini way of looking at Houdini; those were the things that motivated him as well."

The magician sighs.

"But," he says, "I would add that Houdini has achieved something more, some sort of legend, that Copperfield has not, that no other magician has achieved. It is not something that can be put into words, and therefore not something you can achieve by accomplishing more."

Copperfield never stops achieving and accomplishing more. If you show up at the MGM Grand in Las Vegas, he is there, performing two shows a night. If it's Christmas week, he performs three shows a day. In all, he performs more than three hundred and fifty shows per year, still, even after all this time. He is the hardest-working man in Vegas, and, like Houdini, it simply doesn't matter how much he does. He must do more. He must perform magic night after night after night for Vegas tourists drunk on alcohol and gambling losses and the bright lights that never dim.

"Hey, I know how you do that," one drunk shouted at him during a late-night show in Las Vegas. Copperfield tried to ignore the voice, but the guy would not be ignored: "I could do that. Put me on the stage, David!" He had an Australian accent. Bouncers eventually came over to quiet the man down, and he promised to be quiet, but after they left, he again shouted out:

"David Copperfield! I'm a better magician than you are! Put me on the stage."

Finally, the guy was escorted out. The show went on, and Copperfield gave it his all, like he had the night before and the night before that and the night that followed. Why? What compels him? What could drive a man who has made more money and achieved more fame and performed in front of more people than just about anyone in world history to do three shows a night on Christmas week?

"That," one magician says, "is the greatest mystery in all of magic."

I asked Copperfield. Is it the applause? No,

he said. Is it the money? Obviously not. Is it the feeling that he still has more to say? "That's not exactly it," he said. He said he goes on because he loves the process of creating a magic show, loves taking chances, and loves the thrill of making a trick work.

But there must be something more, just like there was something more for Houdini. In the end, I think David Copperfield, more than anyone else on earth, knows what it was like to be Houdini.

ELEPHANTS AND STATUES

David Kotkin was a prodigy. Magic chose him. He was not someone who came upon Houdini and fell in love with the art or ran across a book and wanted to learn a trick. No, magic chose David Kotkin the very first day that he walked into the Tannen's Magic Shop.

Tannen's is the oldest magic shop in New York City and one of the most famous magic shops in the world. Lou Tannen, a redheaded young magician who could sell anything, opened it in 1925. The legend went that Lou Tannen bought his first two magic tricks for a dollar when he was sixteen years old and immediately sold them for a profit. Tannen's storefront has moved numerous times—always to another faceless New York office building on a high floor where only committed magicians will make the effort to find it—but it has always been there to sell tricks, to offer gags, to put on its famous magic summer camp, and most notably, to inspire all those kids and adults who find magic exploding in their minds.

When Hyman Kotkin first brought his son to Tannen's, it wasn't for magic. David wanted a new ventriloquist dummy. He had one, but the

323

eyes on it didn't move. David wanted a dummy with moving eyes, just like the one he saw Paul Winchell use on television.

"Ventriloquism appealed to me because I was an only child," David Kotkin now says as David Copperfield. "I liked the idea of having an imaginary partner. I liked the idea that I could create a friend to talk to."

David Kotkin built up a full act. He wrote his own scripts. He practiced for hours in front of the mirror to make sure that his own lips were not moving. For the jokes, he would go through old *Boys' Life* magazines.

"Who was Snow White's brother?" the dummy would ask.

"I don't know," David said.

"Egg white," the dummy said.

David shook his head and groaned.

"What, you didn't like that yolk?" the dummy asked.

Kotkin's entire ambition—and, as it turns out, his entire life—changed the moment he walked into Tannen's. What a place! He saw all the marked decks, the gaffed handcuffs, the egg bags and disappearing handkerchiefs and linking rings and coin purses and pamphlets offering untold secrets. It felt so exciting and vibrant, and yet David couldn't help but think it also felt oddly familiar. He knew this place. He knew these things. He understood magic from the start. For

David Kotkin, walking into Tannen's and seeing all the magic tricks was like a boy walking into the Barabar Caves in Northern India and finding that he is fluent in Sanskrit.

"Magic came naturally to me," Copperfield says. "I had an instant knack for inventing new things and performing them."

The path was clear and, he admits, not difficult at all. At ten, David became Davino, the Boy Magician. At twelve, he began inventing magic tricks. That same year, he became the youngest ever member of the Society of American Magicians. At fourteen, he invented and marketed a mind-reading pen that could correctly guess any two-digit number. By sixteen, he was teaching a magic class at New York University.

"I was good at magic," he says. "That was my gift."

David Copperfield does not say this arrogantly. He actually feels the opposite of arrogance; he wouldn't have chosen magic to be his gift.

"What you have to understand is my idols were not magicians," he says. "My idols were storytellers, songwriters, filmmakers. Stephen Sondheim was my hero. Walt Disney was my hero. Orson Welles was my hero. I wish I could play the piano like Art Tatum. I wish I could dance like Gene Kelly or sing like Frank Sinatra. I wish I could make people feel like Joan Baez. I didn't think about Houdini.

"But," he says in a resolved voice, "my talent was magic."

That talent was immense. At nineteen, David was the spotlight performer at one of the biggest and most prestigious magic conventions in the world; it was unprecedented to have someone so young perform. How good was he? Peter Samelson, who would go on to create several magical Broadway shows and cofound *Monday Night Magic* in New York, was in the audience that day. After watching the show, he told Jamy Ian Swiss that he was so overwhelmed by David's brilliance that he announced to his girlfriend, "I'm giving up magic."

"David was mind-blowing," Jamy says (and anyone in magic knows the rarity of such a compliment from Jamy, who has higher standards than just about anyone).

Kotkin changed his name to David Copperfield, not out of love for the Dickens classic (he doesn't love the book at all) but because he liked how the syllables sounded together. He has since expressed some regret about the name (for one thing, he has come to believe that Dickens was anti-Semitic). But his sense of showmanship was spot on.

The name David Copperfield, like Harry Houdini, is unforgettable.

After that, Copperfield's rise was spectacular and almost instantaneous. He was twenty when he hosted his first television special: *The Magic of ABC*. The show was meant to introduce a new lineup of the network's shows, but Copperfield was so good that he overshadowed everything else. He was a new kind of television magician. Copperfield had no use for top hats and rabbits and sawing women in half—he wore an all-white suit and began with a big musical number where he danced and dropped playing cards into the hats of eight women dancers.

"Hi," he said to the camera, "I'm David Copperfield. Ever since I was born, uh, twenty years ago, television has been a part of my life. It was my babysitter, my schoolbook, my best friend, and my first love. So, I guess you could call me a full-fledged member of the TV generation."

That was how Copperfield introduced himself to America, and his timing was impeccable. Magic was becoming a big deal on television. The pioneer was Doug Henning, a Canadian magician with big hair, a hippy, 1970s way of talking, and a powerful sense of magic history. Henning had made his splash on television by channeling Houdini and performing his own version of the legend's Chinese Water Torture Cell escape. After that, he performed a series of famous Houdini illusions. Later, Henning wrote a book about Houdini.

Copperfield didn't emulate Houdini. He

modeled himself on Gershwin and Astaire and Fosse. Months later, he got his own television special, *The Magic of David Copperfield*. He was introduced by his hero, Orson Welles.

"The real star tonight," Welles said, "may be fairly new to magic. But you're going to be seeing a lot of him, and for a long time, in bright lights. I refer to the fantastic, the formidable, the entirely flabbergasting Mr. David Copperfield."

"I'm very different from Houdini," Copperfield says. "He was all about the challenge of escaping. Nothing can hold him. People would watch and wonder, *Will he get out this time?* It was very much about his persona, about him beating odds. I have tried for something else. I have wanted to bring people in. When I flew, I wanted to make them feel like they could fly too."

Copperfield's opening performance in his first special describes his ambition. In the illusion, he was a young boy sitting in his childhood bedroom. He pulled out a yellow scarf and then, seemingly to his own surprise, he made it disappear. A woman, the family nanny, rushed into his childhood bedroom.

"What happened to my yellow scarf?" she screamed. "Oh, look at this room, it's a mess! Your parents pay me good money to keep this clean and you mess it up with your magic tricks? You should be studying your schoolwork instead of all of this magic nonsense. I don't see how you can be wasting your time making things disappear. You ought to be taking all of this junk and making it disappear . . . for good. I'll never know why anyone would want to be a magician!"

This was Copperfield's story. The nanny was playing Copperfield's mother, Rebecca, a non-dreamer who was born in Jerusalem, moved to the United States, and became an insurance adjuster. Sensible. She had no use for *meshugas* such as show business and ventriloquism and magic.

"She was not very supportive," Copperfield says. "She was really fearful that it wouldn't work out. So, I had my father saying, 'If you love it, go for it,' and my mother saying the opposite."

Copperfield shakes his head.

"But when I found magic," he says, "there really wasn't much of a choice for me."

Copperfield's first special was a hit, and so he did another one, then another, then another. All the while, he followed his muses, building his acts around Hollywood, Broadway, and classic stories. He played a hard-bitten Humphrey Bogart detective, recast the shower scene from Hitchcock's *Psycho*, and did magic as a suave James Bond secret agent. All along, he sang and danced and told jokes. David Copperfield always got the girl.

"He made magic cool," says Peter Shukoff, one of the writers of the YouTube sensation *Epic Rap*

Battles. "I mean, what could be cooler than being David Copperfield?"

Not much, it turns out. He was more than a magician. He was a superhero. He made magic cool. There were David Copperfield action figures. Kids tried to make each other disappear. But, after some years on top, he found what Houdini found: You can't stand still in magic. There's always a bigger illusion, a more astounding miracle to be created and performed. This has been the story of magic since the dawn of history. As long as the imagination buzzes, there's something else out there, something that no one has ever done, something that will blow their minds for good this time.

In David's fourth television special, he made a jet disappear. It seemed a natural next step to him; he had already made a Ferrari levitate and disappear in 1980. Copperfield put a jet on the tarmac at Van Nuys Airport in Los Angeles. Volunteers surrounded the jet, hands held, arms locked together, so that nothing could get in or out. Copperfield put up a giant sheet to obscure the view, but through it you could still see the shadows of the jet and the people. Then, there was some fuzziness—you could see the shadow of the jet and the people were still holding hands—and Copperfield pulled a lever to turn out the lights. He ran in front of the camera and put his arms out.

"NOW!" he shouted.

The screens dropped. The jet was gone.

"It blew up the internet," he says, "and there was no internet then."

Even Copperfield was shocked by the reaction. The disappearing jet became an American cultural phenomenon. Everybody talked about it. Copperfield at first was dismayed that people loved that trick more than his others; it wasn't the sort of magic he loves. One minute the jet was here, the next minute it was gone—there was no arc, no lesson, no romance, no story. But it moved people like nothing he had ever done before.

A few weeks after the jet disappeared, Copperfield was doing a charity event with Frank Sinatra, one of his idols and role models. Copperfield wanted to talk to the Chairman about the music, about the songs, about the movies, about the emotions.

Sinatra only wanted to know one thing.

"Kid," Sinatra asked him, "where did the jet go?"

Copperfield laughed and explained that it would ruin the illusion if he explained it, and Sinatra nodded as if he understood.

"Yeah, okay," Sinatra said. "But, really, where did the jet go?"

In time, Sinatra eased off ("It's okay, kid, you don't have to tell me"), but the reaction of his hero made Copperfield long for something new. All along, he had wanted to be like Sinatra. And now he understood that, in a strange way, Sinatra wanted to be like him.

It was time for David Copperfield to go for the biggest illusion ever. That meant topping the most spectacular illusion Harry Houdini ever did: the disappearing elephant.

Houdini made the elephant disappear on the enormous stage at the Hippodrome in New York City on January 7, 1918. It was an illusion that forever changed the ambitions of magicians.

Oddly, it didn't really seem like a Houdini kind of trick. He was an escape artist, a scrapper, a symbol of freedom, a man who conquered death, an underdog facing insurmountable odds. What did an elephant have to do with anything? Why did he even have an elephant? Why was he making it disappear? None of it seemed to fit into the larger Houdini persona.

But, in a way, Houdini never stopped being the sixteen-year-old boy who named himself after Robert-Houdin and longed to make a magical life for himself. There were times when he rebelled against magic, when he insisted on people calling him an escapologist because, well, magicians were a dime a dozen. In the end, he just loved magic with a depth of feeling that is really quite touching. It was the one thing that turned him back into a little kid. He spent most of his fortune on magic books and posters and secrets. He would break down in tears when he came across props from some of the great magicians of the past. He searched endlessly for the old magicians who had been forgotten. If they were living, he would interview them. If they were dead, he went to their gravesites (though cynics note that he usually had a reporter and photographer with him).

He held tight to the dream of leaving behind the escapes and becoming a real magician, like his childhood hero, held tight to it until quite literally the day he died. He continuously purchased the most wonderful stage illusions, like Robert-Houdin's Crystal Cash Box and Buatier de Kolta's Expanding Die, with the intention of performing them for adoring crowds. And in the last decade or so of his life, he performed illusions more than escapes. He walked through a wall. He created a radio of the future. He even tried to re-create the bullet-catching trick that killed Chung Ling Soo in 1918 (though he backed away from it; future magicians would perform the bullet catch and call it "the trick Houdini was too scared to do").

The disappearing elephant came from the magic inventor Charles Morritt who—as recounted in Steinmeyer's great book *Hiding the Elephant*—offered Houdini an irresistible pitch.

"If you really want to make headlines with your magic," Morritt said, "you shouldn't bother with little tricks, rabbits, pigeons. Make an elephant disappear."

"It'd be worth thinking about if it could be made practical," Houdini said.

"Oh," Morritt replied. "It's practical."

Morritt had an ingenious method. When Houdini saw how it worked, he instantly saw the possibilities and knew that no other magician was worthy of doing it. On that January day at the Hippodrome with World War I slowly blasting to its conclusion, Harry Houdini called to the stage Jennie the Elephant.

"Ladies and gentlemen," he called to the crowd. "Though Jennie weighs over ten thousand pounds, she is as gentle as a kitten."

Jennie didn't weigh ten thousand pounds, not even half of that, but who would begrudge Houdini a little exaggeration when disappearing such a creature? Jennie stomped onstage with her trainer leading the way into a giant box that was already prepared. Fifteen assistants spun the box around so that everyone could clearly see that Jennie was standing inside.

With that, Houdini closed the doors and curtains of the box.

"Watch closely," Houdini told the audience, "for it happens in two seconds."

On the second beat, Houdini's assistants ran to

both the front and back of the box. They opened each side and, as Houdini said, "You can plainly see, the animal is completely gone."

Jennie *was* gone! Everybody could see it—well, no, not everybody. But some people could see it, those sitting at precisely the right angle; they could see all the way through the box. It definitely looked like an empty box. Houdini had done it. He had made an elephant disappear. It was the miracle of the age.

And almost nobody in the audience got it.

"The Hippodrome patrons squinted at the scene," Steinmeyer wrote, "mumbled to themselves, and let go with what seemed a collective shrug, contemplating the next feature on the busy program: a trapeze act. They'd just seen the most gigantic wonder ever presented on a stage yet greeted it with only a deflating smattering of applause."

Why did it flop? Well, there are some good theories. First, as mentioned, this was not really a Houdini act. People came to see Houdini tempt death, defeat danger, not make a few jokes about an elephant. In this illusion, Houdini didn't seem to do anything. Someone else led the elephant into the box. Assistants opened and closed the doors. Where was Houdini's magic in all this? To disappear an elephant so gracefully that everyone could feel wonder—that was not in Houdini's skill set.

Steinmeyer put it less charitably: "Houdini," he wrote, "was a terrible magician."

There was also the aforementioned technical flaw: most people could not see the inside of the box at the end. The Hippodrome stage was enormous (as a stage needed to be for an elephant), and most people in the crowd were too far away or had too sharp an angle to see inside. Was the elephant gone? They either took Houdini's word for it, or they didn't.

Magicians ruthlessly mocked the trick. Servais Le Roy summed up the cruel criticisms by calling the Disappearing Elephant "perfect in its utter weakness."

When I asked Jamy Ian Swiss, one of magic's great essayists and thinkers, about the Disappearing Elephant, he said something fascinating. I had told him that part of my interest in Houdini stems from the fact that he sparks so much wonder in the world, even today. His eyes flashed when I used that word *wonder,* and he shook his head slowly.

"You have to be really careful when talking about Houdini and wonder," he said.

"Why is that?"

"What you have to understand," he said, and his voice rose an octave, accentuating his New York accent, "is that Houdini was not a magician."

"Yes, I have heard people say he was not a good magician—"

"No," he corrected, "that's not what I'm saying. I'm not saying he was not a good magician. I'm saying he was not a magician at all."

He paused to let the words sink in.

"Magic," he said, "is the art of doing the impossible."

"But," I said, "Houdini escaped from everything. People all over the world put him in jail cells and chains and straitjackets, they threw him in coffins, in crates, in bags, they constructed impenetrable boxes of glass and steel and wood and leather, they devised handcuffs that could not be opened except with complex keys turned eight different ways, and he escaped from them all."

"Ah," Jamy says. "That's amazing. But it's not impossible."

That is perfectly stated. People came to see Houdini do the amazing.

But making an elephant disappear, that is impossible.

A cruel joke circulated through the magic world after Houdini performed it: Did you hear Houdini had three people bring a box on stage, put an elephant in it, made it disappear, and then he needed twenty men to roll the box offstage. It wasn't true, but it endured. The Disappearing Elephant was a brilliant illusion, a breakthrough in magic, but Houdini did not live long enough to see the impact. As the years went on, it grew larger and larger in magicians' minds. How far could a magician go? How much could he or she make an audience believe?

These were the questions on the mind of David Copperfield.

"When Houdini vanished the elephant, it was the biggest thing ever done," David Copperfield says. "The next biggest thing after, more than fifty years later, was to vanish an airplane."

"And then?" I ask him.

"And then," he says. "It was the Statue of Liberty."

The reaction to the disappearing jet surprised Copperfield. But he knew exactly what he was doing with the Statue of Liberty. On the night he made it disappear, Copperfield himself called it "The Illusion of the Century." He was right. Decades later, Joshua Jay was asked to put together a college-basketball style bracket of the greatest magic tricks ever, and he ranked the Statue Disappearance as the most influential illusion of our time.

It was Jim Steinmeyer who invented the ingenious method. He, like the Disappearing Elephant inventor Charles Morritt, knew the illusion could work. He also knew that it faced the same obstacle that the Disappearing Elephant faced in 1918.

Who would ever believe that the Statue of Liberty had disappeared?

To pull it off required a magician who was larger than life.

"Tonight, we're on Liberty Island," David Copperfield began. "People come here by boat, and I made the trip quite frequently during this past year, getting ready for tonight. A couple of weeks ago when I was on the boat, a young sightseer about seven years old came up to me and said, 'Are you David?' He said he saw me make a car disappear. And then he said he saw me make the jet plane disappear.

"I thanked him and watched as he looked up at the Statue of Liberty, then at me, then back to the statue, then back to me. Finally, he looked me right in the eye and said, 'Are you thinking what I think you're thinking?' Well, that's what I was thinking all right. And tonight, he and I and you are going to find out if it can be done. Can the Statue of Liberty really disappear?"

Well, can it? The setup was a complicated affair: there was some scaffolding, a live audience, a helicopter, and various spotlights. And with dramatic music playing in the background, Copperfield, wearing a silver bomber jacket he would later regret, had a screen raised. He went to one knee and appeared to concentrate deeply. He then stood up and turned and raised his hands, asking for the screen to be lowered. The Statue of Liberty was gone. "The entire thing, it just disappeared," a woman told the show's host.

"What happened to it? I have no idea. It was fascinating to watch."

Steinmeyer's method is so ingenious that a quarter century later, people still talk about it, argue about it, race to YouTube to study, and guess how it was done.

And like Houdini's elephant, it was not a huge hit at the moment it happened. Sure, people watched—it was the fifteenth-rated show of the week—but the buzz afterward was muted compared to the jet disappearance. Magicians were uniformly unimpressed.

"For an illusion to work," Doug Henning said, "it must create a sense of wonder, and that's what was lacking there. After all, when you watch a magician, it shouldn't be just like trying to figure out a puzzle, because then who cares?

"Now, there was no wonder in the Statue of Liberty illusion because he attempted to do something so large that it stretched the credibility of the audience to the point where most people didn't believe any of it anymore. They thought it was trick photography or something like that and, again, if that's what it is, who cares?"

There it is: the amazing and the impossible.

Did Copperfield think that he could make most people believe he made a 305-foot, 450,000-pound statue disappear? No, he didn't. But like Houdini, he wasn't going for a single moment. He was going for history. He was going for something that would last forever—and he was right. Disappearing the Statue of Liberty is legend, the boldest endeavor in magic history. It put Copperfield in the pantheon of magic.

"Can an illusion be too amazing?" Copperfield said in response. "Yes. That's why I would never walk on water. Nobody would believe it."

"David is famous for making the Statue of Liberty disappear," Steinmeyer says. "But almost no one has seen it or even bothered to go back to watch the videotape. Houdini, of course, benefited from the reputation of the elephant. If you watch Copperfield's stuff, you'll see lots of 1980s indulgences that make it truly silly and a museum piece. I particularly like him concentrating, fingers to temples, as he makes it disappear. Really?

"Those tricks are about headlines, not about the actual accomplishment."

Copperfield does not avoid Statue of Liberty talk, but he would prefer to move on. "I don't look backward," he says. And he doesn't. He performs a strange and surprising new act in Las Vegas built around his discovery of a military card that showed his father had been stationed in Roswell, New Mexico, just when there was a famous UFO incident.

"It all begins in truth," he says.

Copperfield connected details and conceived of an elaborate thirty-minute magic performance that features Copperfield, his father, and an alien named BLU. This is Copperfield as storyteller using magic to express regret (Copperfield was not there to say good-bye when his father died), chase memories (here is his chance to go back in time and see his father again), and spread love (BLU's message to the world is that love can save us all), and, sure, to have a cute blue alien tell a few off-color jokes. When Copperfield began performing it, the act was mocked and loathed. Copperfield remembers reading TripAdvisor reviews—can you imagine a billionaire who owns islands looking at TripAdvisor reviews?— that said things like, "I didn't come to Las Vegas to see a puppet show."

Copperfield never gave up on the alien illusion, though. He worked it, reworked it, and he reworks it still, twice a day most days, three times on Saturdays and around Christmas. More people like the show now. Some still don't. He goes on, three hundred and fifty shows a year. Houdini was like this too. What is behind the mystery? What does Copperfield feel that Houdini felt? Maybe it's this: You can make an elephant disappear. You can even make the Statue of Liberty disappear. But the show goes on, and there's always more magic to be done.

EPIC RAP BATTLE II

[Harry Houdini]

So, abracadabra, you billowy bitch
Man, you look like a pirate on a Las
  Vegas strip
I'm swallowing needles and spitting out
  evil
You couldn't escape from a flash paper
  bag
I'm badder with patter and matter of fact
You can't match all my skill if you sawed
  me in half

[David Copperfield]

You failed at making movies and you
  failed at making kids
You should stick to what you're good at
  and lock them lips
Here's a tidbit that might drive you nuts
I bought half your shit, and I keep it
  locked up
Got the slim fingers that were built for
  sleights
You're a chunky stuntman; dressed in
  tights

You talk shit about your hero; that ain't
right
But you can look up to me now; I know
you like heights
       —*Epic Rap Battles of History*:
"David Copperfield vs. Harry Houdini"

When Peter Shukoff and Lloyd Ahlquist first came up with the *Epic Rap Battles of History* YouTube concept—making videos of famous people in history rapping insults at each other, some three billion hits on YouTube so far—they asked fans to choose the combatants. Their first video featured bombastic conservative talk show host Bill O'Reilly facing off against Beatle and peace activist John Lennon. They made it for two hundred dollars. A few people watched.

But their second video—also on a two-hundred-dollar budget—matched Darth Vader against Adolf Hitler. Millions watched. It happened that quickly. Their video was even banned in numerous countries including Germany and Poland. They had a worldwide hit on their hands.

From the start, they knew at some point they would have to do Houdini.

This was particularly personal for Shukoff.

"Absolutely, Houdini was one of the most popular suggestions right away," Shukoff says. "And it never really stopped. It's remarkable, everybody knows him. He's a verb, man. A cat gets away, a dog tries to get out the window like my dog is trying to right now, it's a Houdini. He's like Napoleon or something.

"We knew we would do Houdini. I couldn't wait, really, because I love magic. I began as a high school magician. But the challenge was finding who he would battle. Who was big enough to go against Houdini? The suggestion we kept getting was Harry Houdini versus Harry Potter. I really wanted to stay away from that. Harry Potter, it seemed, was already a character in people's minds. Anything we would do with him would be fake and weird. I just could never figure out who to put in there with Harry Houdini."

In time, they came upon the obvious but inspired choice: Copperfield. Peter and Lloyd, you should know, really get into their rap battles. They investigate. They research. They work with costumers and video and props people to make everything feel as authentic as possible. For Harry Houdini versus David Copperfield, they were able to sneak in so many wonderful little details about both men. They get into Houdini's Needles trick, point out Copperfield has the largest Houdini collection in the world, and have Copperfield go after Houdini for attacking Robert-Houdin. They got so into it that Lloyd, who plays Houdini in the video, insisted on having his wife, Josie, play Bess.

"We think a lot about our characters," Peter says. "With Houdini, we decided he would be a little cranky and he would be entirely unimpressed with David Copperfield. More than that, he'd be bothered and annoyed by David Copperfield. I feel sure that's true."

This might have been Peter's favorite of the series. He too fell under Houdini's spell as a boy. He remains a member of the Magic Castle in Los Angeles. And he has spent quite a lot of time thinking about Houdini and Copperfield.

"It's hard to say for sure who was better," he says. "I think if you had them perform back-to-back, it would have to be Copperfield, right? I mean Houdini wasn't the greatest magician. Howard Thurston was better. Houdini mainly did just one thing: he escaped. It was great, it was incredible, it has lasted all these years. But Copperfield can do any kind of magic. He did the big things like the Statue of Liberty. He does the small things like the dancing cane. I tried to do that in the video. It's really hard.

"Copperfield, you know, he's one of the best ever, one of the greats. He's done all the big illusions, but truth is, he could be standing right in front of you and do something that just blows your mind. Plus, he's unflappable. He's just cool."

Copperfield was so cool, he let Peter and Lloyd

know how much he enjoyed the video even though there he takes a few shots in it.

"That was a real thrill," Peter says. "You know what, it's silly to compare them. They are each of their time."

He pauses. Yes, it is silly to compare them. It's silly to compare anyone to Houdini.

And yet . . .

"After the video came out," he says, "I was surprised how many times we got the question, 'Who is David Copperfield?' Maybe that shouldn't be surprising. I mean, there are a lot of kids who watch these videos. It has been quite a few years since Copperfield has been on television. They didn't grow up with him like so many of us did. I guess I shouldn't be surprised."

I ask Peter how many people didn't know Harry Houdini.

"Oh," he says, "they all knew Houdini."

TORTURE

NOTHING SUPERNATURAL

"Ladies and gentlemen, I take great pleasure in introducing my latest invention, the Water Torture Cell. Although there is nothing supernatural about it, I am willing to forfeit the sum of one thousand dollars to anyone who can prove that it is possible to obtain air inside of the Torture Cell when I'm locked up in it, in the regulation manner, after it has been filled with water.

"Should anything go wrong when I'm locked up, one of my assistants watches through the curtain, ready to rush in, demolishing the glass, allowing the water to flow out in order to save my life . . . I honestly and positively do not expect any accident to happen. But we all know accidents will happen—and when least expected.

"Harry Houdini, October the twenty-ninth, nineteen hundred and fourteen, Flatbush, New York."
—From one of the few known recordings
of Harry Houdini's voice

HOUDINI UPSIDE DOWN

In April of 1911, Harry Houdini performed in an odd play at the Hippodrome in Southampton. Admission was a guinea, an outrageous price for a theater ticket in those days—by 2018 inflation, it was roughly the equivalent of one hundred and nineteen pounds, or one hundred sixty-six dollars. One person showed up.

The play was called *Challenged, or Houdini Upside Down*. The plot was pretty thin. It begins with a multimillionaire sportsman, Tim Connor, lounging around the Eccentric Athletic Club with a newspaper editor (Henry Jones) and a former swimmer from Australia (Bob Matthews). They presumably were doing what millionaire sportsmen, newspaper editors, and former swimmers might do in such a situation: talking about Harry Houdini and how he was impossible to hold prisoner.

"Then you think this great Houdini invincible, eh, Jones?" Connor, the sportsman, sneered.

"I've known him for ten years now," Jones the newspaper editor replied, "and I honestly think the man does not live who can tie him or box him up so he can't escape."

"Well, my dear old pal," Connor replied, "don't think me conceited when I tell you I can hold him. Little me! And I'm so sure of it, I'll bet him a cool thousand pounds I can hold him."

The swimmer Matthews finally jumps in: "Hurrah!" he says. "Some excitement at last."

At this point, the plot turns to the question of whether Houdini would dare accept Connor's devious and dangerous challenge. Jones, Houdini's man to the end, shouts out: "He's a fair and square showman, a gentleman and a sport . . . Now let me hear your blooming challenge!"

Connor points at the aquarium across the room.

"My idea," he said, "is to put this Houdini fellow into that aquarium, head first, understand me, head first, with his feet in the air, then put a cover on, fasten his feet to this cover, and lock him in."

Matthews, the famous swimmer, was the first to understand the horrors of this challenge.

"Why," he shouted, "it's nothing short of murder!"

Harry Houdini knew from the start that the Chinese Water Torture Cell—or, as he called it, the Upside Down—would be his masterpiece. He began conceiving it in 1908, when he first felt audiences pulling away from him. He thought day and night, pondering everything he had learned about escape and danger and how to take spectators to the very edge.

"The Water Torture Cell," he explained to a

reporter, "was constructed by myself not in a day, an hour, a week, or a month. It took years of calculation to bring it to its present state of perfection. The actual construction of it took two full years. Another year was required to give me sufficient courage to attempt same. Can you blame me?"

The Chinese Water Torture Cell added two key elements to his legendary Milk Can escape. First, he added glass in front so that people could actually see him underwater. Second, and most important, he entered into the Torture Cell upside down.

"Houdini looked at the milk can," says Jamy Ian Swiss, "and said, 'Okay, what's good about this? The drowning. The claustrophobia. The water. The seal on top. How can I think of something that has all that but is also different?'

"And that's Houdini's genius. That's what it is: *genius*. How do you present an escape from your own device? The milk can, the water torture cell, he built it. Why would people believe that he could not escape from something that he himself built? But he had people inspect it. No trap doors. No secret compartments. They could see the water. Then he went in upside down. He took away the possibilities one by one until there were none left."

The Upside Down—USD is how he referred to it in his diary—is a box of steel and mahogany and glass. Anyone who sees the cell today, in David Copperfield's museum, has the same reaction: it's tiny. The entire cabinet is roughly five and a half feet tall. It is so small, you feel yourself suffocating just a little when you see it. That's the Chinese Water Torture Cell's brilliance: it is immaculately crafted to cut deep into our fears.

"Imagine yourself," Houdini said, "jammed head foremost into a cell filled with water. Your hands and feet unable to move, your shoulders tightly lodged in this imprisonment. Can you blame me for fearing to trust myself in the apparently deadly embrace of this unheard-of contrivance, which smacks of the Dark Ages?"

For the performance, Houdini invited eight or ten or even a dozen people on the stage to inspect the Torture Cell. He encouraged them to look closely; he knew that his secret was invisible. He asked them if there were any trap doors below. When people complained (as he wanted them to) that they could not see below the cell, he smiled. "Choose any part of the stage," he said, "and I'll have the cell removed to it."

When the cell was in place, Houdini shouted: "Begin!" He stretched out on the stage and allowed his legs to be locked into a block. All the while, volunteers dumped buckets of water into the cell, in full audience view. Through the glass, everyone could see the water level rising until the tank was entirely filled. Houdini was then lifted up by the ankles and held upside down above the water. This was when people could see the block at his feet was actually the water cell cover.

Houdini was lowered slowly into the Torture Cell. Water cascaded from both sides. He continued to be lowered until the cover was in place and Houdini's head was at the bottom of the cell. People could see his face staring out at them; it was a haunting picture. Then a curtain draped around the cell.

And the music began—an old parlor song: "The Diver."

He is now on the surface gasping for
    breath
So pale that he wants but the stillness of
    death
To look like the forms, he has left in the
    caves
Silent and cold 'neath the trembling
    waves
        Silent and cold 'neath the trembling
        waves

People held their breaths too. The escape always took so long, just long enough for everyone to believe something must have gone wrong. Finally, the curtains would shake, just a little, and the audience would rise in anticipation.

Then after a couple of electrifying seconds, Houdini jumped through the curtains, soaking wet, somehow defeated and triumphant all at once. People went mad. He bowed his head and soaked in the applause.

"I believe," he said, "it is the climax of all my studies and labors."

Houdini loved the Upside Down deeply, but he was nervous about it. He wasn't nervous about performing it (though he often said he was), but instead about someone stealing the idea from him. Within weeks of him performing the Milk Can, imposters began doing their own versions. There were so many imposters, even Houdini could not unmask them all.

And that's when he came up with yet another flash of genius. He knew that you could not copyright magic tricks in 1918.

But you could copyright plays.

So, for one day only, Harry Houdini performed *Challenged, or Houdini Upside Down*.

You must want to know how the play ended. Connor did challenge Houdini to escape from the aquarium. Their exchange on this is particularly choice.

HOUDINI: Well, now, what am I
  supposed to say?
CONNOR: You are supposed to say: "Yes,

I will accept the challenge." And just
to make it interesting, I'll bet you a
thousand pounds on the side you can't
escape from the aquarium under our
conditions, as set forth in the challenge.
HOUDINI: I never bet, Mr. Connor.
CONNOR (*slyly*): Only sure things, eh?
HOUDINI: I think your remark is entirely
uncalled for, sir. Now I *will* accept your
challenge, and your bet of a thousand
pounds as well.

The "I never bet" line is priceless. All Houdini
ever did was bet. He backed every escape, every
trick, every challenge, and even his late-life
efforts to expose spiritualists with money wagers.
He wagered one hundred pounds to anyone who
could find a trap door in his Prison Cell and
Barrel Mystery, two hundred dollars to anyone
who could prove that it's possible to draw breath
while hanging upside down in the Water Torture
Cell, and even a thousand dollars to anyone who
could prove that the airplane crash in his silent
film *The Grim Game* was not genuine.

When he first invented the Milk Can, he
performed it exclusively for Bess. In his diary, he
wrote: "She saw me do the can trick, thinks it's
great. I offered her ten dollars if she could tell
me how it was done. She failed to fathom trick.
GOOD." He bet his own wife that she couldn't

figure out the secret. Houdini was part magician, part daredevil, and all gambler.

In the play, no surprise, Houdini did escape from the aquarium, and even the doubting Connor was forced to admit: "The Great Houdini is indeed a marvel." Houdini accepted the thousand-pound check but announced, "Ladies and gentlemen, I make it a practice never to take side bets, but I was practically forced into this bet. I wish to inform you that I will have much pleasure in handing this check for one thousand pounds to the home for Poor and Aged Actors and Artistes."

This led the people on the stage and one person in the crowd to shout, "Three cheers for Houdini!"

The curtain fell: the play was performed and copyrighted, and Houdini immediately let every other magician on earth know that his Water Torture Cell was protected by a "Special Licence from the Lord Chamberlain."

Almost no one in Houdini's time attempted the Water Torture Cell, but it probably wasn't the copyright that dissuaded them. Magicians have always stolen, borrowed, and reproduced tricks. The truth was that almost nobody knew how he did it.

THE EMPATHY OF ESCAPE

I watch my daughters' hands. They are clutching the sides of the armrests on their chairs and squeezing so hard that I can see the blood rushing to their fingertips. They have never understood this Houdini obsession, never why our house overflows with Houdini posters, shelves of magic books, Houdini coins and dolls, spare handcuffs, a Houdini bobblehead, a beer stein in the shape of Houdini's milk can, and a teddy bear that was released as a celebration of the Houdini postage stamp.

But now, our oldest, Elizabeth, grips the side of her chair as if it is falling from the sky, and that is nothing compared to Katie, the thirteen-year-old, who has a less acerbic disposition and is so nervous that she is on the verge of tears.

On the stage, Andrew Basso performs his own version of the Chinese Water Torture Cell. There is no curtain to hide behind. He is dangling upside down and underwater and in full public view. A digital clock shows the elapsed time. We are told that if he does not escape by the three-minute mark, he could die. The clock winds closer to 3:00.

As I look around the arena—this is in Charlotte, at the national tour of *The Illusionists*, more than one hundred years after Houdini introduced the Upside Down—the same scene replays on every row. Men and women, girls and boys, all races, all ages intently watch the stage, their faces white with fear, their hands clenched on the armrests at their sides.

At the precise moment, a few miles away, Kristen Johnson also performs the Chinese Water Torture Cell in Charlotte, though she performs the escape a bit differently. For one thing, she performs it outside, at the Queen City Fair, and the wind blows so hard that the sign behind her stage, the one that reads "Lady Houdini," flaps so wildly it threatens to take the whole stage away.

Families gather around Kristen. The air smells like popcorn. To her left is a carousel and to her right is an open field where cars park. Kristen has handcuffs locked on her, and she gets into the water cell. Her husband, Kevin, locks the top on. There is no clock here to give the audience that sense of doom. But people feel it anyway.

Kristen tries to pick the locks, but she does not seem to be doing very well. Kevin walks over to the cell to check on her, looking nervously through the glass. She almost imperceptibly signals that she is okay, and he begins to pace. A bubble emerges from Kristen's mouth and then another. She has one of the locks off, but there are two more. She seems to be straining. Kevin checks on her again. Some people in the audience might know that a few years earlier, Kristen tried the Water Torture Cell escape at halftime of an NBA game. She could not get the locks picked in time and was deprived of oxygen for so long that she had a hypoxic seizure and had to be pulled from the tank. She survived, but it became a YouTube moment. Kristen never forgets.

"The lights go out," Kristen says. "The body seizes up. The airways lock off. And you have to get to the surface before the seizure ends or you will, in fact, drown."

The people at the fair begin to feel uncomfortable. She has been in the water for a long time.

"Is she okay?" one little girl, younger than our daughters, says to her mother. The mother nods but seems unsure. Kristen works away at the lock. She has one more handcuff to go. She runs out of air.

"Is it fun to perform the water torture escape?" I had asked her hours earlier.

"No," she said. "It is not."

Andrew Basso grew up in Borgo Valsugana, a tiny village in northern Italy. He says it is the sort of place familiar to anyone who grew up away from anything exciting and thrilling and risky. One day, the circus came to this town where nothing ever happened, and Andrew remembered it so vividly, a splash of color in his gray existence.

"I remember this giant tent," he recalls, "and I remember entering, smelling the food, the animals, seeing people flying in the air. It was all very different, very strange, very fascinating. The lights! The colors! And then I saw the show, all these people dressed differently from anyone I had ever seen, and they all were doing these incredible things, each with their own special skill.

"I went home and found tennis balls and taught myself to juggle. I was obsessed. Sometimes my father would take me to the little square of my little town, and I would perform on the street. I wanted to be a circus man, climbing anywhere and everywhere, juggling,"

There is such a strong connection between juggling and magic that, in the earliest written accounts, they are almost interchangeable. The history of magic literature goes back to 1584, when two books—in England, Reginald Scot's *The Discoverie of Witchcraft* and in France, Jean Prevost's *Clever and Pleasant Inventions, Part One*—set off the age of magic. In those books, magicians were called jugglers. There is a thread that connects the art forms: in both, a performer spends countless hours perfecting a trick that will leave the audience breathless.

But there is a difference: a juggler can only

stretch the imagination so far because a juggler is bound by what is possible. A magician sheds those limitations. Andrew remembers the precise moment that juggling fell away for him and magic took hold. His family went to a fair in a nearby town, and he saw his mother walk up to a street magician.

"Let me describe my mother to you," he says. "She is very beautiful. Her name is Clara. She is like Morticia Addams. She is very pale with long flat hair and big eyebrows. And she is very serious. If you don't know her, you think she's going to kill you. And she always wears black. Can you picture her in your mind?

"There's this guy at a table, this magician. I remember nothing of what he looks like or what he was wearing. I only remember that he sees my mother, and he grabs her hand. He pulls her closer. The guy had three cups and three balls. And he was making the balls disappear. He was making the balls penetrate right through the cups. This is the oldest magic in the world, yes, but I had never seen it before. It was not the magic that captured me. No, the magician grabbed my mother's hand, and he put one of the balls in it, and then he closed her fist tight around it. He told her to wish. And when she opened up her hand, there were two balls in it.

"To see my mom's face—it was a complete transformation. It went from seriousness to total wonder. She was in awe. That for me was a picture, the only thing I remember. That was my life-changing moment. If he is able to do that, I want to be able to do that."

When Andrew came upon Houdini, as was inevitable, he felt the connection. "He was in handcuffs, and he had this intense look, and I remember thinking that he was very familiar to me," he says. "I thought, *Did I meet this guy? I know this guy. How do I know this guy? It is not possible.* Even now, I cannot explain this.

"And because I felt close to him, I wanted to escape like him. I was already doing magic, working with cards, making coins disappears, but escape . . . this was something else. I had friends tie me up. I freed myself. That feeling of satisfaction, that sense of freedom, of victory, I had never felt anything like it."

Kristen Johnson began as a clown. She learned that from her mother, Sunny, who had played Cuddles Z. Clown for most of Kristen's life. Sunny opened up her own entertainment business, Clowns Etc. (Slogan: "There's Always Room for a Smile!"), in Carmel, Indiana, and in college Kristen worked for the company, putting on clown paint, painting kids' faces, folding balloons, and doing small bits of magic here and there. She knew that wasn't going to be her life; Kristen did not see herself as an entertainer.

She graduated, got a job in a human resources department at a major tech company, and left the stage behind.

Then Sunny got cancer.

"They removed a foot and a half of her colon," Kristen says. "She made it, but the surgery, the anesthesia, all of it did a number on her. I left my job to run her business. And I started performing again as part of that. Eventually that was all I was doing."

She performed at birthday parties, orchestrated fashion shows, and dressed up like costume characters. Soon after, she met Kevin, and they hit it off.

"My mom said, 'Good, another performer,' " Kristen says. "So, she started getting him performing too, doing birthday parties and things like that."

Kristen and Kevin did not expect this to become their lives. She had a good job in HR. He had a good job in sales. But all at once, as a complete shock to both of them, they came to the conclusion that they wanted to be entertainers. "I'm going to be a magician," Kevin announced one day. "I'll help you," Kristen said. They put together a show and started their own entertainment business, Living Illusions, spending most of their time entertaining at Christian fundraisers and church gatherings.

"Kevin is the magician," Kristen says. "He's

the guy. He's articulate and engaging; if you needed an MC, Kevin was your go-to guy. The guys think he's cool. The girls think he's hot. And me? I had no showmanship. I was just jumping in and out of boxes and, like, 'ta da!' "

Then Kristen did her first rope escape. That's when she started to think about Houdini. She didn't know much about him, only the stuff everybody knows. But when she freed herself from the rope that the first time, *Wow, what a rush*. She felt alive in a whole different way. What other escapes could she do? Houdini was the road map. What did he do? He began with ropes, so she did too. He moved on to handcuffs, so Kristen escaped from handcuffs. What next? Straitjackets? Kristen escaped from straitjackets. She began pushing the edge, trying to surpass Houdini. She escaped a straitjacket while dangling upside down from a rope like he did and then freed herself from the rope itself.

"I love giving people something they don't expect," she says. "The coolest moment for me is when I've escaped from something, and everyone starts to applaud, and then they stop and realize that the coolest part still hasn't happened. That's why I love the straitjacket escape. I get out and everyone thinks, *That's it*. But that is the easy part."

Soon, people began calling her Lady Houdini. She is hardly the first. In 1922, an escape show called Lady Hudini and LaSalle gained enough popularity that Houdini caught wind of it. "There is no such person as Lady Houdini, the wife of Harry Houdini being known as 'Mrs. Houdini,'" he said grumpily. Houdini was unmoved by the counterargument that the Lady had separated herself by removing the *o* from Houdini.

Esme Levante—the daughter of the magician the Great Levante—was known briefly as Lady Houdini, as was Florence Kazan, whose specialty was the upside-down straitjacket escape. A woman with the already interesting stage name of Dell O'Dell also called herself Lady Houdini; she later traveled with her own circus and was one of the pioneers of magic on television.

With such a long history of Lady Houdinis, Kristen did not particularly want the name. "I would have never decided to call myself that on my own," she says. But everywhere she went, that's what people called her, so she gave up fighting.

"Well," she says, "it is a perfect description of everything the show is. When I try to explain what I do, people don't always get it. But when they hear Lady Houdini, they understand."

All escape roads lead eventually to the Water Torture Cell, there's no way around that, so Kristen began performing her own version of the escape at halftime shows, at county fairs, and in small arenas everywhere. She performed it hundreds and hundreds of times, in full view of the audience. She doesn't love the escape. She doesn't even like it. It's dangerous, and it's hard, and she isn't crazy about how she looks doing it.

"It's not magic," she says. "They see exactly what I'm doing. They see that I'm picking the locks. They see that I'm holding my breath. They see how much I have to do before time runs out. Houdini performed the Water Torture Cell with a curtain surrounding him. That was how it was done at that time, when any brush with death was a big deal. I would love to do it that way, but you can't in today's world."

Kristen smiles.

"In today's world if there's a curtain," she says, "there's a trick."

The digital clock behind Andrew Basso moves past 2:30 on the stage. The people at the fair feel time running out on Lady Houdini. Everyone knows it will turn out okay. Everyone knows it might not turn out okay.

"Let me tell you about my first time in front of a live audience," Andrew says. "I went into the tank, and after thirty seconds I already started feeling my diaphragm contracting. I didn't even start the escape yet. It was over before it started. I gave the signal, the emergency signal, I started to swallow water, I was losing consciousness, and they got me out. They got me out fast.

"And at that moment, all I remembered was that a teacher had once told me that if you have a very bad experience, the brain remembers it. It memorizes that bad experience, and it will never allow you to be put back in that position again. I couldn't let that happen, so as soon as they pulled me out, I was shouting, 'I have to do it again! I have to do it again!'

"A half hour later, they made an announcement: On my request I was going to do it again. I performed the escape, and the audience cheered like crazy—it was the loudest cheer I ever had. It was so loud the manager said, 'Can you do that again?' I said, 'What, are you crazy?'"

On this night, like on just about every other night, Andrew and Kristen escape. Kristen Johnson has escaped more than two thousand times. Andrew Basso had escaped even more. Everyone intuitively knows that this is a show, that they got out last night, and they will get out tomorrow night, and they will get out tonight too.

And yet, the power of Houdini's invention is that the danger always feels close and overpowering and real. On the stage, the clock passes 3:00, and there is no air in the room, and Andrew picks the final lock and emerges from the tank, triumphant. At the fair, Kristen gets the last lock picked, and then she leaps through the lid of her tank, and the huge crowd that had come over to see what was happening all shout in unison.

People do cheer, yes, but the feeling is more exhausted relief. I look at my daughters, and the color is only just beginning to come back to their faces.

"The Water Torture Cell," Andrew says, "is more than a magic trick. Houdini understood this. It attacks our inner feelings. It steals our basic needs for air and freedom. It touches something deep inside us today, just as it did one hundred years ago, just as it will one hundred years from now."

THE SECRET

Do you want to know how Houdini did it? As I'm sure you noticed, this book does not give away Houdini's methods. This is not that kind of book. But there's something fascinating about the way Houdini performed the Chinese Water Torture Cell, something that cuts to the very heart of Houdini's character. So, let me repeat the question.

Do you want to know how Houdini did it?

Do not answer too quickly. At the heart of magic is that question: Do you *really* want to know?

The secret, in magic, often feels like a letdown, something less magical than you expected. Sometimes it's a piece of thread. Sometimes it's a gaffed coin. Sometimes it's a mirror in just the right place. Penn and Teller do this trick they call Honor System, loosely based on Houdini's double-box escape. They have two boxes on stage, one is a typical wooden crate, the other a transparent Plexiglas box with a cover that goes over the top like the cover of a gift box. You can see through the Plexiglas box. Teller gets into the box and it is locked. Everyone can see Teller inside. That box is then put into the wooden box, which is also locked.

Then comes the part that makes the trick wonderful. Penn begins to play a song on his bass guitar, and he tells the audience that Teller will emerge and finish the song on his vibraphone. And he says that if you want to know the secret, all you have to do is keep your eyes open. He promises that you will see exactly how the trick is done.

But he offers another option as well: You can close your eyes until the moment is right. And when you open them, you will experience the true wonder and mystery of the illusion.

Most people keep their eyes open. Who doesn't want to know the secret? But when they do, many of them are disappointed because the method, while ingenious, isn't especially fun, not compared to the wonder of someone escaping from two boxes. And some people do close their eyes. Some of them leave the show and tell people around them: "Don't explain it to me. I don't want to know."

And so now . . . you have a choice.

With magic, you always have a choice. I wanted to be sure that this book reveals no methods (other than our wild guess at how Houdini did that crazy Mirror Cuffs escape), but if you want the secrets to anything you read in here, there are literally hundreds of places you can go: books, magazines, websites, YouTube videos, etc. You can find out how to make an elephant or the Statue of Liberty disappear, saw a woman (or a man) in half, or solve a Rubik's Cube by throwing it into the air. The answers are readily available if you want to look.

"Do you want to know how Houdini escaped the Water Torture Cell?" Jim Steinmeyer asks.

I shrug. I'd heard and read many theories on it. But this is the master explaining.

"Do you really want me to tell you?" he asks. "I will. But you have to say you want to know."

"I want to know," I say to Steinmeyer.

It's not too late to skip ahead to the next chapter.

Before we get to the secret, let's talk for a minute about magical secrets. Steinmeyer has always found magicians' outrage and obsession about them to be a little bit silly. He doesn't think people should just expose how a trick is done. Magician Max Maven says it best: it's just plain rude.

But Steinmeyer thinks magicians are too concerned about their secrets because, he believes, those are not at the heart of real magic.

"Magicians guard an empty safe," he famously wrote. "There are few secrets they possess which are beyond a grade-school science class, little technology much more complex than a rubber band, a square of black fabric or a length of thread."

What makes the magic, Steinmeyer says, is what surrounds the secret. Penn and Teller do a wonderful demonstration of this too. Teller does an illusion called the Red Ball, which is a gorgeous magical set piece that goes back more than one hundred years to a Nebraska magician and Houdini friend named David P. Abbott. Teller makes a large red ball come to life.

And before he even begins, Penn tells everyone that it is done with a single piece of thread.

For three and a half minutes, Teller then has the red ball follow him, leap into his lap, refuse to move, and finally jump through a hoop. For Penn, revealing the single piece of thread is what makes the trick work. Penn originally hated it. "The whole plot," he told the *Las Vegas Weekly*, "is he has a ball that can do shit." Penn realized that if he just told the audience at the start that it was all done with one piece of thread, that would become the plot. And instead of people thinking, *Okay, this is cool, but I don't get it,* they would think, *He can't possibly be doing that with one piece of thread.* (In fact, many magicians do believe that Penn is lying and that the method actually involves something more than one piece of thread.)

Teller, though, is going for something else. He has worked on the Red Ball for so many hours, he lost track somewhere along the way. Performing it is an obsession, and he wants it to be so flawless, so perfect, that the audience feels the impossible.

"Sometimes," Teller told *Esquire*'s Chris Jones, "magic is just spending more time on something than anyone else might reasonably expect."

All of this brings us back to Steinmeyer's reveal of the Chinese Water Torture Cell. There are, as you might expect, various ingenious mechanical devices on the cell, a trick panel, a glorious method to open that panel, a feint that no one sees. If you want to know the full method for how Houdini gets out, you can try to find Patrick Culliton's rare book, *Houdini: The Key*, where he goes over it in scholarly detail—though I will warn you that it might be easier to escape from the cell than to find the book. The cell itself is an amazing piece of machinery.

But, here's the thing: the cell is not the secret.

Are you ready?

"I found this out twenty-five years ago," Steinmeyer says. "It astonished me when I first found out, and it astonishes me now. Every single time Houdini did it, every time he was locked in that thing, someone got him out. It was usually his assistant Jim Collins who, while preparing the cell, actually freed Houdini. It happened right in front of the spectators. Houdini didn't operate the mechanism or let himself out. He left it to someone else.

"It blows my mind. I have never worked

with an escape artist who would do it that way. Everyone I have worked with wants to be upside down in that tank and wants to feel something and check something and know they can get out on their own. But Houdini would be let out of it every night. That was a revelation to me. I don't know how that makes you feel. But for me, it's extraordinary. If Houdini had that much trust, that much faith, if he was willing to put himself in others' hands every night, there's nothing he couldn't do."

INESCAPABLE DEATH

THE DUTIFUL SON

Dash, it is tough, and I can't seem to get over it. Sometimes I feel alright, but when a calm moment arrives, I'm as bad as ever.

—Houdini letter to his brother roughly a year after his mother, Cecilia, died

On a July day in 1913, Harry Houdini took his mother and two of his brothers to the grave of Mayer Samuel Weiss. This was a tradition, something Houdini would do whenever he was to leave on a long European tour. This time, though, Houdini acted strangely. He told his mother, Cecilia, that he would lie down in the dirt next to his father so that he could say he slept in that plot before his mother. Hardeen put a stop to it, asking Houdini to stop being morose. Two days later, as he prepared to board the ship for Bremen, Germany, Cecilia grabbed him and hugged him tighter than usual and whispered in German, "Ehrich, perhaps I won't be here when you return."

And nine days later, on July 17, Cecilia Weiss died, while Houdini was in Copenhagen performing for members of the royal family. When he was told, he fainted. When he woke up, he ordered that an emergency message be sent to his brother: Do not hold the funeral until I return. It is Jewish tradition for the burial to be within one day of the death, but Houdini insisted that tradition be broken, and Cecilia's body be preserved until he could sail home. He left immediately.

Houdini left so suddenly that his loyal assistant Jim Collins was left to deal with the broken contracts. According to one newspaper story, he was jailed in Stockholm for impersonating Houdini on the stage.

Houdini made it back to the United States in a week. When he saw his mother's face in the casket, he broke down. Houdini was, in his own words, "a mother's boy." It would be difficult to overstate how true this was. He referred to Bess and Cecilia as "my two sweethearts." Ken Silverman found an odd letter Houdini wrote to Bess a couple of years before Cecilia died that demonstrates his devotion:

> I love you as I shall never again love any woman, but the love of a mother is a love that only a true mother ought to possess, for she loved me before I was born, loved me as I was born and naturally will love me until one or the other passes away in the Great Beyond, not passing away but simply let us say "gone on ahead."

When Cecilia died, Houdini was shattered, and it is fair to say that he never was the same again. "I who have laughed at the terrors of death," Houdini wrote to Hardeen, "who have smilingly leaped from high bridges, received a shock from which I do not think recovery is possible."

In the weeks after Cecilia's death, Houdini stopped working for the first time in his adult life. He visited his mother's grave every day of the first month after her death and began collecting her letters to turn into a scrapbook. She filled his every thought.

"After dinner I go alone to Cypress Hills and visit the family plot," he wrote in his diary. "Bleak and windy. It is six months and five days since Mother went to sleep. I certainly feel lonely."

Even after leaving New York and going overseas to perform, Houdini could not overcome his depression, could not shake the darkness. He spent his free time in Europe visiting graveyards. In Monte Carlo, he took particular interest in a graveyard dedicated to those who lost everything gambling and committed suicide.

"A terrible feeling pervades the first time one sees the graves," he wrote in his diary. The details of the cemetery seemed to obsess him. He filled his diary with gruesome details.

"More suicides in winter than in summer."
"When a body is found, money is stuffed

in the pockets to cause the belief that money affairs did not cause the deed."

"Suicides are buried for seven years, then dug up, placed in boxes and saved in this manner for future reference in case relatives wish to take bodies away."

"Saw grave of man and wife who committed suicide together."

He talked for the first time about leaving show business and retiring to a quiet life.

But, still, he was Houdini, and though he never fully shook the gloom, he eventually threw himself back into his work becoming, if anything, more manic and prolific and intent on achieving fame. He wrote books (or, at least, engaged with ghostwriters), and he appeared in movies. He created and performed some of his most famous illusions, including the disappearing elephant, the walking through walls, and the aforementioned Radio of 1950 illusion.

That's my favorite of his big bits of magic. In it, Houdini would bring a giant radio on the stage and open it to show there was nothing inside but coils and glass tubes; radio itself was a little piece of magic in 1925.

"I would like to present my original conception of what radio will be like in twenty-five years," Houdini told the audience. "Tune into any station and get the girl you want."

He paused and in his best comedic spirit said, "No gentlemen, it is not for sale."

Houdini then twisted the dials as he looked for KDKA in Pittsburgh. When he found the station, the announcer's voice said, "Miss Dorothy Young, now doing the Charleston." And like that, Houdini's assistant Dorothy Young began to emerge, first showing leg and then climbing out. When she reached the stage, to the hoots and hollers of the crowd, she danced the Charleston.

"Often I would go over my allotted time for the dance," Dorothy wrote, "but the audience loved it, applauding even more, and Houdini never reprimanded me."

I love that illusion because, even though it never became famous, it was so different from anything else Houdini did. Houdini thought himself a funny person. He often invented jokes; these were almost always built on groan-worthy puns. But that humor didn't often come through. "I'm sure he was very funny," magician Dorothy Dietrich says. "If you study him closely, you see it."

After Cecilia died, Houdini tried to become the graceful magician he had dreamed of being when he first began. He tried again and again to leave behind the escapes and the chains and the danger and launch a real magic show. He had a little bit of success with that at the end of his life, but, in a larger sense, audiences never did embrace the

385

lighthearted version of Houdini. They adored the small, muscular man who could escape from anything, the daredevil who put his life on the line, the fighter who took on all challengers.

And, as it turns out, even after Cecilia died, Harry Houdini did have one fight left in him.

SPIRITS OF THE NIGHT

Let me make an admission: I don't care much about spiritualism. I don't care much about Houdini's late-life exposure of mediums. There are many people, countless people, who are obsessed by this chapter of his life, who can't hear enough about his great battle with the medium Margery, his friendship and bad blood with Sherlock Holmes author Arthur Conan Doyle, and his hunger to speak again to his mother after her death. I get it. Houdini reached new levels of fame and notoriety when he took on spiritualism and dedicated his life to exposing mediums as frauds. The last years were filled with controversy and threats and triumphs; in many ways this was the battle Houdini was born to fight.

But I can't lie: It bores me. I prefer the escapes. I'd rather talk about the magic.

In 1914, Houdini performed a little parlor magic for a group of people on the SS *Imperator*, which was sailing to the United States from Germany. He did a couple of card tricks, changed the colors of handkerchiefs, and probably performed his most beloved small illusion, the Needles. The group, which included former president and American icon Teddy Roosevelt, loved it.

Then came the final act. Houdini announced

that while he did not normally do such things, he wanted to do something special in the president's honor. A séance. He handed out pencils and paper and asked each person to write down a single question for the spirits to answer. He saw Roosevelt struggling to write with no table. Houdini haphazardly handed him an atlas to use for support. Roosevelt wrote down his question, placed it in an envelope, and, like the others, handed it to Houdini.

"I am sure there will be no objection if we use the colonel's question," Houdini said, to applause. Houdini took Roosevelt's envelope and placed it between two slates, the sort that mediums used to communicate with the spirits.

"State your question," Houdini said.

"Where was I last Christmas?" Roosevelt asked.

Houdini nodded. He then pulled apart the slates. There was a map of Brazil on them. And the River of Doubt—where Roosevelt had vacationed over Christmas—was highlighted.

Roosevelt was stunned.

"Tell me the truth, man to man," he said. "Was that genuine spiritualism or legerdemain?"

And Houdini smiled.

"It was hocus-pocus," Houdini said.

He had planned it out for weeks. He had conversations with Roosevelt, put carbons on the atlas that Roosevelt had been using and took a gamble that Roosevelt was so preoccupied by his extraordinary journey on the River of Doubt that he would certainly ask a question about it.

Houdini used the story to explain just how the mind of a medium works, how cleverly and deceitfully they can manipulate the mind and how convincing they can be.

John Cox has collected (and debunked) countless Houdini myths through the years, but he believes the most pernicious one is that his obsession with spiritualism began when he tried to connect with his mother in the afterlife.

The myth starts on a particular night when an unfortunate séance was performed by Lady Doyle, wife of Sherlock Holmes creator Sir Arthur Conan Doyle. The Doyles and Houdinis were vacationing together in Atlantic City at the height of their famous friendship. Sir Arthur worried about his friend and knew that he had not recovered from the death of Cecilia. The Doyles were fervent spiritualists, and even though Sir Arthur was aware of Houdini's skepticism, you do sense that he was trying to provide comfort when he approached Harry on the beach and announced that Lady Doyle had been sensing his mother reaching out through her. She wanted to do a séance that very night. And Houdini, probably more out of respect for his friend than anything else, agreed.

Houdini had long been both fascinated and repelled by spiritualism, a fact that the myth misses. You might recall that a young Harry and Bess had performed as spiritualists in a medicine show back in Kansas. He found the whole episode so distasteful—"Bad effect," he wrote in his diary—that he actually delivered his first "exposé of Spiritualism" in a church in St. Joseph, Missouri, in 1897, long before he had become successful and almost sixteen years before Cecilia died.

And once he did become hugely successful, people were desperate to say he was a master of the black arts. Doyle used to drive him crazy by saying that Houdini was not a magician at all but a highly skilled and talented medium. He was not the only one.

"Houdini is enabled by psychic power, though this he does not advertise, to open any lock, handcuff, or bolt that is submitted to him," a quack named James Hewat McKenzie wrote in his surprisingly popular book *Spirit Intercourse, Its Theory and Practice.* "The force necessary to shoot a bolt within a lock is drawn from Houdini as the medium, but it must not be thought that this is his only means by which he can escape from his prison, for at times his body had been dematerialized and withdrawn."

Houdini hated that stuff, and not just because of his aversion to spiritualism. Whenever someone credited his escapes to some sort of mystical power, they were failing to credit Houdini himself. He was not above taking credit, now and again, for having supernatural gifts, but he would make a point in all of his shows that everything he did, everything, was done naturally.

Still, Houdini was so taken by his friendship with Sir Arthur Conan Doyle that when they were together, he claimed to be open to all possibilities. It wouldn't have been possible to stay friends any other way because Sir Arthur was, in the words of Jim Steinmeyer, "a crackpot."

The séance was set. The Houdinis and Doyles sat at a table, and the shades were pulled. Arthur wore black, Harry white. Sir Arthur began by bowing his head and asking for a sign. Houdini bowed his head and tried to turn off everything in his mind but thoughts of his mother in the beyond.

Lady Doyle asked if Cecilia was present. Her hand knocked the table three times, meaning yes. Houdini concentrated harder. There was a part of him that always did want to believe. "According to Bess," Ken Silverman wrote, "he often woke up in the night and raised his head, asking, 'Mama, are you here?' "

Lady Doyle began to write furiously a message that she said came from Cecilia. By the time she was done, Lady Doyle had scribbled fifteen pages from Cecilia Weiss to Harry Houdini.

When she handed the letter over, Sir Arthur saw a man deeply moved and felt sure his friend had become a believer. (Anyway, that's what he told reporters afterward.)

Sir Arthur could not have more spectacularly misread Houdini and, as a result, his friendship with Houdini more or less ended that day. Yes, they would see each other, they still corresponded—sometimes in friendlier terms, but more often not—but Houdini felt humiliated by the experience. He knew instantly that the letters were fraudulent because Lady Doyle had placed a cross at the top of the first page, an odd thing for a rabbi's wife to put on top of her letter. Lady Doyle also wrote in English; Cecilia spoke almost no English at all and always corresponded with Harry in German. Also, nothing about the words, nothing at all, sounded like Cecilia Weiss.

There can be no question that the séance did have a dramatic impact on Houdini's life.

"As I advanced to riper years of experience," he later wrote, "I was brought to a realization of the seriousness of trifling with the hallowed reverence which the average human being bestows on the departed, and when I personally became afflicted with similar grief, I was chagrined that I ever should have been guilty of such frivolity and for the first time realized that it bordered on crime."

Not long after, Houdini freed himself from

Sir Arthur's friendship and began to attack fake mediums everywhere. The myth is that it was Houdini's disappointment in not being able to reach his mother in the afterlife, but Houdini already knew that. No, it was the clunky and shameful methods to fool people that offended Houdini.

There are those who believed then and now that the whole spiritualism crusade was an act. Houdini's star was beginning to fade a bit by the late 1910s, and his war on mediums got him back into the news and in some cases won him even bigger headlines than he'd ever had before.

"I don't buy it," Jamy Ian Swiss says. "I think Houdini was too devoted to exposing fakes and frauds to think it was just a play for promotion. He believed he was doing a great service. And I think he was too."

There is much more to tell about Houdini's great battles with the spiritualist community, his appearance before Congress, his ongoing feud with Sir Arthur, but as I said from the start, my mind is already wandering to other things, particularly to the story of Houdini and the great actress Sarah Bernhardt.

Bernhardt was the daughter of a French courtesan and a wealthy customer. Her father—it is still unclear who he actually was—did not appear in her life but was financially generous, paying for Sarah to go to a boarding school and then a convent. She wanted to a be a nun but the Duke of Morny—half-brother of Napoleon and one of her mother's lovers—suggested that she become an actress instead.

Sarah Bernhardt became the star of her day. Some thought her an extraordinary performer. The poet and novelist Victor Hugo, for instance, wrote that she had a golden voice, though his view might be slightly colored by their torrid love affair (Hugo was forty-three years older). The British writer Lytton Strachey wrote, "She could contrive thrill after thrill, she could seize and tear the nerves of her audience, she could touch, she could terrify, to the top of her astonishing bent."

Others, like critic George Bernard Shaw, were less impressed: "I could never, as a dramatic critic, be fair to Sarah Bernhardt," he wrote, "because she was like my Aunt Georgina."

Her popularity, though, was unquestioned. She was the most famous actress of her time. And she was extraordinarily eccentric. She traveled around with her own coffin. She toured America with an alligator she called Ali-Gaga. She wore a dead bat on her hat. She was famously promiscuous. And, like Houdini, she willfully created a story for herself that blurred truth and reality.

"Legend remains victorious in spite of history," she once wrote.

In 1905, Bernhardt suffered a severe knee injury. The pain never went away and about a decade later she had no choice but to have the leg amputated. Soon after, she met Houdini for the first time.

Houdini made one of his classic entrances into her life. In 1917, a group of New York actors held a celebration to honor Bernhardt. It is unclear what group was doing the honoring—newspapers referred to them as "the actors and actresses of America"—but it was probably the New York Players Club, a private social club founded by Edwin Booth, brother of future Lincoln assassin John Wilkes Booth. In the ceremony, the Shakespearean actor John Drew spoke eloquently about Bernhardt's career, and he handed her a bronze statue with Bernhardt's likeness. It was a lovely night with much applause.

Shortly afterward, Bernhardt got a three-hundred-fifty-dollar bill. They expected her to pay for the statue.

She was outraged, as you would expect, and sent back both the bill and the statue. The story made the papers, and Houdini saw it. His publicity genius began whirring. Almost immediately, he sent a $350 check to the company for the statue and wired Bernhardt to ask if she would allow him the honor of buying the statue and returning it to its rightful owner. Bernhardt accepted the noble gesture. The newspapers all wrote at great length about Houdini's generosity.

This pleased Houdini to no end.

From Kellock's biography *Houdini: His Life Story*:

> Within a fortnight, Houdini had received from clipping bureaus 3,756 newspaper clippings warmly commending his action and coupling his name with Bernhardt's. They averaged fifteen lines in length. A newspaper columnist, estimating the advertising at the pure reading-matter rate of a dollar a line, calculated that Houdini secured publicity worth $56,340 for an outlay of $350.

That, right there, was Houdini.

They met in person soon after at Keith's Theater in Boston. Houdini performed some close-up magic for her and invited her to sit in his car and watch as he escaped from a straitjacket while dangling one hundred feet over Tremont Street. More than twenty-five thousand people watched along with Divine Sarah.

When he finished, she was so taken by the experience that she asked for a favor.

"Houdini," she said, "you are a wonderful human being. You must possess extraordinary power to perform such marvels."

Houdini undoubtedly accepted this as truth.

"Houdini," she then said, "won't you use your power to restore my limb?"

396

He was dumbfounded. He stammered as he thought of how to answer.

"You are asking me to do the impossible," he said.

"Yes," she said. "But you do the impossible."

Houdini asked if she was jesting, to which Bernhardt replied in French:

"*Mais non, Houdini, j'ai jamais été plus serieux dans ma vie.*"

But no, Houdini, I've never been more serious in my life.

He felt tears come to his eyes. And he said, no, he could not bring back her leg, because his magic was not real. A photograph was taken of the moment, Houdini standing outside the car and looking straight ahead. In the background, you see Sarah Bernhardt looking down at him, her face ashen and sad. There is the amazing. And there is the impossible.

THE PUNCH

I've mentioned Joshua Jay many times, but it seems that there has never been a formal introduction. Josh is—well, why don't you see for yourself. We are on the campus of Bryn Mawr College, just outside of Philadelphia at Tannen's Magic Camp. It is the most famous magic camp on earth. David Copperfield went here. David Blaine went here. Jen Kramer went here. Josh stands in front of the campers, boys and girls of all ages, and tells them, "The next great magician, the person who is going to change the face of magic, is in this room right now."

Josh is tall and self-possessed and has that sort of Jimmy Stewart/Tom Hanks everyday good looks. He, like Copperfield, was a magic prodigy. His father, Jeffrey, a dentist in Canton, Ohio, showed him a card trick when Josh was nine or so. It was a good card trick, a difficult one that divides the black and red cards, and Josh was blown away. He asked his father how it was done. Jeffrey smiled and said that a magician never reveals secrets.

Josh went up to his room, spent hours working out the mechanics of the trick, and then came downstairs and performed the trick flawlessly for his slack-jawed father. It went quickly from there. At sixteen, Josh wrote his first magic book, *A Teen's Routines*. The next year, he won first place at the World's Magic Seminar. His senior thesis at Ohio State later became *Joshua Jay's Amazing Book of Cards*, which has been translated into four languages. Soon after, he was named Close-Up Magician of the Year. He is in the *Guinness Book of World Records* for a complicated card memorization feat with a complicated name: Most Selected Cards Found from a Shuffled Deck in One Minute.

His magical life, certainly through the eyes of the boys and girls at Tannen's Magic Camp, looks dreamlike. He has performed on dozens of television shows, including *The Tonight Show*, and he collaborated with HBO's *Game of Thrones*. His magic inspires the people at Pixar and Google, and he is guest lecturer at the University of Chicago. He has written numerous books, but he's also one of magic's most prolific publishers. He and his business partner Andi Gladwin annually put on Magifest, America's oldest magic convention, in Columbus, Ohio.

Beyond all of that, his focus has been his show in New York where he performs the most intimate show in magic for twenty people every night.

And his focus also has been on traveling the world. He has performed in more than one hundred countries, and he goes out of his way to take every job that will take him to a new and exotic place. To the kids here at the camp, his life is beyond a dream.

So they rush up to him, and they surround him, and they hand him their decks of cards and ask him to do something impossible, and he turns four aces into four kings, four kings back into four aces, and these kids, many readily and even joyfully admit that they fell into magic because they feel awkward and misunderstood. To them, Joshua Jay is the coolest guy on earth.

And none of them would guess that Josh has spent countless hours—probably more hours than anybody anywhere—obsessing over the death of Harry Houdini

There are some people who still believe that Harry Houdini died in the Chinese Water Torture Cell. This comes from the movie *Houdini*. The myth was so pervasive that John Cox used to carry around a Houdini biography with dog-eared corners marking the pages that proved Houdini did not die that way. Even when he would show people the proof, they refused to believe.

Maybe people want to believe it because that was a more heroic ending.

The real ending is more ironic than heroic.

"It is 1926," Josh says, and he's beginning the story. "Houdini is tired. He has been on tour for months. He lost his mother, and he is still aggrieved about that even though it has been more than a decade. He is mentally tired. He is physically tired. He twisted his ankle badly, broke it, that was when he was performing the Chinese Water Torture Cell.

"Where most people would take off, rest a little, recover, Houdini cannot. He has sold out shows across Canada and the Northeast United States. He must trudge on. He is doing very physical shows, and it is taking a lot out of him. He's older now. His hair is thinning. He's putting on a little weight. His ankle is bothering him. Every night, after the show, he sits and puts his ankle up."

If the words sound practiced, it is because they are. Josh does a lecture he calls "Tragic Magic." He studies magicians' deaths. He collects them, actually. Sometimes he will just say, "Oh, I added one this week." Magical deaths are his obsession.

It is an ultra-specific obsession—even more so than you might think. He's not interested in deaths of all magicians. For instance, Tommy Cooper, a British comic magician, died onstage in front of a live television audience in London. But he died of a heart attack unrelated to the act and, as such, this falls outside of Josh's scope of interest. The magician has to die because of the magic.

"Why do I spend so much time thinking about magicians' death?" he asks. "I've thought about it. I think it's like this: What I have, at the end of the show—what I will have at the end of my life—are the tricks. These things I've invented and shared with the audience are my contribution to magic. They are my contribution to the world. They are the comfort I have that some part of me lives on.

"But there's a massive insecurity here too, and I'm far from alone in this. What if my magic doesn't live on? I came across magicians who have died in the service of the thing I hold most sacred in the world: magic. I want to remember them. I want others to remember them."

"Everyone remembers Houdini," I say.

"Yes," he says. And then he says something surprising. He says, "Did you know that Houdini unknowingly inspired more magical deaths than anyone else?"

It's true. There are a dozen such cases, and Josh believed there are more. In 1930, for instance, a thirteen-year-old boy in Australia named Graham Egan was practicing a Houdini rope escape in his bedroom when he slipped off a trunk and accidentally hanged himself. Fifty-seven years later, James Keller, a nine-year-old boy in Illinois, put on a pair of handcuffs and went into the family clothes dryer to do a Houdini escape. He died of asphyxiation.

The most heartbreaking of the Houdini deaths is probably that of Genesta, a traveling escape artist. He escaped from Houdini's milk can so many times that one newspaper account reported that it had to be fake. Before his escape in Frankfort, Kentucky, though, the can was dropped by his assistants as they unloaded it from the truck, jamming the mechanism he used to get free. Genesta started the escape, couldn't get out, and an assistant had to smash the can with an ax and pull him out. His heart had stopped. They raced Genesta to the hospital where, according to reports, he was revived for a few seconds. His last words were: "That was the only time I failed to escape the milk can."

Genesta died in the arms of his wife.

"These are pretty gruesome stories," I say to Josh.

"Yes," he says.

We return to 1926 and an exhausted Harry Houdini. He is performing in Montreal, at the Princess Theatre, and two students from local McGill University want to interview him for the paper. As worn down as Houdini feels, he could never turn down publicity, so he sits in a robe and leans back on a couch and apologizes for reclining. Samuel Smilovitz, a local Jewish student who admires Houdini, sketches his likeness, while Jacques Price interviews him. Smilovitz will never forget how yellow Houdini's skin looked, how sunken his eyes. He is slightly shocked by how much life had taken out of his hero.

"A third student walks in," Josh recounts.

"He's a little bit odd physically; he's six-foot-five and thin as a rail and has a big concave in his midsection. The student has the unusual name of J. Gordon Whitehead. He has terrible posture. He looks nothing like a student; the others are twenty years old, twenty-one. Whitehead is thirty-two years old."

Right away, Whitehead grabs hold of the conversation, making Smilovitz and Price feel uncomfortable. Whitehead seems intent on provoking Houdini right from the start. He begins by asking about biblical miracles. "I don't discuss those matters," Houdini replies.

And then Whitehead brings up something entirely out of the blue: Whitehead asks Houdini if he maintains a standing challenge for anyone to punch him in the stomach. It sounds like a Houdini challenge. But is it?

"Scholars can't even point to the actual place where Houdini made this challenge," Josh says. "But I'll grant that it is in line with something Houdini might have said: 'I will absorb a blow in the stomach from anyone in the audience.' We might not be able to find that precise challenge. But it is pure Houdini."

There must be something to it because Don Bell—author of the exhaustively researched *The Man Who Killed Houdini*—reports that Houdini is challenged with stomach punches at least two other times while visiting Montreal.

Whether or not Houdini initially issued the challenge, he does accept it. He is Houdini, after all.

"Houdini begins to stand up off the pillows," Josh says, "and as he rises, he is not flexing. He's not ready for the blow. Whitehead delivers three severe blows to the stomach, and then, as Houdini falls over, several more, up to seven successive blows before Houdini, the wind knocked out of him, raises his hand and says quietly: 'That will do.' "

That will do. Those three words are among the most poignant Houdini ever spoke. He is in agony after the punch, but of course he hides that from everyone. It is likely that he is already suffering from appendicitis. If he will just tell someone about the pain, it would require a fairly simple operation even in 1926. But he does not tell. He cannot tell. Houdini has never admitted weakness. He performs that night. He performs the next.

"The next night, during intermission, he lays down on the couch in a cold sweat," Josh says. "After the show, he is a wreck, barely able to stand, entirely unable to put on his clothes by himself. On the train out of Montreal, he is in such agony that someone sends a wire ahead, to have a doctor meet the train in Detroit. The doctor sees signs of appendicitis and insists that Houdini be checked into a hospital immediately. Houdini refuses."

Instead, Houdini goes to the hotel in Detroit. He shivers under covers. His temperature during the day is 102 degrees. By showtime, it is up to 104. Houdini still performs. He makes it through the first act, but only barely, and he collapses during intermission. He is revived and goes back out for the second act. He collapses again. He is taken back to the hotel where a doctor, Charles Kennedy, insists on taking Houdini to the hospital. Even now, as he dies, Houdini refuses. Finally, he is taken to the hospital, and Kennedy performs the emergency surgery.

And it is too late. It is October 25, 1926. Kennedy releases a statement to the papers.

"We have great doubts for Houdini's recovery," it says.

Did the punch kill Houdini? People in Houdini World will argue that question forever. There are those who believe that the punch either caused or exacerbated Houdini's appendicitis, though the science on that is in dispute. The more common theory is that Houdini already had appendicitis, and that the punch probably did not exacerbate it—though it might have so embarrassed Houdini that it caused him not to report the agonizing pain that he was feeling.

If he had reported it, he probably would have lived for years longer.

I ask Josh how he would sum up Houdini as a magician.

"On the basis of both skill and originality," he says, "Houdini gets average marks. His harshest critics are wrong; he wasn't terrible or entirely unoriginal. He was knowledgeable, and he cared, and all correspondence points to a man who worked hard on the material. But his most devoted fans are not right either: he was hardly an artist in these areas.

"What Houdini was, well, he was an indescribable and unrepeatable alignment of the stars, this thing that happens when rare talent (which he did have) meets ambition and drive (which he certainly had) meets just the right circumstances. The result is a kind of once-in-a-generation superstardom. Think Bob Dylan. He was talented, yes, but he was the right person at the right time, the icon of a generation, the symbol of a movement. It's bigger than artistry, bigger than talent. Houdini was that kind of superstar."

He pauses for a moment.

"You ask why I care about Houdini's death so much," he says. "Well, I don't think Houdini would be Houdini if he didn't have the strange death. He was gone too soon, when he was still at his peak. There's something about people dying young. Houdini will never grow old."

THE END

The dying took longer than even the doctors expected—six days—but Houdini had always fought death more or less to a draw.

"I'm going to lick this thing," Houdini told friends.

"Houdini is Recovering!" the newspapers dutifully reported.

"Houdini temperature drops below 100 for the first time."

"Houdini has a restful night."

None of these was true. There were no trap doors this time, no handcuffs to disengage, no locks to pick, no assistants to set him free. Houdini was dying, and the doctors knew it. In a straitjacket, coffin, or water torture cell, Houdini may have been invincible, but inside the hospital room, he was a fifty-two-year-old man, and the poison had spread beyond the power of antidotes.

Two days before Halloween, Dr. Charles Kennedy walked into the room to talk with Houdini; the men had grown fond of each other. Kennedy was particularly taken by how kindly Houdini treated everyone in the hospital, and he loved hearing of Houdini's adventures, his exposure of spiritualists, his impossible escapes all around the world. On this day, though, Houdini was quiet.

"Doctor," he finally said in barely a whisper, "you know I always wanted to be a surgeon. But I never could. I have always regretted it."

"Why, Mr. Houdini," Kennedy said in horror, "that is one of the most amazing statements I have ever heard. Here you are, the greatest magician and the greatest entertainer of your age. You make countless thousands of people happy. You have an unlimited income, and you are admired and respected by everybody, while I am just an ordinary dub of a surgeon trying to struggle through life."

Houdini smiled wanly. "Perhaps those things are true, doctor," he said. "But the difference between me and you is that you actually do things for people. I, in almost every respect, am a fake."

Houdini died two days later. It was Halloween. According to the papers, he spoke his final words to his brother Hardeen. Houdini said: "I can't fight anymore."

This final Kennedy story—told in 1950, almost a quarter century after Houdini died—like so much in Houdini's life, might not be true. By then, Bess was gone. Vaudeville was gone. Within a dozen years, Kennedy himself would be dead.

I, in almost every respect, am a fake. Did Houdini really say that? And if he did, what did he mean? We don't know. It was the last secret of his life.

The greatest newspapers around the world all ran long and warm stories about Houdini in the days after his death, and that is something Houdini undoubtedly would have appreciated. One particular editorial appeared in newspapers across the United States that I think would have pleased him.

"Houdini was more than a magician," it read. "He was a dramatist, a scholar, a preacher, and a fighter . . . He played for the world and fought for the world."

But the greatest tribute might have been from Houdini's rival Howard Thurston.

"Life was a serious proposition with Houdini," Thurston said. "He was an indefatigable worker of insatiable ambition, an aggressive enemy and a loyal friend. As a showman, he was in a class with Barnum. In force of character, he resembled Roosevelt."

Two thousand people crowded into the Elks Ballroom on West Forty-Third Street for his funeral. Hundreds of flower arrangements filled the ballroom, and thousands of telegrams poured in from all over the world. "Houdini possessed a wondrous power that he never understood and which he never revealed to anyone in life," Rabbi Bernard Drachman said during Houdini's eulogy.

At the end of the funeral, one of Houdini's pallbearers, *New York Evening Post* theater critic Charles Dillingham, looked hard at Houdini's casket. He turned to one of his fellow pallbearers.

"Wouldn't it be funny if he weren't in there," he said.

THE AFTERLIFE

The 1953 Tony Curtis movie *Houdini* did much to revive the legend of Harry Houdini, but more than anything, it rewrote his death.

That movie took many creative liberties—"Generally speaking," the magician Milbourne Christopher wrote, "if any phase of Houdini's life is shown on screen, you can be sure it didn't happen the way it's pictured"—but the death rewrite was the big one. This was done very much on purpose. The producers did not think that a hero like Houdini should die because he got punched in the stomach.

Instead, they portray him dying in the Chinese Water Torture Cell, which they renamed the "Pagoda Water Torture Cell." The final scene of movie shows the crowd calling to Houdini, pleading with him to try to escape from the cell. Houdini's friends beg him to leave; they believe even trying the escape is suicide.

"They're never satisfied," his assistant Otto tells him. "Ignore them."

"I can't," Houdini says as he looks back at the crowd.

"You have given them enough!" Otto shouts, but Houdini does not hear him. He cannot hear anything but the sound of the crowd. In this way, they got Houdini exactly right.

"Get the torture cell ready," he announces.

He is lowered into the tank, and for a moment he is motionless, as if he's trying to dematerialize. Soon Houdini has run out of breath. Bess shrieks. Otto races in and smashes the glass with an ax, gallons and gallons of water pour out. Houdini is pulled out.

"I'll come back Bess," he says with his last breath. "If there's any way, I'll come back."

The camera then pans to a poster of the Great Houdini. And the movie ends.

This is the ending that haunted and mesmerized audiences so much that it overtook the truth, but Joe Notaro discovered that it was not the original ending. He came upon two other versions. Houdini

414

dies in the Pagoda Cell in all three. But in one of the two alternate endings, the camera then closes in on Bess sitting alone in a room, and we see a vase crash to the ground. She reaches down to clean it up and comes across a note Houdini had left behind.

Roses are red
Violets are blue
Even after I'm dead
I'll still love you

You can see why that ending died on the cutting room floor.

And then there is my favorite ending. For one thing, it shows Houdini getting punched in the dressing room, though with entirely made-up details.

After he dies, ten years go by, until another Halloween night. We come across an older Bess, and she sits alone. Midnight strikes, and a waltz begins to play, a Hungarian waltz. Their song. Bess sways slowly to the music as the movie fades to black. She is waiting for him.

THERE IS NO DEATH

Yes, I went to a Houdini séance. If you're going to write a Houdini book, you have to go to at least one, right? There are hundreds of them every year, all around the world.

Yes, it is ironic; Houdini spent the last years of his life as America's leading skeptic, telling everyone how phony séances are. And yet, he has inspired more séances than any person in modern times.

Bess is the one responsible. She relentlessly promoted him in the years after his death, refusing to let people forget him. Every year, on Halloween night, she would make headlines by going to a séance and trying to connect with her husband one last time.

It is not entirely clear why she did it. Maybe she believed in the possibilities of talking with Houdini again, but probably not. Bess lived a difficult life after Houdini died. She grew deeply depressed and fell for a series of shady men. She smoked heavily and was an alcoholic; her niece Marie Blood told John Cox that Bess died of tuberculosis.

But she did love being in public. She, like her husband, longed for fame.

Shortly after Houdini died, Bess talked openly (and often) about how he had promised that he would return from the dead and leave her a message if he could find a way. Houdini was so dedicated to the idea of speaking to Bess after he died that they worked together to develop a specific message, so she would know it was truly him. This would become known as the Houdini Code.

The first word of the code was "Rosabelle," the name of the girl in the song "Rosie, Sweet Rosabel." The name in the song and the name in the code are spelled differently, but Houdini never was much of a speller.

Rosie, Sweet Rosabel,
I love her more than I can tell
O'er me she casts a spell,
My charming, black-eyed Rosabel.

Bess claimed it was the song they danced to on the day they decided to get married at Coney Island. The song meant so much to them both that Houdini had Bess's wedding ring engraved with the word "Rosabelle."

Anyone who knew anything about Houdini probably could have figured out "Rosabelle." After that, though, the Houdini Code contained a series of words that seem to have no connection:

Answer
Tell
Pray
Answer
Look
Tell
Answer
Answer
Tell.

The words had to be said exactly so to spell out the code that Harry and Bess had perfected for their mind-reading illusions. Each word represents a number. Pick one, any number. Okay: 693.

Six is represented by "Please."

Nine is represented by "Look."

Three is represented by "See."

Bess would ask someone in the crowd to pick a number and whisper it in her ear. Then she would shout out something like "Please look inside your heart and see this number." And Houdini would know the number 693.

The Houdini Code words represented the numbers 2–5–12–9–5–22.

Now, you just look to see what the corresponding letters spell:

Answer (2 = B)
Tell (5 = E)

Pray-Answer (12 = L)
Look (9 = I)
Tell (5 = E)
Answer-Answer (22 = V)
Tell (5 = E)

The Houdini Code spelled "Believe."

Many mediums tried to convince Bess that Houdini spoke through them, but none got the code right.

Which leads us to the bizarre story of a bizarre medium named Arthur Ford. He claimed to have learned of his psychic powers during World War I, where he would hear the names of soldiers just days before they were killed.

As the years went on, Ford would claim the ability to go into a deep trance and be controlled by a spirit named David Fletcher. Ford convinced enough followers that he opened the First Spiritualist Church and gained the enthusiastic endorsements of many people in the spiritualist community, including the ubiquitous Sir Arthur Conan Doyle, who called him "the next apostle of the age."

Ford was a particularly charming and con-vincing con artist: William Kalush and Larry Sloman also make the compelling case in *The Secret Life of Houdini* that Bess fell hope-lessly in love with him. On January 6, 1929—just twenty-six months after Houdini's death—

Ford came to Bess's home. Bess was resting on a cot; she had fallen in a drunken stupor during a party on New Year's Eve and was in terrible shape.

Ford pulled the shades of the house. There were two reporters in the room, one a woman name Rea Jaure, who would play a significant role in the saga, the other John Stafford, an editor of *Scientific American*. There were a few of Bess's friends there too.

Ford went into a trance and his control, Fletcher, spoke:

"The same man who came Saturday night is coming again," Ford/Fletcher said. "He says, 'Hello, Bess, my sweetheart.' He says he wants to repeat the code you used in your mind-reading act with him."

At this, Bess sat up a little bit on the cot.

"First of all, he says, 'Rosabelle.' Do you know what that means?"

"Yes," Bess said softly.

"And now the words. Answer . . . tell . . . pray . . . answer . . . look . . . tell . . . answer answer . . . tell. Is that right?"

"Yes," Bess whispered again. "It is."

"Thank you, sweetheart. Now take off your wedding ring and tell them what Rosabelle means."

At this point, Bess got off the cot. She took off her ring. And she began to sing.

Rosie, Sweet Rosabel,
I love her more than I can tell,
O'er me she casts a spell,
I love you, my sweet Rosabel.

Bess was crying by the time she finished the song.

"Thank you," Ford/Fletcher/Houdini said. "That was the first song I ever heard you sing. You sang it in our first show. Remember?"

Bess could barely speak, she was sobbing so deeply. "Yes," she said.

"The message I wanted to give you, wife, is 'Believe, Rosabelle.' . . . Now, I am happy that I have got the message through. All those who have lost hope must lay hold of the truth and there is no death."

Like that, the séance was over. Bess Houdini confirmed that it was all true. And Houdini's return became front-page news:

"Houdini Talks with Wife (?)"—*Ames Daily Tribune*

"Woman Certain She Got Spirit Message from Harry Houdini"—*Minneapolis Star*

"Spirit of Houdini Talks with His Wife"—*Detroit Free Press*

"And There Is No Death"—*Honolulu Advertiser*

This triumphant "He's back" version of the story lasted for two days. That's when Rea Jaure, the woman reporter in the room, broke the real story: It was a fraud. She admitted to writing her article the day before the séance, after Bess herself had told her what was going to happen. Jaure said she had been to several parties with Bess and had met a man named, yes, David Fletcher. She claimed that whole thing had been a stunt to publicize a national tour featuring Arthur Ford and Bess Houdini.

Jaure also said that she got Ford to admit the whole deception, and that conversation was recorded on Dictaphone by two of her editors.

Arthur and Bess probably made a poor decision when they invited an honest reporter to the séance. They tried for a time to discredit her, with Ford insisting he had never met Jaure. An angry letter under Bess Houdini's name appeared in the newspapers denying that she would ever be part of a ruse:

> When the real message, the message Houdini and I agreed upon, came to me and I accepted it as truth, I was greeted with Jeers. Why? Those who denounce the whole thing as a fraud claim that I had given Mr. Arthur Ford the message . . . When anyone accuses me of giving the words that my husband and I labored so long to convince ourselves the truth of the communication, then I will fight and fight until the breath leaves my body.

She probably didn't write the letter. One of the better theories is that it was written by, you guessed it, Sir Arthur, who had called the Ford séance "the classical case of after-death return." Even after it became clear that it was a hoax, Sir Arthur held firm. "Surely," he wrote, "it cannot be dismissed as if it never occurred."

Pretty quickly everybody got bored by the whole thing; even Bess dismissed the episode, though she never did admit giving Ford the code (Kalush and Sloman report that she did shyly tell friends, "He was such a handsome young man"). But she kept on going to séances. On the ten-year anniversary of Houdini's death, a longtime carnival barker and magical bon vivant named Edward Saint—he and Bess had become partners and were even perhaps secretly married—led what was called at the time "The Final Séance."

"Yes," Saint said in his distinctive voice, which was recorded for posterity, "hundreds of alleged psychics and mediums have written in and stated that Houdini has appeared to them in some form or other. In Chicago they say he walked boldly into a room. In Kansas City, Houdini was said to have written a long letter to Mrs. Houdini. In Long Beach, Houdini was said to have hypnotized a medium and then delivered a message through her. In New Zealand, he drank a cup of tea. And in Santa Monica, he escaped from several pairs of handcuffs by dematerializing his hands.

"These things may be! Surely it is not for Mrs. Houdini to decide. But we all believe, and many prominent psychics agree, that if Houdini has appeared all over the world in spirit form, under every kind of manifestation, and doing this many times every week of every year of the last ten years, then we believe that the Great Houdini will, on this last authentic séance, come to the little silver-haired widow, the little lady who for thirty-three years stood by the side of her beloved Harry, listening to the applause of kings and emperors."

Alas, Houdini did not show.

"Mrs. Houdini," Saint said at the end of the séance, "the zero hour has passed. The ten years are up. Have you reached a decision?"

"Yes," Bess said. "Houdini did not come through. My last hope is gone."

But it was not gone. Hope is never gone. The séances continue, all year round but particularly around Halloween, in parlors and dining rooms and museums and in a special room at the Magic Castle in Los Angeles. The séances are kitschy and silly and most done in jest; nobody expects Houdini to return. But still . . .

"I really have seen some things that I can't explain," says Dorothy Dietrich. She and Dick Brookz now run the Original Houdini Séance, the one that they say has been passed down from Edward Saint (though this, like all things

Houdini, is controversial, as a man named Bill Radner runs what he has trademarked as "The Official Houdini Séance").

"What do you mean by things you can't explain?"

"Let's just say," Dorothy says with a wink, "the Houdini story isn't over yet."

THE GRIM GAME

Dorothy Dietrich and Dick Brookz keep apologizing for the cold. We are sitting and shivering in a one-hundred-twenty-five-year-old house on Main Avenue in Scranton, Pennsylvania. That is Main Avenue, not Main Street. It's an important distinction. Scranton also has a Main Street. People make that mistake all the time.

This is the Houdini Museum (of Scranton, Pennsylvania).

Of all the people in Houdini World, even the mysterious Patrick Culliton, nobody works harder to keep Harry Houdini going than Dorothy and Dick. They develop their plans in this museum.

They chose to build it here in Scranton because—well, because they moved here. Houdini's connections to the area are pretty limited, though he did once expose and humiliate a particularly inept Scranton spiritual medium named George Valentine ("I never saw such awkward work in all my life," Houdini grumbled as if it wasn't worth his time), and a local newspaper, the *Scranton Republican*, used Houdini to advertise their classified ads ("It Doesn't Take a Houdini . . . to turn spare rooms into cash!").

Dorothy and Dick moved to Scranton after the New York real estate prices got too high—they tell a story that seems to suggest they were priced out of town by Donald Trump. In any case, they looked around at various newspapers to find a new place to live and were taken in by the charm of Scranton.

"We bought different newspapers and drew concentric circles around New York," Dick says. "Finally, we hit the Poconos and Scranton. And in the Scranton papers, there were two papers then, you opened it up, and here's the pictures of a couple getting married, and there's this headline in the paper: 'Joey's Bike Got Stolen.'"

Dorothy: "That's the big crime on the front page. Joey's bike got stolen from the porch. They have a description of the bike and a phone number."

Dick: "Somebody's gotta find Joey's bike."

Dorothy: "And get it back to him. And inside was a picture of this other boy getting his Eagle Scout Award. And we're like: This can't be real. This has got to be a made-up place."

Soon after moving to Scranton, they found a house that they turned into a theater and Houdini Museum.

That was thirty years ago. The museum walls are now covered with Houdini posters and photographs and various other things they have spent a lifetime collecting. The cabinets are filled with rare books and magical artifacts and toys that connect back to Houdini. In one of the rooms, there is a stage where they perform magic when the museum is open.

The museum is not open today.

"I'm sorry it's so cold," Dick says for the eighth or ninth time, and you can see his breath. "We turn off the heat when the museum is closed. You wouldn't believe what it costs to heat this place."

On the table nearby is their latest idea: a Monopoly game based on the life of Houdini. It is somewhat awkwardly called "Houdini-opoly," but it is lovingly made, with a board that displays all the details of Houdini's life. All of them. You would never expect anyone to get this much Houdini information on one Monopoly board.

Even better than the board, though, are the player pieces. These include:

An elephant (to disappear),
A wooden milk can,
A Metamorphosis chest (sort of),
Two magic top hats,
A rubber playing card (that doubles as an eraser),
A rubber robot eraser (because Houdini fought a robot in *The Master Mystery*),
Two dogs (Houdini liked dogs),
A tiny pair of handcuffs,
An eyeball (unclear why).

But we are not here to see Houdini-opoly. We are here to see *The Grim Game*. In the late 1910s, Houdini began to star in some movies, sensing before many others did that movies were going to take over entertainment. He had a pitch-perfect sense of where pop culture was heading. Late in 1918 and early in 1919, *The Master Mystery* came out as a fifteen-part serial. It was notable for Houdini's fight with the Automaton, the first human-robot fight in movie history. It did well enough for Houdini to quit escaping and move to California and become a movie star.

Houdini made four more films. In *Terror Island*, he played Harry Harper, an inventor who fought cannibals on an island in the South Seas. He also starred in *The Man from Beyond* as Howard Hillary, a man who had been frozen in ice for a century but returned to find his love. Later, Houdini wrote, starred in, and directed *Haldane of the Secret Service*, where he was a Secret Service man named Heath Haldane.

Harry Harper. Howard Hillary. Heath Haldane. What do all these movies have in common? They all featured repetitive *H* names—and critical disdain. Of his acting, *Variety* wrote, "The only asset he has in the acting line is his ability to look alert." The terror and danger in the movies, *Billboard* reported, often "caused the audience to laugh outright."

But, if nothing else, Houdini had *The Grim Game*.

Until he didn't.

For almost one hundred years, *The Grim Game* was little more than a whisper, a sigh, a tall tale that Houdini junkies would share with each other at magic conventions. Everyone insisted it was, by far, Houdini's best and most spectacular movie, the masterpiece of his life. But almost nobody had actually seen it. The film disappeared, like the majority of silent films. Only the breathless newspaper ads for *The Grim Game* survived:

> SEE him dive between the wheels of a speeding motor-truck and fool his pursuers!
>
> SEE him climb the side of a prison and crawl for a rope to the end of a flagpole swaying far from earth!
>
> SEE him on the brink of a gorge, fight a terrifying battle with his foes!
>
> SEE him leap from the roof of a skyscraper and release himself from a straight-jacket while hanging head downward on a rope!
>
> SEE him risk his life in a deadly bear trap and set himself free!

Houdini fans were dying to see it. In addition to the exclamation-point thrills, *The Grim Game* was known because of an actual plane crash that happened during shooting. Houdini's character, Harvey Hanford (yep, more *H* names) jumped from one plane to another in midair, the most daring airplane stunt ever attempted on film. But it almost became deadly as the planes accidentally crashed into each other during the stunt.

It was briefly the talk of Hollywood. Houdini, it will not surprise you, offered a thousand dollars to "any person who can prove that the airplane collision was not real," a bet he couldn't lose because it was real.

Even so, Houdini did employ some skillful misdirection: What he failed to mention is that he was not on either plane when the crash happened. His double, Robert E. Kennedy, had actually performed the stunt, though, to be fair, Houdini wanted to do it but had been injured during an earlier shot, and the director refused to let him do it.

The Grim Game was a big deal. But it disappeared, probably in July 1920, when there was an explosion in the Famous Players–Lasky film vault in Kansas City. Thousands of films were destroyed, totaling an estimated one million dollars in damage. Insurance had refused to cover the vault because celluloid films were so flammable in those days, and so they were never replaced. Most of the *The Grim Game* reels died in that fire.

And after big silent films went out of style, the surviving reels were lost or destroyed. For years, there was only one known copy, and it was owned by Bess Houdini. Then, that copy went missing. It was widely assumed that *The Grim Game* had been lost forever.

But Dorothy Dietrich and Dick Brookz knew it wasn't lost. They had seen it. The last remaining copy belonged to their friend, an odd and stubborn former juggler named Larry Weeks. Nobody knows how Weeks obtained it; Dick says Larry changed the story every time he told it. But Weeks definitely had a copy; he screened it for friends like Dorothy and Dick.

They tried for years to buy *The Grim Game* from Weeks, but it never went anywhere. Weeks briefly would show interest, a deal would almost be struck, and then he would pull out. Dick in particular tried to convince him that *The Grim Game* was a national treasure and should be seen by the world. This had no impact on Weeks; he claimed to be the world's biggest Houdini fan and, as such, trusted no one else to own the film.

In early 2014, Rick Schmidlin—a noted silent-film scholar who had made his name restoring the Lon Chaney horror film *London After Midnight*—came to Scranton to visit his mother. Dorothy and Dick told him about the lone copy of *The Grim Game*. What followed is disputed— Dorothy and Dick have one version of the story,

Schmidlin another—but all agree that in time Schmidlin reached out to Weeks.

"How much?" was the first thing Schmidlin remembers Weeks saying. They eventually agreed on a price.

After months and months of tireless work by Dorothy, Dick, Rick, and others, *The Grim Game* came back to life at the Turner Classic Movie Festival, though Larry Weeks died before the premiere. It was a sensation. Patrick Culliton called it one of the most moving moments of his life. John Cox was overwhelmed. "It was so much more of an emotional experience than even I expected," he says. "I felt like, in some ways for the first time, I got to see the real Houdini."

The Grim Game is unquestionably the movie that best captures Houdini's persona and charisma. This is in part because the other movies are so terrible, but, beyond that, *The Grim Game* has a little bit of magic. The plot is basic and absurd: Three men decide to frame Houdini for murder and kidnap his fiancée. To clear himself and save the girl, Houdini has to escape from chains, free himself from prison, and, yes, wriggle out of a straitjacket while hanging upside down. The intricate plot points necessary for the straitjacket upside down escape—they had to put Houdini in the straitjacket, then tie his legs with a rope that was attached to something, then push him off the building so that he was dangling upside down—are part of what make *The Grim Game* over-the-top and wonderful.

The powers of *The Grim Game* even softened the hardened Houdini heart of Mike Caveney.

"I showed up," Mike says, "and people like John and the other Houdini people said, 'What are you doing here? You don't belong here.' But I always have been told that to understand the power of Houdini, you need to see *The Grim Game*. And I wanted to see it in full, on the big screen, in a packed theater.

"And when he got out of the straitjacket, there was cheering. It was wonderful. The guy was not young. But he was still doing stunts that were just nuts. I'm really glad I saw it. I walked out there thinking, *I get it.* That's the Houdini who captured the country's imagination. He was Superman."

Dorothy and Dick watched proudly. They had played an enormous role in bringing Houdini back to life. There in the Houdini Museum (of Scranton, Pennsylvania), they show me *The Grim Game* on a 15-inch MacBook Pro, and though they have each seen it dozens of times, and it's utterly freezing in here, they watch every minute with me. And we all cheer.

"There are all those people who say Houdini couldn't act," Dorothy says. "You get them to watch *The Grim Game* and then tell me he's not a great actor, not a great magician."

Believe it or not, *The Grim Game* is not the craziest Houdini story involving Dick and Dorothy. No, for that you have to go to Houdini's gravesite in Queens.

On October 24, 2011, a story appeared in the *New York Times*. The headline read:

"Houdini Returns. (Of Course.)"

For almost seventy years, there was a bust of Houdini at his grave, located in a Jewish cemetery in Queens called Machpelah. His gravesite has been a pilgrimage for countless Houdini fans, particularly around Halloween when magicians come to break their magic wands over his grave or leave behind handcuffs, playing cards, coins, and photographs. Vandals have come too, as have kids looking to party and tourists wanting to leave behind a mark. It all became so ugly that in 1994, Machpelah closed down around the holiday.

True fans, however, have tried to preserve the sanctity of the gravesite. David Copperfield, for example, paid to have replacement benches put there after the originals had been destroyed. But, over time, it didn't seem like anyone could keep up with the vandalism, particularly the constant stealing or defacing of the Houdini bust. The Society of American Magicians, sick of replacing it, finally decided to have it removed in 1993.

Ten years later, police found one of the stolen

Houdini busts at someone's home and put it back on its pedestal. "This is going to make news around the world," Houdini collector Sidney Radner said. But the bust was stolen again the next year.

Then in 2011, a miracle happened. Nobody knew how but a brand-new Houdini bust appeared at the gravesite. This was not a cheap imitation; it was well made, bolted into place so firmly that it could not be easily stolen. Nobody had any idea where it had come from. The Society of American Magicians had not put it there, nor had the Machpelah Cemetery. No donor came forward to take responsibility. The whole thing was a crazy mystery.

Here's the secret: The trick was pulled off by Dick Brookz and Dorothy Dietrich.

"We thought it should be done," Dick says. "And, so, why not us."

How they did this is a marvelous and winding story. They actually broke into the cemetery—"We were absolutely ready to be arrested," Dorothy says—were caught, and then they somehow talked the grumpy cemetery operator David Jacobson into letting them install the new bust. If you are ever in the Scranton area, you must go to the Houdini Museum and visit. They happily will tell you the whole thing.

I had that question: Why does Houdini live on?

And the answer is simpler than I thought: He lives on because people will not let him die.

THE UNMASKING

In 1908, when Houdini was at the height of his powers and fame, he wrote a book called *The Unmasking of Robert-Houdin*. That book's legacy is as complicated as the legacy of the man who dedicated so much of himself to write it.

"I asked nothing more of life," Houdini wrote in the introduction, "than to become in my profession like Robert-Houdin . . . Alas for my golden dreams! My investigations brought forth only bitterest disappointment and saddest disillusionment. Stripped of his self-woven veil of romance, Robert-Houdin stood forth, in the uncompromising light of cold historical facts, a mere pretender, a man who waxed great on the brainwork of others, a mechanician who had boldly filched the inventions of the master craftsmen among his predecessors."

For hundreds and hundreds of pages, Harry Houdini cut away at the character and legacy and heart of the magician who had set him on his path and inspired his name. Houdini called Robert-Houdin a fraud, a thief, a liar, and a subpar magician. He wrote (falsely) that the famed *Memoirs of Robert-Houdin* was proven to be the penwork of a brilliant Parisian journalist.

"At times," the magician Maurice Sardina

wrote of Houdini's *Unmasking*, "so much spite, jealousy and vindictiveness are displayed that the reader is disgusted."

Many have called the book a patricide. Houdini, this theory goes, had become so famous and successful that there were no more worlds left for him to conquer, no more enemies left to vanquish, and all that was left was to destroy the memory of the Father of Modern Magic and of his own dreams. It is interesting that Houdini dedicated *The Unmasking* to his own father, Mayer Samuel Weiss.

"The only thing left for Houdini," wrote Christian Fechner, a French film director and a magic scholar, "is to kill the father."

The Unmasking is not only a book about Robert-Houdin. In fact, despite the title (which Houdini might have regretted), it's not even mostly about Robert-Houdin. Houdini spent much of the book remembering old magicians, the ones he believed had been unfairly drowned out by Robert-Houdin's fame. Houdini traveled the world to find them, and then he told their stories.

There is one particularly touching account of how he sought to interview a magician named Wiljalba Frikell. He was long forgotten by the time Houdini came for him, but Frikell was, for a time, one of the most famous magicians in the world. He was a big-stage magician, but he did not need props or big illusions to amaze. As the legend goes, he once lost all of his equipment in a fire just before a show, yet he left the audience spellbound using just playing cards, coins, and handkerchiefs.

Frikell eventually grew disappointed, and he disappeared. Houdini searched for him obsessively, at one point hiring a photographer to take photos of anyone who came out of a house where he was rumored to live. When he found Frikell, Houdini stood outside the house and pleaded with his wife to let him in. She sadly refused.

"Frau Frikell heard my pleadings with tears running down her cheeks," Houdini wrote. "And later I learned that Herr Frikell also listened to them, lying grimly on the other side of the shuttered window."

Houdini would not give up. He sent Frikell letters. He sent newspaper clippings. He had a box of Frikell's favorite Russian tea delivered to the house. Finally, Frikell gave in and invited Houdini to come at his earliest convenience.

"I rang the bell," Houdini wrote. "It echoed through the house with a peculiar shrillness. The air seemed charged with a quality which I presumed was the intense pleasure of realizing my long-cherished hope of meeting the great magician. A lady opened the door and greeted me with the words: 'You are being waited for.'"

He walked into the parlor. There was a man

439

sitting there, and it was Wiljalba Frikell, no question about it, wearing his finest clothes. Frikell was surrounded by some of the medals he had won through the years and the clippings and programs that marked his magical life. He had prepared for the visit. Frikell smelled of the cologne that he had splashed on his face just moments earlier.

But Wiljalba Frikell was dead. He had died moments before Houdini arrived.

"We stood together," Houdini wrote, "the woman who had loved the dear old wizard for years, and the young magician who would have been so willing to love him."

Sure, this could be another Houdini exaggeration. But the point is that to Houdini, *The Unmasking* was more than merely an attack on Robert-Houdin.

"*The Unmasking* was perverse," Jim Steinmeyer says. "It's sad. There's really amazing research in that book, original research about many magicians like [Bartolomeo] Bosco and Phillippe, wonderful original research. And then he's got to bitch-slap Robert-Houdin for things he doesn't understand. It's a shame, really."

In the end, what is impossible to miss about *The Unmasking* is that every single complaint Houdini has about Robert-Houdin—every single one—was true about Houdini. Again, and again, Houdini ascribed his own failings and flaws in his words about his first hero. He wrote that Robert-Houdin had a ghostwriter pen his famous memoirs. This was not true, but Houdini hired ghostwriters for every book he wrote. "When you see something Houdini *actually* wrote," Steinmeyer says, "you are struck by how dumb and laughable the prose."

Houdini wrote that Robert-Houdin was not an especially skilled magician. This is what people said of Houdini in his time and continue to say today.

Houdini accused Robert-Houdin of being a bully. Houdini was a bully.

Houdini wrote that Robert-Houdin took credit for illusions he did not invent. Houdini took credit for everything.

Houdini wrote that Robert-Houdin was a supreme egotist—nothing more needs to be said.

He attacked Robert-Houdin for not seeing through other magicians' secrets when he himself was fooled often; he was even fooled in the very book that inspired him, fooled by Torrini, a fictional character Robert-Houdin had invented.

But perhaps nowhere did Houdini seem more blind to his true self than when he accused Robert-Houdin of creating a myth more beautiful than reality.

"Yes, you can point to the rather obvious, and slightly annoying, observation that Houdini was projecting himself on Robert-Houdin," Jim

Steinmeyer says. "But I think that misses that there's a deep hurt expressed in the book. I think that Robert-Houdin turning his career into a glossy document, emphasizing the appearances in front of royalty and leaving out the rather dirty, nasty details about tours and theaters, about rude audiences and ineffective promoters, he gave magicians—and Houdini—an extremely misleading impression about mid-Victorian magic."

In other words, Houdini believed in the romanticized and idealized version of magic that Robert-Houdin had breezily written about. It had been the image that made him chase magic in the first place. Houdini believed in this magical world of Robert-Houdin, and when he realized the world did not exist—realized that Robert-Houdin had made it up—he lashed out.

"I think that Houdini felt betrayed," Steinmeyer says.

A few months before Houdini died, he wrote a letter to Harry Leat, an English magic dealer and publisher of a small and sometimes controversial monthly pamphlet called *Leat's Leaflets*. In part it read: "Regarding my *Unmasking of Robert-Houdin*, time has proven I was one hundred percent correct. The only mistake I did make was to call it the name I did when it should have been called 'the History of Magic.' "

People in magic still argue about the letter.

Some think that Houdini was expressing regret over the vicious way he attacked Robert-Houdin. Others think he was simply flexing his ego again by stating that his book was so good and all-encompassing, it deserved a bigger title.

Either way, *The Unmasking* feels like the closest Houdini came to writing an autobiography. It is the man in full color.

One question people have asked me again and again: "Do you like Houdini?" The answer is, "Yes, very much, but it's complicated," just like the man was complicated. *The Unmasking of Robert-Houdin*, like Houdini himself, is both cruel and profoundly decent. It's impossibly sloppy and also filled with stories and quotes that would have been lost to history without Houdini's exhaustive efforts. It is an all-out attack, Houdini at his most vengeful, and yet it is also a love letter to magic and forgotten magicians, as sentimental as Houdini could be.

"The secret of showmanship," Houdini wrote in *The Unmasking*, "consists not of what you really do, but what the mystery-loving public thinks you do."

AFTERWORD:
HOUDINI'S GHOST

Now, in the end, we seek our own Wiljalba Frikell. It is time for me to find Patrick Culliton. Yes, he made it clear from the very start that he had talked all he wanted to talk about Houdini, that he wanted to be left alone. I understood that. I searched in vain for his books. I searched for months for someone who might vouch for me. And finally, I gave up and moved on. There were too many other people to talk with, too many other stories to tell. I left Patrick Culliton behind in the collection area where writers store all their regrets.

And finally, I asked the real question: *What would Houdini do?*

He would never give up so easily.

Hi Patrick,

I apologize for writing again and understand if you just delete this email immediately. I certainly understand that you have moved on and am sheepish even about this email. But Houdini certainly never held back, and I know I would regret it if I didn't at least once more ask if you might have time to talk. I promise this will be the last email. Thanks for listening.

Joe

He responded with an odd email. He said that I would get a lot more out of his book *Houdini: The Key* than I would out of talking with him. I quickly wrote back and said that I couldn't find his book anywhere and would happily pay whatever price to get it.

He wrote back again: "I'll meet you at the Magic Castle to sign one over."

"Magic is a kind of healing thing," Patrick Culliton is saying. We are sitting in the lower level of the Magic Castle, where the wonderful magician Shoot Ogawa is about to give a lecture on a trick called the coin matrix. Patrick doesn't perform much magic, but he often goes to lectures like this.

"In some ways," he says suddenly, "it's very frustrating to be around the best in the world all the time. All the fucking time. When you think about it, I guess that most magicians, including most of the great ones I know, have some kind of issues. You know, they were a lonely kid, or they were a nerd, or they had some tragedy in their life . . ."

He shakes his head.

" . . . or, you know, whatever their story happens to be."

The Magic Castle is the unofficial name for the clubhouse of the Academy of Magical Arts. It is an old house just a couple of blocks away from Hollywood Boulevard. I think the best way to explain the power of the place: In here, magic is treated seriously, and it is treated like art. There are no snickers and no apologies in the Magic Castle. Irony is frowned upon. To get in, men must wear jacket and tie. Women wear formal dresses from every era of the last one hundred years. Children are not allowed except for the weekend brunch. No one here believes that magic is only for children. Drinks are never to be placed on the felt tables.

It is a holy place for magicians and magic lovers. Celebrities and fans mingle in these rooms, all connected by the same quest: to catch a little wonder.

There are so many traditions here, it's hard to keep up. The first time you come, you are supposed to approach the golden owl on the bookshelf and say, "Open Sesame." A bookshelf slides open. Inside, magic is everywhere— close-up magic, big illusions, table magic, comedy magic. No photos are allowed. And, this is quite serious: exposing tricks can get you expelled from the club.

"Did you ever meet Muhammad Ali?" Patrick asks suddenly, and I find that he often speaks suddenly, with quick turns and unexpected transitions. I tell him that, yes, I met Ali twice in my life as a sportswriter. One of the most cherished memories of my life was having the former heavyweight champion of the world, the Greatest, tap me on the shoulder and show me a magic trick. He made a handkerchief disappear.

"Did he show you how it was done?" Patrick asks.

And I remember: Yes, he did show me. I thought the trick was over and began to applaud or show some sign of gratefulness when he tapped me on the shoulder and told me to look again into his hand. There was a fake thumb. Inside the fake thumb was the handkerchief.

"Yes," Patrick says. "Muhammad had this belief. It was against his religion to fool anybody. But he still loved to do magic. Looking back, I think he did more good than harm, but, you know, they gave him a lifetime membership in the Castle here. And then they kicked him out because he wouldn't stop exposing. I tried to talk to him. I said, 'Muhammad, part of magic is fooling people.' But what could you do? You couldn't tear him and his belief apart."

Patrick says he has been around the Castle

more or less since the beginning of the place in 1963. The Castle, Patrick says, brings him to life. "There are only two times I feel complete," he says. "One is in front of a camera or in front of an audience, when I'm performing. And the other is here."

He was destined to be a star. Everybody said so. As a senior in high school, Patrick got the lead role in *The Music Man*. This was not like getting the lead role at a regular high school. This was Hollywood High. Two of the original Mouseketeers went to the school at the time. John Clifford, who founded the Los Angeles Ballet, played a supporting role in the play. Rory Flynn, the daughter of Errol Flynn, was at the school as were actors like Barbara Hershey, Meredith Baxter, Mimsy Farmer, and Linda Hart.

"It was like Broadway," Patrick says. When he got the lead, his future seemed assured.

By this time, he had already developed a more than moderate interest in Houdini. He found a Houdini book in his junior high library in 1956, and he fell in love. He wanted to read everything he could, he collected old photos and posters and magical things. Once, when he was sixteen, he met the great magician Harry Blackstone and asked about Houdini. "He didn't want to hear some punk asking about Houdini," Patrick says. "He was sweet to me, but he did tell me exactly how much he wanted to talk about Houdini. I can still hear him: 'Oh yeah, let me tell you about your friend Houdini.' That was about as far as that went."

But Houdini was secondary to his path to stardom. Right out of high school, he began getting television parts. He won a small role on *The Big Valley*, and he played several different roles in the television shows *The Time Tunnel* and *Voyage to the Bottom of the Sea*.

"I just want to be a bush-league star," he joked to a reporter.

But, in truth, he didn't want that. He wanted the biggest prize. He had ambition, big dreams. And he had talent. Everybody said so.

Acting was all-consuming. The nights, the auditions, the drinking, the lights, the loving, the fighting, it was all a big, beautiful blur. He won a role in *The Beguiled*, with Clint Eastwood and Geraldine Page. Pat Culliton knew where he was going, until he went to war.

"Vietnam stole my career," he says. "And Vietnam stole my life."

I ask Patrick how he met Muhammad Ali. He says that when he got back from Vietnam, he heard "The Battle Hymn of Lt. Calley," a song—sung to the tune of "Battle Hymn of the Republic"—that idealized William Calley, the US Army officer who was court-martialed after the murder of civilians at My Lai.

"I was so disgusted by that song," Patrick says. "So disgusted. It glorified him. It sickened me. I had just gotten back from Vietnam, and I knew what it was, I understood what it was. I had lived it. I felt badly for Lieutenant Calley, but what he did, it was horrible. It was how people blow it in war.

"Meanwhile, here was Muhammad Ali. He didn't go to war. He conscientiously objected. He didn't run. He stood up, said he would not fight, said he would pay whatever price it took. Well, they took away his ability to make a living. They took away his championship. They threatened to put him in jail. But he stood strong. He didn't fight."

We are sitting in the downstairs area of the Magic Castle, and to our right a man is showing another a card trick. He pulls one card from the deck and shows it to the spectator. It is an eight of clubs.

"I wrote 'The Ballad of Muhammad Ali,'" Patrick says. "I still sing this song. I still sing the last line."

And he sings the last lines.

And freedom is a battle
And the fight is never done
And how you learn to live
Is how you've lost or won
And if one man is enslaved

Then no man is free
So, it's good to have you back
Muhammad Ali

"I'm no songwriter," he says, and his eyes are wet. The eight of clubs has disappeared and reappeared and in the spectator's jacket pocket. There is so much pain.

There were few parts waiting for him when Patrick returned home. He realized that directors and casting agents seemed nervous around him; that was how he knew that the war had changed him. He felt rage about all of it—Vietnam, the fickleness of Hollywood, what he'd lost. He drank more. This was around time when he got into the fight with David Carradine, the one where he almost fell off the balcony, and he tells that story and laughs a little. What difference did it make? Living? Dying? It all seemed about the same.

I think back to that Carradine quote: "Patrick was a shell-shocked Vietnam vet and half-crazed a lot of time."

"Yes," Patrick says, and he says no more about that.

On March 24, 1974—and Patrick will never forget the day—he went into his old boxes and pulled out all of his old Houdini stuff. A couple of friends were coming over, and he wanted to share with them his childhood passion. He had not looked at some of it in years, all of these photographs and books and magic tricks but was surprised how much he remembered about Houdini, how much he still knew, and how easily he could do some of Houdini's sleight-of-hand tricks.

At some point, someone asked him Houdini's birth date.

"March 24, 1874," he said instinctively.

"Hey," one of his friends said, "that's exactly one hundred years ago today."

Patrick smiles now. "What would life be without coincidences?"

An idea sparked that day. It took a little time to evolve. Patrick wasn't getting much work, but he knew so much about Houdini, and he needed to perform so he created a one-man show about Houdini. He played the college circuit. The show was a lecture and a little bit of magic. He performed the Needles. He escaped from a straitjacket. He told Houdini's story.

"At the time, no exaggeration, I probably talked to six hundred people who had seen Houdini perform or actually knew him," he says. "I really didn't think about what I was doing, didn't think about where it would take me. I just kept on going, kept on talking to people, kept on researching, and at a certain point everybody realized, 'Huh, Culliton knows more about Houdini than anyone else on earth.' "

It was more than that. At some point, he admits, it was hard to tell where Houdini's life ended and Patrick's life began. While getting a divorce from his third wife, he started telling people, "I'm writing a book."

"Was I writing a book?" he asks now. "Did I even know how to write a book?"

Either way, he did write one, *The Tao of Houdini*, which he saw as the autobiography Houdini never wrote. He went deep into the archives and found every single word Houdini ever wrote about himself and put them together. While researching, he came across so many Houdini secret methods that he wrote a second book, *The Secret Confessions of Houdini*, which broke down exactly how he did his tricks and escapes. He packaged them together into a set he called *Houdini Unlocked*.

The set will probably cost you a grand on the internet, if you can find it at all.

Then he wrote the big book, *Houdini: The Key*, the one he brought for me in a nice blue vinyl case. The book is so enormous that I wonder if I will have to check it for the plane ride home.

"I worked on the book for three years, basically never leaving my computer," he says. "I looked bad. I smelled bad. I stopped shaving. My friends used to pop their heads in to see if I was all right, and I'd talk about what I was doing and give them a friendly good-bye as I shoved them out the door. These were my best friends. They just wanted to know: Is he still alive?

"I was alive. I invested all I had left in my tank. I designed every bit of this book. And inside, it's everything. All the secrets. All the keys."

I give Patrick two hundred ninety-five dollars for the book—well, I give him three hundred and tell him to keep the change, but he refuses—and I tell him that I couldn't find the book anywhere at any price. He nods. The first printing was 278— that corresponded with Houdini's New York address at 278 West 113th Street.

"First printing?" I ask.

"Yes," he says, "I did a second printing. This is part of that."

"Oh," I say. "How many are in that?"

He smiles. "One hundred and thirteen, of course."

"This book," Patrick writes in the opening, "is dedicated to all the finks, rats, squealers and thieves who sought to learn and tell Houdini's secrets, and to those who kept those secrets alive until I could write them down."

It's not exactly right to call *Houdini: The Key* a book. You know how in the movies sometimes an author will put his or her unbound typewritten pages outside, and the wind will catch them and send them all flying into the air, and the poor author will chase after them, running and leaping and trying to get hold of each page? It's like that—*The Key* is Houdini's life dispersed and scattered in the wind. "Everything is in there," John Cox says, "but it's Patrick. So, it's not always easy to find what you're looking for."

Our time is running short, and I try to get Patrick to talk a little about Houdini. He seems willing enough. But every time he begins to go into Houdini, something stops him, and he jumps to something else. He starts to talk about Houdini's death, and then suddenly he is talking instead about a small role that he had in the television movie *Outrage*, with Robert Preston. Patrick felt a special bond with the legendary actor because Preston was most famous for playing Professor Harold Hill in *The Music Man*, both on Broadway and on film, and that was the same role Patrick played in high school, the role that promised infinite possibilities before the war.

"So, I have to tell you this," he says, and he tells the story of the day that Yul Brynner died. Brynner had performed in *The King and I* more than forty-five hundred times in life, dying at the end of each show.

"So, I see Preston and I ask him, 'Did you see that Yul Brynner died?'" Patrick says. "And do you know what he says to me? He says, 'Well, he certainly had enough practice.'"

• • •

We walk together, room-to-room, through the Magic Castle. Magic is all around us. I ask Patrick why Houdini has lasted all these years. He thinks about it.

"Part of it is the phonetics of the name," he says. "You never forget it. HOO-DEE-NEE. It's the most remarkable name, isn't it?"

We pass someone making a coin disappear from his right hand and reappear in his left.

"And then there are people who are just different," Patrick says. "You know, there's something about them, no words for it. I met James Dean. I didn't even know who he was then—*East of Eden* had just come out. I didn't know that. I was ten. But there was something about him."

A man we pass takes an entire deck of playing cards out of his mouth.

"Of course, there's also the way he died," Patrick says. "On Halloween. That's a big deal. Bess kept his name alive for so many years with all the talk about him coming back. The Tony Curtis movie was a big deal—I got to know Tony Curtis a little bit. Sweet guy. And, you know, there's the whole idea of escape, I'm sure everybody has told you that. People talk a lot about that. I don't know. I guess we all want to escape something."

Patrick excuses himself to go to the restroom,

and I watch him slowly, painfully walk away. I pull out the book—it is so heavy—and I look at his inscription. It is on the last page, beside a sketch of himself with his hands out in that classic magical pose, as if he is trying to make the reader disappear.

> To Joe,
>   Wishing all the best on your endeavor-
>   But especially the book you are writing
>   About WONDER—a Houdini specialty.
>   Patrick Culliton
>   +
>   (of course)
>   Houdini's Ghost

"You know," Patrick says as he returns, and he grabs my hand, "it rankles me that I never made my mark as an actor. It hurts me, even now. I should have . . . but you can't change things. It rankles me that I've never been a good magician, not by the standards I would like, not by the standards of some of the people you see in here. It rankles me that Vietnam . . ." He trails off, and then begins again.

"A few years ago, my wife got hired to play Mary in *The Music Man*, at a dinner theater in Sarasota, Florida," he says. "The place was called the Golden Apple Dinner Theater. It's closed now. Anyway, they lost their Harold

Hill, which, as you know, was the part I played in high school. I wrote the producer a letter. I said, 'Listen, if these kids let you down, just remember that us old pros are here to bail you out.'

"And you know what? He hired me. He paid me less than he paid my wife. But I got to be Harold Hill again eight times a week for ten weeks. It was just like high school."

His smile makes him look many years younger.

"And I remember once, I had a particularly good performance," he says. "There were only a few of those out of the ninety-one shows, but an actor knows when it's all working, when everything clicks. I had one of those shows. We had laughter from the first line, and I just kept them going.

"But here's the best part. My kid was also in the show, he was ten, and afterward, it was such a good show, I was feeling so good, and I took that old line from *The Champ*, you know, I said, 'Well, you proud of your old man now?' "

At this, Patrick Culliton, Houdini's Ghost, begins to cry.

"And my kid said, 'You know, you've always been my hero, Dad.' "

He then sobs and sobs, happy tears, sad tears, all the tears.

"That's amazing," I say to him, and I realize we are still holding hands from our long-ago handshake, and neither of us will let go. I guess we all want to escape something.

"It is amazing," he says. "Because I'm no hero."

ACKNOWLEDGMENTS

I write this in my small office and realize that I might have gone a bit overboard on the Houdini stuff. I am surrounded by eight Houdini posters, three Houdini photographs, a blueprint of a diver's suit that he used, two Houdini bobblehead dolls, two more Houdini action figures, a Houdini paperweight that was given out at a minor league baseball game, a Houdini PEZ dispenser, three sets of handcuffs, two Houdini teddy bears, and a beer stein that looks like Houdini.

My wife and daughters are convinced I only wrote this book as an excuse to buy the merch.

I plead the fifth on that.

Everything about writing this book was pure joy. It emerged from a strange place. As a longtime sportswriter, I am often approached to write about sports (my first four books were sports books), and someone I respect asked me to write a book about Babe Ruth. That is well-covered ground—my friends Jane Leavy and Leigh Montville are among the many who have wonderfully told his story—but I thought about why the Bambino still fascinates so many people.

I decided that it comes down to that word: Wonder. Ruth comes from that time, before twenty-four-hour news coverage and social media

461

and a creeping cynicism, when we unabashedly allowed ourselves to feel awe and wonderment. Ruth, with his myriad addictions and general over-the-top lifestyle, would be treated very differently now. Is that bad? No, of course not. But I was curious: What have we lost through the years? What have we held on to?

I wanted to write about *that,* but I realized that Babe Ruth was not the right person for me to tell that story.

Enter: Harry Houdini.

I was a lifelong Houdini fan when I began this project, but I came in knowing almost nothing about magic. I knew exactly zero people in magic. It was, in many ways, like writing my first book because I was starting from square one. And it would have been impossible without the help of literally hundreds of amazing people in and around magic who did not just offer advice and insight but went out of their way to guide me, protect me, and save me from my own worst instincts. I could not possibly thank them all here—I hope they see themselves in the book—but I would like to highlight five specifically.

First, there's the most famous magician in the world, today's Houdini, David Copperfield. He embraced me and my project at the very beginning, and I cannot be more grateful. There's a moment in the writing process that I think many authors will find familiar, that moment when you realize: "Okay, yes, this will actually become a book!" That happened for me when David Copperfield invited me to Las Vegas to tour his museum and spend some time with him.

Second, there's John Cox, founder of the Wild About Harry website and my compass for this project. Nobody knows more about Houdini than John, but more, he allowed me to see (and hopefully capture) the emotion that Houdini still stirs in people.

Jim Steinmeyer is one of the world's great thinkers about magic. He made it clear the very first time we talked that Houdini is not his favorite topic, but he was still there to offer incredible insights and new directions every time I asked. We exchanged dozens of emails through the book-writing, and each one he wrote felt like a finished essay. I diminished them by only using parts of them. I could not have written this book without him.

Fourth, there's Dorothy Dietrich and Dick Brookz. What a couple. I cannot begin to explain how much richer my life is (and how much richer this book is) because they took me into their lives and shared their amazing stories.

And, I want to thank Joshua Jay. Being an old sportswriter got me nowhere in the magic world—those two circles do not overlap much on the Venn diagram—but Josh, in addition to being one of the world's great sleight-of-hand magicians, is also a huge basketball fan. That helped. Josh opened up this book in countless ways and vouched for me with so many of the people who appear in its pages. It's an honor to call Josh a friend.

My editor at Avid Reader, Jofie Ferrari-Adler, took a chance on this book when it was nothing more than a hint of a dream, and I am deeply indebted to him. Associate editor Julianna Haubner was joyfully relentless with her edits and improved this book immeasurably. Sloan Harris has been my agent for approaching twenty years now, though at this point he's much more friend than agent. It will take me years to thank all the other friends who supported me throughout but let me begin with Dan and Debby McGinn; Tommy Tomlinson; Alix Felsing; Brian Hay; Jim Banks; Jonathan Abrams, Mechelle Voepel; Jen Kramer; Mike Schur, and Mike Vaccaro. I promise to get to the rest of you.

Finally, there is the family, beginning with my in-laws, Cecil and Judy Keller, and my parents, Frances and Steven Posnanski. This book was particularly hard on my wife, Margo, and our daughters, Elizabeth and Katie, who for two years endured an endless stream of Houdini stories, watched every magic video and show available, and rolled their eyes every time another package with Houdini memorabilia showed up on our front porch. Their love and inspiration live in every word.

One memory stands out above all: Elizabeth, a junior in high school, chose to be Houdini for her school history project. You haven't lived as a parent until you've sat with your daughter in front of a computer and scoured the Internet to buy a straitjacket.

A SELECTED BIBLIOGRAPHY

I just counted: I referenced 212 different Houdini and magic books in the writing of *The Life and Afterlife of Harry Houdini*. I read more than a thousand newspapers and magazine articles. I watched dozens of documentaries, films, and television shows. I will be honest: I did not intend to do quite that much research on the man as this book is as much about magic today as it is about our hero, but what you find is that once you start going down the Houdini rabbit hole, you really don't want to come up for air.

In addition to the selected bibliography I list below, I want to make mention of the amazing Ask Alexander, the search engine on magic provided by Conjuring Arts. It saved my life repeatedly.

Numerous websites, including John Cox's Wild About Houdini (wildabouthoudini.com), The Houdini File (houdinifile.com), The Magic Detective (themagicdetective.com), Harry Houdini Circumstantial Evidence (harryhoudinicircum stantialevidence.com), Harry Houdini: His Life and Art (thegreatharryhoudini.com), and Patrick Culliton's site (houdinisghost.com) were essential.

Here's a selected list of the books that played a significant role in my research:

Bell, Don (2004): *The Man Who Killed Houdini.* Georgetown, Ontario. Vehicule Press.

Ben, David (2006). *Dai Vernon: A Biography.* Chicago: Squash Publishing.

Brown, Bob (republished 2017). *Houdini.* New York: Roving Eye Press.

Cannell, J. C. (1931). *The Secrets of Houdini.* London: Hutchinson & Co. Limited.

Cartlidge, Ron (2002). *Houdini's Texas Tours 1916 & 1923.* Austin, TX: Ron Cartlidge Publications.

Cervon, Bruce and Burns, Keith (1992). *He Fooled Houdini: Dai Vernon, A Magical Life.* Tahoma, CA: L&L Publishing.

Christopher, Milbourne. (1969). *Houdini: The Untold Story.* London: Cassell.

Christopher, Milbourne. (1973). *The Illustrated History of Magic.* New York: Crowell.

Cox, John (2014). *A Brief History of Houdini's Water Torture Cell.* Los Angeles: Wild About Houdini Press.

Cramer, Stuart and Meriwether (1962). *The Secrets of Karl Germain.* Cleveland: Emerson.

Culliton, Patrick and T. L. Williams (1992). *Houdini's Strange Tales: A Collection of Fiction by Harry Houdini.* Los Angeles: Kieren Press.

Culliton, Patrick (2011). *Houdini: The Key.* Los Angeles: Self-published.

Erdnase, S. W. (1902). *Artifice Ruse and Subterfuge at the Card Table: A Treatise on the Science and Art of Manipulating Cards* (later republished as *The Expert at the Card Table*). Self-published.

Ernst, Bernard M. L., and Hereward Carrington. (1932). *Houdini and Conan Doyle: The Story of a Strange Friendship*. New York: Albert and Charles Doni, Inc.

Fitzsimons, Raymund. (1980) *Death and the Magician: The Mystery of Houdini*. New York: Atheneum.

Fechner, Christian (2002). *The Magic of Robert-Houdin: An Artist's Life*. Bolougne, France: Editions F.C.F.

Fleishman, Sid (2006). Escape: *The Story of the Great Houdini*. New York: Greenwillow Books.

Frost, Thomas (1876). *The Lives of the Conjurers*. London: Tinsley Brothers & Catherine Street, Strand.

Gibson, Walter and Young, Morris N. (1953). *Houdini on Magic*. New York: Dover.

Gibson, Walter B. (1976). *Houdini's Escapes and Magic*. New York: Funk & Wagnalls.

Gibson, Walter B. (1976). *The Original Houdini Scrapbook*. New York: Sterling Publishing.

Gold, Glen David (2001). *Carter Beats the Devil (A Novel)*. New York: Hyperion.

Goldston, Will (1927; republished 1999).

Sensational Tales of Mystery Men. London: José Antonio González.

Gresham, Douglas H. (1988). *Lenten Lands: My Childhood with Joy Davidman and C. S. Lewis*. New York: HarperOne.

Gresham, William Lindsay (1959). *Houdini: The Man Who Walked Through Walls*. New York: Holt, Rinehart and Winston.

Gresham, William Lindsay, and Bret Wood (2013). *Grindshow: Essays of William Lindsay Gresham*. Lakewood, CO: Centipede Press.

Harrison, John (2009). *Spellbound: The Wonder-Filled World of Doug Henning*. New York: BoxOffice Books.

Henning, Doug (1977). *Houdini: His Legend and His Magic*. New York: Warner Books.

Hardeen. *Life and History of Hardeen: 20 Years of an Eventful Career on Stage*. Promotional Material.

Houdini, Harry (1906). *The Right Way to Do Wrong: An Exposé of Successful Criminals*. Boston: Self-published.

Houdini, Harry (1908). *The Unmasking of Robert-Houdin*. New York: The Publishers Printing Co.

Houdini, Harry (1920). *Miracle Mongers and Their Methods*. New York: E. P. Dutton & Company.

Houdini, Harry (1922). *The Adventurous Life of a Versatile Artist*. Promotional Pamphlet.

Jay, Joshua, Ed. (2014). *Magic in Mind: Essential Essays for Magicians.* New York: Vanishing Inc.

Jaher, David (2015). *The Witch of Lime Street: Séance, Seduction and Houdini in the Spirit World.* New York: Crown Publishers.

Johnson, Karl (2005). *The Magician and the Cardsharp: The Search for America's Greatest Sleight-of-Hand Artist.* New York: Henry Holt and Company.

Kalush, William and Larry Sloman (2006). *The Secret Life of Houdini: The Making of America's First Superhero.* New York: Atria Books.

Kalush, William and Larry Sloman (2007). *The Secret Life of Houdini Laid Bare: Sources, Notes and Additional Material.* New York: Atria Books.

Kellock, Harold (1928). *Houdini: His Life Story by Harold Kellock from the Recollections and Documents of Beatrick Houdini.* New York: Harcourt, Brace & Company.

Kendall, Lace (1960). *Houdini: Master of Escape.* Philadelphia: Macrae Smith Company.

Kuzmeskus, Elaine M. (2015). *The Medium Who Baffled Houdini.* Chula Vista, CA: Aventine Press.

Lamont, Peter and Jim Steinmeyer (2018). *The Secret History of Magic: The True Story of the Deceptive Art.* New York: TarcherPerigee.

Lead, Brian and Roger Woods (1987). *Houdini the Myth Maker: The Unmasking of Harry Houdini.* Self-published.

Lead, Brian (1988). *Laughing at Locksmiths: The Legend and Legacy of Harry Houdini.* Limited publishing for International Brotherhood of Magic convention.

Loomis, Bob (2016). *Houdini's Final Incredible Secret: The True Story of How Houdini Mystifed the Creator of Sherlock Holmes.* Self-published.

Lutes, Jason and Nick Bertozzi (2007). *Houdini: The Handcuff King.* New York: Hyperion.

McNab, Bruce (2012). *The Metamorphosis: The Apprenticeship of Harry Houdini.* Fredricton, New Brunswick: Goose Lane.

Meyer, Bernard C., M.D. (1976). *Houdini: A Mind in Chains.* New York: E.P. Dutton & Co. Inc.

Montague, Charlotte (2018). *Houdini: The Life and Times of the World's Greatest Magician.* London: Chartwell Books.

Moses, Arthur (2006). *Houdini Periodical Bibliography.* Humble, TX: H&R Magic Books.

Rapaport, Brooke Kamin (2011). *Houdini: Art and Magic.* New Haven: Yale University Press.

Rauscher, William V. (2000). *The Houdini Code Mystery: A Spirit Secret Solved.* Pasadena, CA: Mike Caveney's Magic Words.

Richards, Leann (2011). *Houdini's Tour of Australia*. Self-published.

Rinn, Joseph (1950). *Sixty Years of Psychical Research: Houdini and I Among the Spiritualists*. New York: The Truth Seeker Company.

Robert-Houdin, Jean Eugène (1859). *Memoirs of Robert-Houdin: Ambassador, Author, and Conjurer, Written by Himself.* Philadelphia: Geo. G. Evans.

Saltman, David (2018). *Houdini Unbound: Espionage in Russia (A Novel, Based on True Events)*. New York: Hudson River Books.

Scot, Reginald (1584; republished 1972). *The Discoverie of Witchcraft*. London: Dover.

Silverman, Kenneth (1996). *Houdini!! The Career of Ehrich Weiss: American Self Liberator, Europe's Eclipsing Sensation, World Hand-cuff King and Prison Breaker—Nothing on Earth Can Hold HOUDINI a Prisoner!!!.* New York: Harper Collins Publishers.

Silverman, Kenneth (1996). *Notes to Houdini!!!* New York: Kaufman and Greenberg.

Steinmeyer, Jim (1998). *Art & Artifice and Other Essays on Illusion*. New York: Carol & Graf Publishers.

Steinmeyer, Jim (2003). Hiding the Elephant: *How Magicians Invented the Impossible and Learned to Disappear.* New York: Carroll & Graf Publishers.

Steinmeyer, Jim (2011). *The Last Greatest Magician in the World: Howard Thurston Versus Harry Houdini & the Battles of the American Wizards*. New York: Penguin Group.

Sugar, Bert Randolph (1976). *Houdini: His Life and Art*. New York: Grosset & Dunlap.

Swiss, Jamy Ian (1994–2001). *Jamy Ian Swiss Book Reviews*. *Genii Magazine*. Self-published.

Tait, Derek (2017). *The Great Houdini: His British Tours*. Barnsley, South Yorkshire: Pen & Sword.

Young, Dorothy (2003). *Touring with Houdini*. Ocean Grove, NJ: Penrod Press.

ABOUT THE AUTHOR

Joe Posnanski is the #1 *New York Times* bestselling author of six books, including *Paterno* and *The Secret of Golf*. A longtime columnist for *Sports Illustrated*, *NBC Sports*, and *The Kansas City Star*, he was twice named the best sports columnist in America by the Associated Press Sports Editors. He lives in Charlotte, North Carolina, with his family.

PHOTO CREDITS

Books are produced in the United States using U.S.-based materials

Books are printed using a revolutionary new process called THINKtech™ that lowers energy usage by 70% and increases overall quality

Books are durable and flexible because of Smyth-sewing

Paper is sourced using environmentally responsible foresting methods and the paper is acid-free

Center Point Large Print
600 Brooks Road / PO Box 1
Thorndike, ME 04986-0001 USA

(207) 568-3717

US & Canada:
1 800 929-9108
www.centerpointlargeprint.com